IMAGES
of America

CHICOPEE
1950–1975

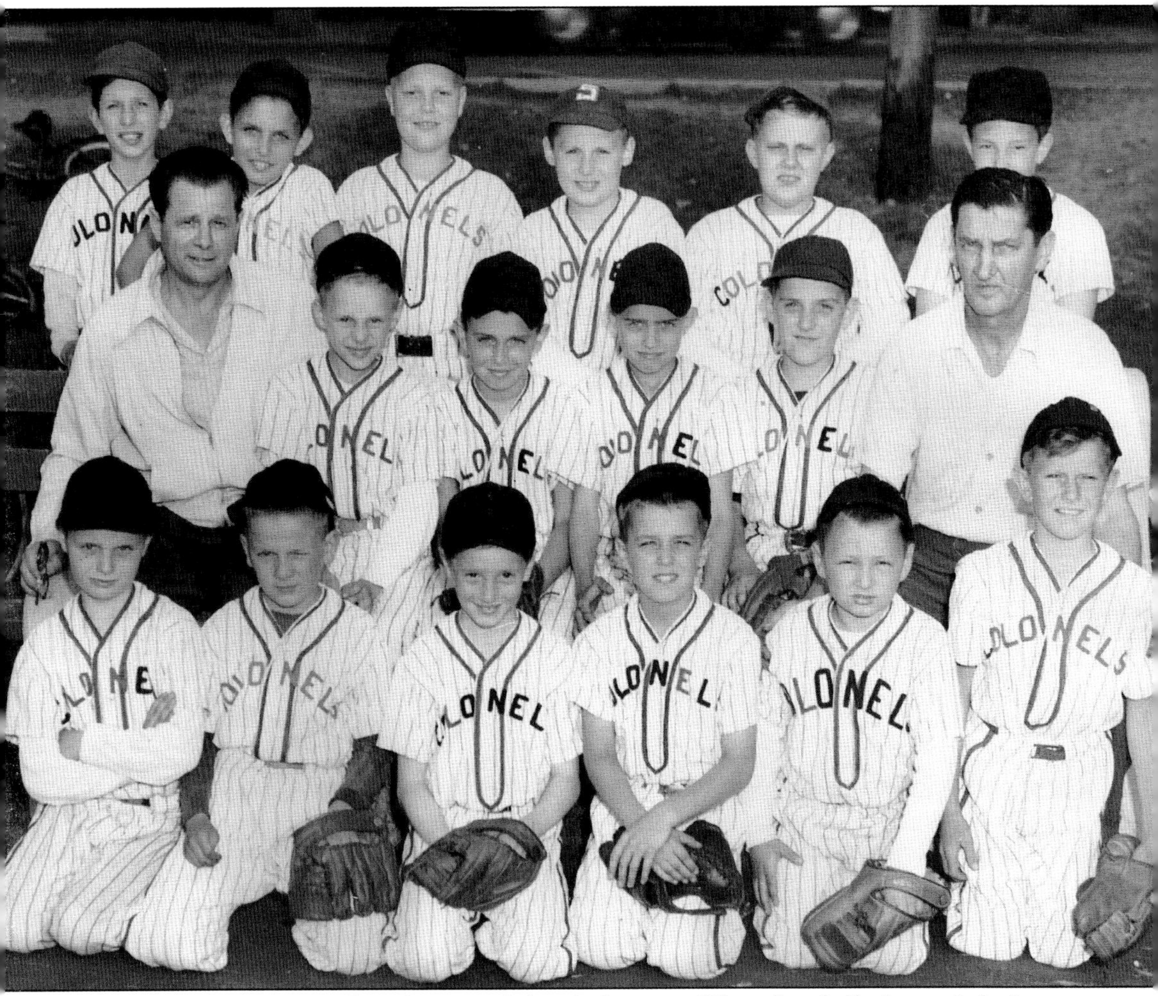

Pictured in 1956 are the Chicopee Colonels Peewees. These baseball-playing baby boomers would arrive in high school just in time for the turbulent 1960s. During the post–World War II era, a new generation of young athletes would bring glory and fame to the little mill town at the junctions of the Connecticut and Chicopee Rivers. Alexander Vyce (second row, third from left) would pitch the Chicopee High School Pacers to a record third-straight division-one state baseball championship in 1963. (Courtesy of Anne Jendrysik.)

ON THE COVER: On May 18, 1967, the Iowa Caravan, a delegation of Midwest Chamber of Commerce members, arrived at Westover Air Force Base. Mayor Demers (dark suit, left) was on hand with Chicopee Chamber of Commerce members to welcome the visitors. (Courtesy of the Chicopee Chamber of Commerce.)

IMAGES
of America

CHICOPEE
1950–1975

Stephen R. Jendrysik

ARCADIA
PUBLISHING

ISBN 978-0-7385-7661-9

Published by Arcadia Publishing
Charleston, South Carolina

Printed in the United States of America

Library of Congress Control Number: 2011931592

For all general information, please contact Arcadia Publishing:
Telephone 843-853-2070
Fax 843-853-0044
E-mail sales@arcadiapublishing.com
For customer service and orders:
Toll-Free 1-888-313-2665

Visit us on the Internet at www.arcadiapublishing.com

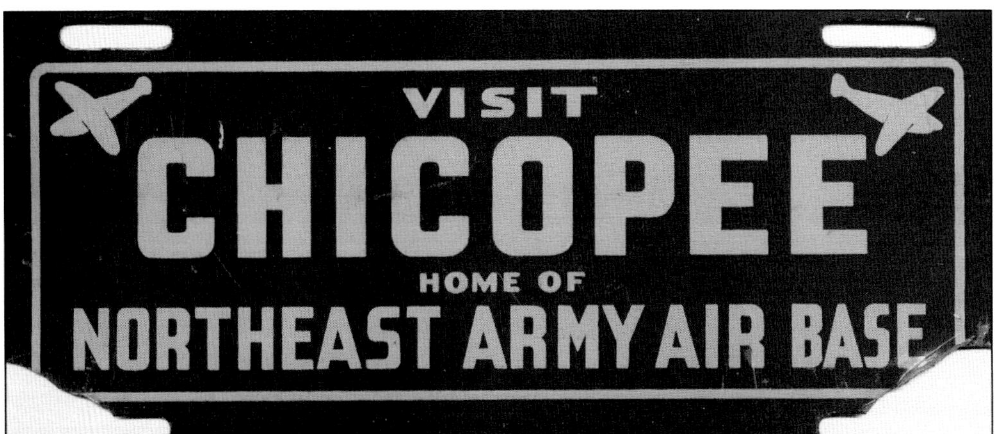

On January 13, 1948, the Northeast Army Air Corps Base in Chicopee, Massachusetts, was redesignated as Westover Air Force Base. The following year, the Defense Department merged the Air Transport Service (ATS) and the Naval Air Transport Service (NATS), creating the Military Air Transport Service of the US Air Force. Westover would become the new command's northeast center. (Westover plate courtesy of the Edward Bellamy Memorial Association.)

Contents

ACKNOWLEDGMENTS

This project has been in the works for nearly four years. Not unlike my three previous efforts, I initially encountered a shortage of appropriate images. Jeff Groleau came to my rescue with his father's personal collection of photographs from Westover Air Force Base. Ron Groleau's primary interest had been the extraordinary achievements of individual US Air Force pilots during the post–World War II era. Peter Gallagher at the *Springfield Republican* newspaper provided several images and was most helpful. Chet Kobierski allowed me to borrow images from his personal and family collections, and Fairview historian and photographer Raymond Burke provided several photographs.

The Peter Bardon Collection, the *Chicopee Herald*, the *Star Press* Collection (photographers: Dick Boisvert, Warren Messenger, and Michael Prystupa), the Walter Mrozinski Collection, the William Santos Collection, the "Bud" Schubach Collection, the St. Stanislaus Holy Name Society Collection, and the Ted Szetela Collections of the Edward Bellamy Memorial Association Archives provided images for the book.

Chicopee's post–World War II history is the double-edged story of the benefits garnered from a diversified industrial base and the location, within its city limits of a vital seven-square-mile federal military facility. The Strategic Air Command's (SAC) actual interaction with the local community was marginal. Within the parameters, the base functioned as a small independent city.

Additionally, I am most appreciative for the technical assistance provided by Alison Kobierski, Dr. Mark Jendrysik, and Dr. John Kozikowski. For the use of their archival materials, I thank the Chicopee Historical Society, the Chicopee Public Library, the Connecticut Valley Historical Museum, the Elms College Library, the MacArthur Memorial Archives, the Chicopee Chamber of Commerce, and the Westover Air Reserve Base. The majority of the images used in the book are from the archives of the Edward Bellamy Memorial Association Incorporated unless otherwise noted.

For willingly sharing their vintage pictures, I am grateful to Michael Baron, Joan Boratis, Pat Burden, Edward Connors, Francine Jasinski Hayward, Anne Jendrysik, Linda Jordan, Helen Kitovich Kennedy, Chester Kobierski, Barbara Leyden, John Moran, William Nieckarz Jr., Joseph Pasternak Jr., Steffi Strycharz, Alexander Vyce , and Joanne Zaskey.

Most importantly, I want to thank my best friend and life partner, my wife, Barbara, for her forbearance and continuing encouragement of her husband's lifetime obsession with the history of Chicopee.

INTRODUCTION

The original meaning of Chicopee is "place where water rushes." By 1831, there were two giant dams, two waterpower canals, and two manufacturing communities on the Chicopee River. In 1950, the city's diversified industrial base was in the midst of an unprecedented postwar expansion. The seven leading local companies that employed more than 10,000 highly skilled unionized workers were A.G. Spalding & Bros. (sporting goods), American Bosch Company (fuel pumps), General Instrument Corporation (formerly the F.W. Sickles Company, radio and television components), Johnson & Johnson Company (the parent company of Chicopee Manufacturing Company, Chix Brand textiles), Moore's Drop Forging Company (Craftsmen tools), Savage Arms Company (sporting rifles and shotguns), United States Rubber Company (formerly Uniroyal, Fisk automobile and truck tires). All were engaged in business on a global scale.

On September 19, 1939, Chicopee mayor Anthony J. Stonina was sitting at his desk wiping away tears. The city's chief executive had just finished reading a letter from the US War Department. The community's agricultural Tobacco Plains had been selected as the site for the Army Air Corps Northeast Base. In 1942, the facility was named to honor the memory of military aviation pioneer Maj. Gen. Oscar Westover and was already the largest air base in the country. In 1945, several Congressional committees were planning the demobilization of the nation's military facilities. Westover Field was never even considered for the closing list. The original seven square miles of the Westover Air Force Base were flat. The base's elevation varied by less than two feet, and the facility's location 100 miles inland destined Chicopee to permanently be a "City with Wings."

In 1956, Westover Field became the home of the 99th Bombardment Wing, the 450th Air Refueling Wing, and the 814th Combat Support Group of the 57th Air Division of the Eighth Air Force. Westover was being reconstructed to meet the needs of the Strategic Air Command's nuclear mission. A Combat Operations Center was built deep in the Mount Holyoke Range. Runways were expanded, and two new maintenance hangars were built. At the Stony Brook Reservation, armament bunkers were constructed to store nuclear bombs.

For 18 years, it was an almost daily event: sonic booms, vapor trails, and the unnerving roar of eight Pratt & Whitney jet engines hurtling the B52 Bomber, the free world's most awesome offensive weapon, into the clouds over the old Pioneer Valley. At its peak, the base was an integral part of the New England economic community. Employing approximately 5,000 military and 850 civilian personnel, the facility had an annual payroll of $57 million. In the region, the Air Force was spending more than $1 million a month to purchase goods and services.

During the tension-filled years of the Cold War, the little city was the fastest-growing community in western New England—a fact not lost on the local citizenry. Westover Field's considerable impact on Chicopee, Massachusetts, is understood and appreciated. Initial misgivings long ago faded into a symbiotic relationship, which continues to this day.

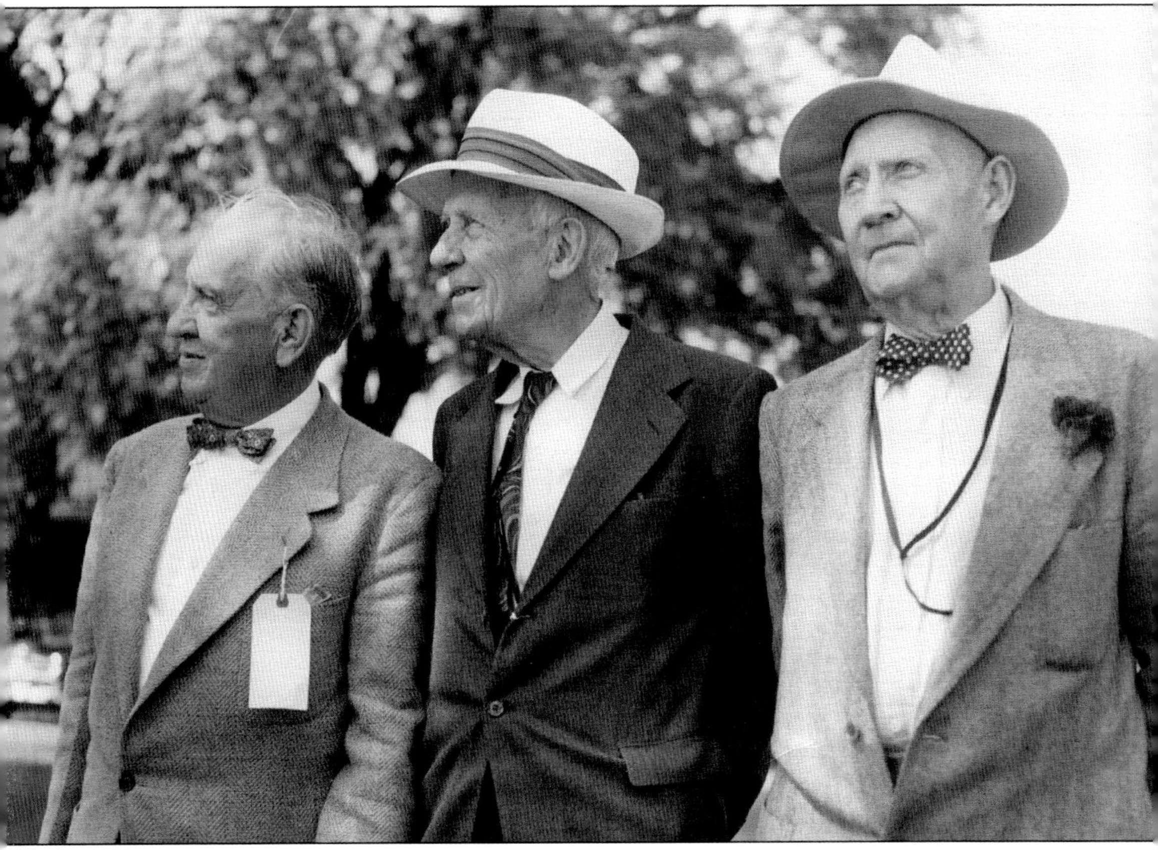

Shown from left to right, A.E. Roberts (74), Archie Brooks (86), and E.S. Bemis (78)—three original members of Chicopee's Oxford Country Club—attend a Professional Golfer Paddy Berg exhibition match at the club on June 7, 1951. (Courtesy of John Pajak.)

One

The Forgotten War
1950–1956

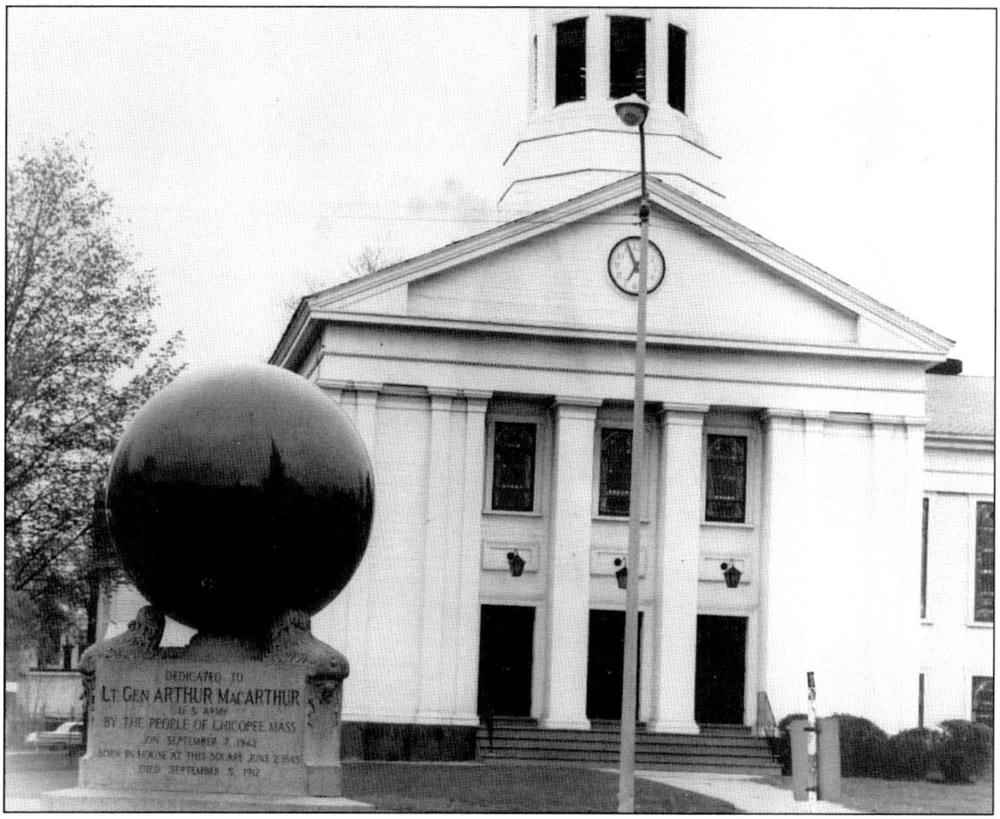

On September 7, 1942, in the middle of the street at the junction of Broadway, East, and Belcher Streets, the city dedicated a memorial honoring Lt. Gen. Arthur MacArthur who was born in 1845 in the Belcher Homestead in Chicopee Falls. In 1951, his son Gen. Douglas MacArthur would visit the birthplace of his father.

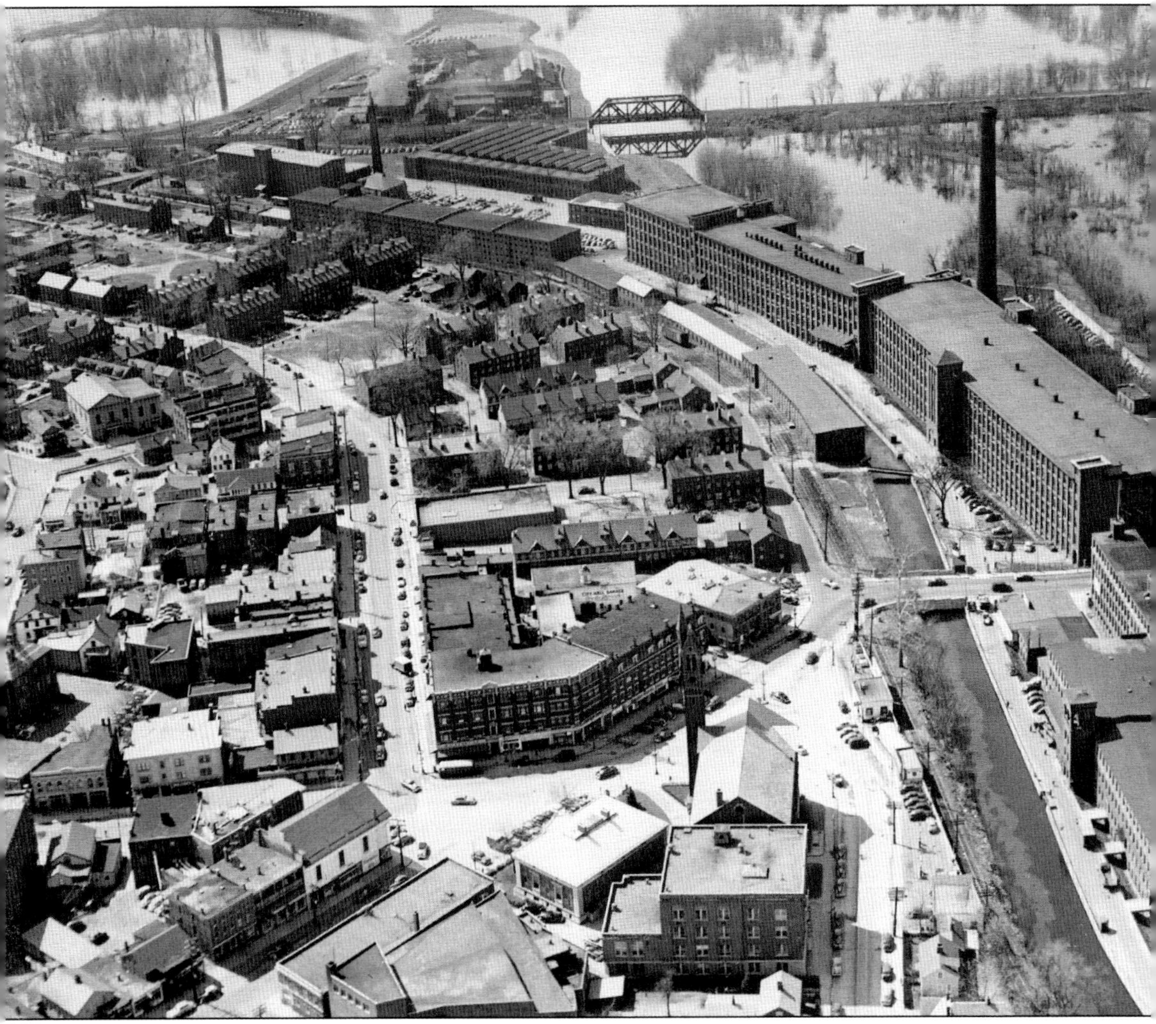

The center of Chicopee was unchanged for decades. It was a classic New England manufacturing community with a network of waterpower canals constructed in the 1820s by immigrant Irish labor. The Boston Associates capitalized the construction of the textile mills, which prospered for nearly 100 years. The company used more than 15 million pounds of cotton annually to manufacture the famous Anchor brand of cotton cloth. The company served a global market. The Dwight Anchor brand of sheeting was the Cadillac of cotton sheets, while the Star brand was the nation's best-selling bedsheet. In 1924, the banking house of J.P. Morgan & Company of New York established operational control of the mills. In three years, Morgan interests shut down the entire operation. The company moved to Alabama, idling 2,000 Chicopee workers. During the decade of the 1950s, the tenement buildings constructed by the Dwight Manufacturing Company in the 19th century would be replaced by new retail stores and the parking lots necessary to accommodate the unprecedented increase of downtown traffic.

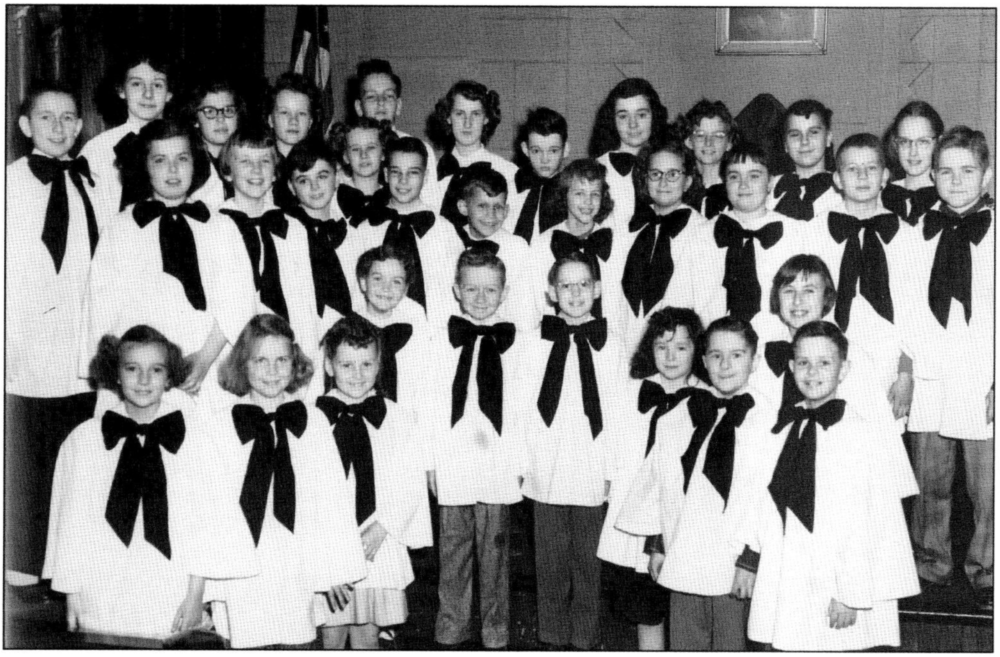

In 1950, the bright faces of these baby boomers are the result of a successful concert by the Children's Choir of First Methodist Church of Chicopee Falls. The church was first established in 1822 when a group of young people gathered in a room at the Chicopee Manufacturing Company, the community's first textile mill.

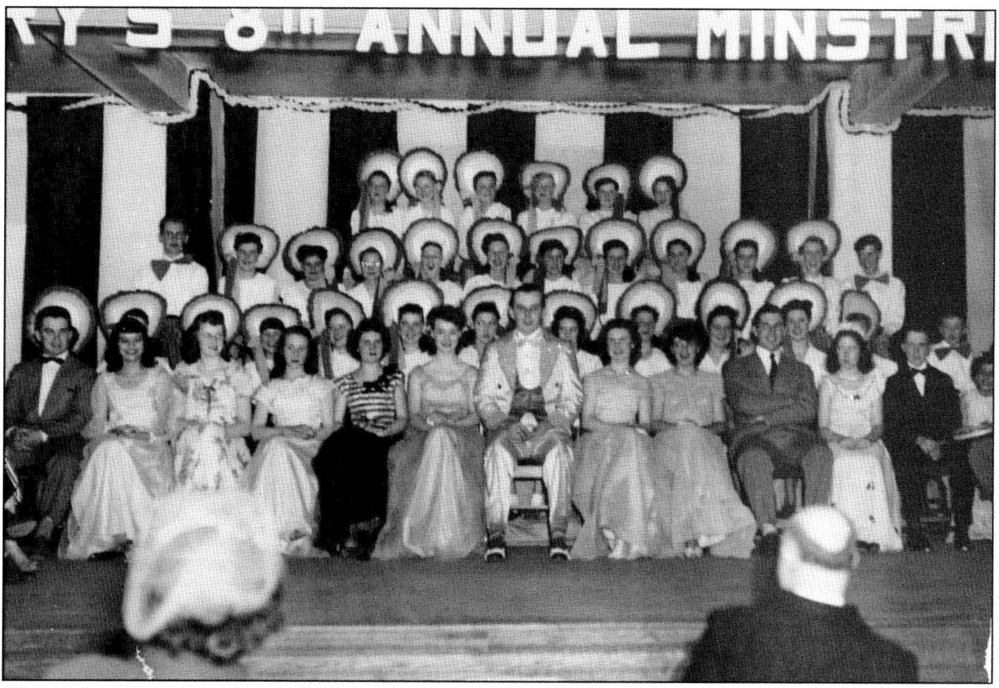

The minstrel show had been a staple of community entertainment since the turn of the century. Here in 1950, the entire cast of the Eighth Annual St. Mary's Parish Minstrel Show is pictured. The three-day event at the Willimansett Parish always sold out.

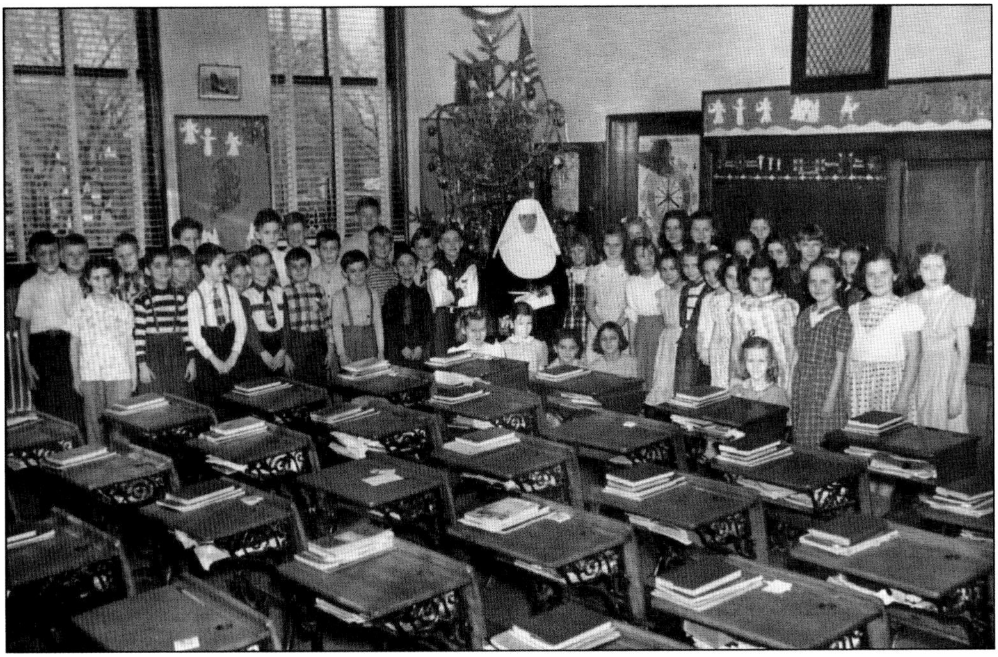

In Chicopee, there were seven Catholic elementary schools and a girl's high school, four French Canadian parishes, three Irish Catholic churches, and three ethnic Polish churches. In the 1950s, St. Stanislaus School on Front Street had the largest enrollment. In 1950, Sister Veronica's fourth-grade class takes time out to pose with the classroom Christmas tree.

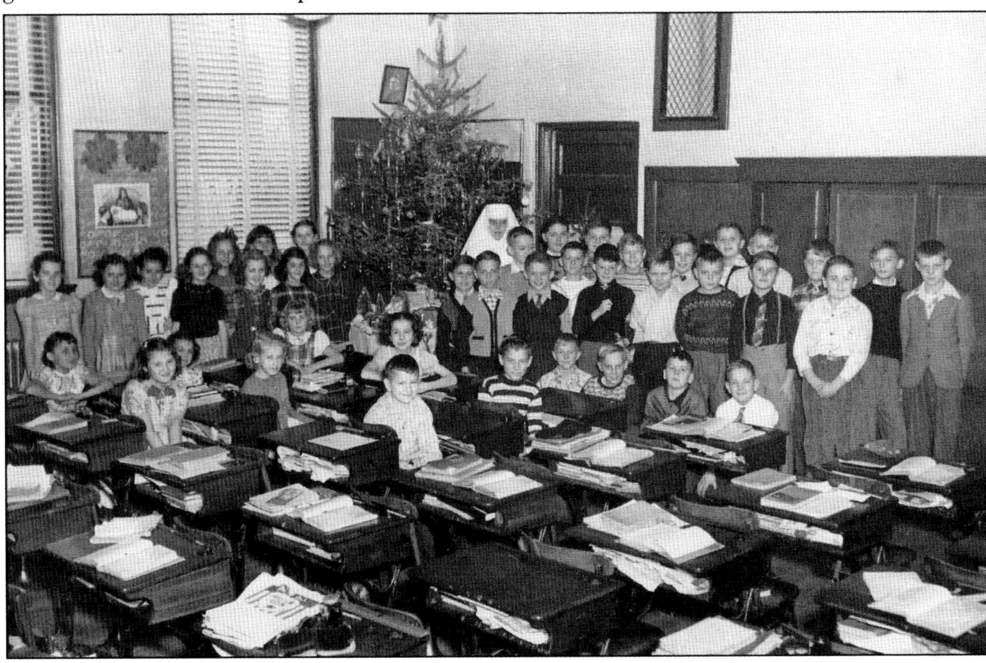

Sister Marietta was the young and very popular fifth-grade teacher at St. Stanislaus School. The teaching sisters made parochial education in the 1950s a viable alternative for working families. The ethnic makeup of the city was reinforced by the presence of a Catholic school in walking distance for most students.

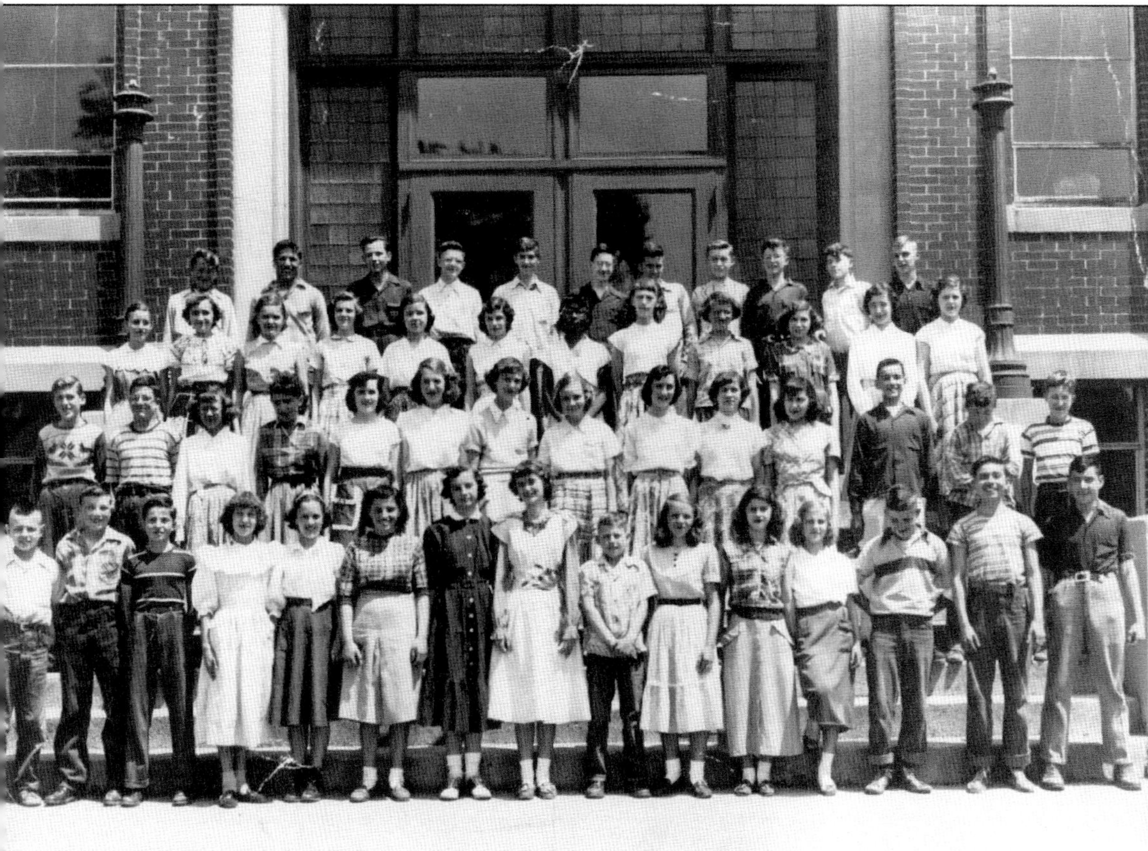

The Patrick E. Bowe School on Hampden Street was the community's top-rated elementary school. In 1950, there were 4,912 students enrolled in the Chicopee Public Schools. There were eight ethnic Catholic parochial schools throughout the city with an enrollment of more than 3,000 pupils. The parochial schools in Chicopee include Holy Name Irish Elementary and High School, Assumption French School, St. Stanislaus Polish School, Mount Carmel French School, Holy Mother of the Rosary Polish National School, and St. Jeanne D'Arc French School. For decades, these students went on to attend Catholic high schools in the neighboring communities of Holyoke and Springfield and Catholic boarding schools around the country. In the 1950s, more than 80 percent of the eighth-grade parochial school graduates went to Chicopee High School. That year, 113 students graduated from Chicopee High School. In the next seven years, the number of high school graduates would double.

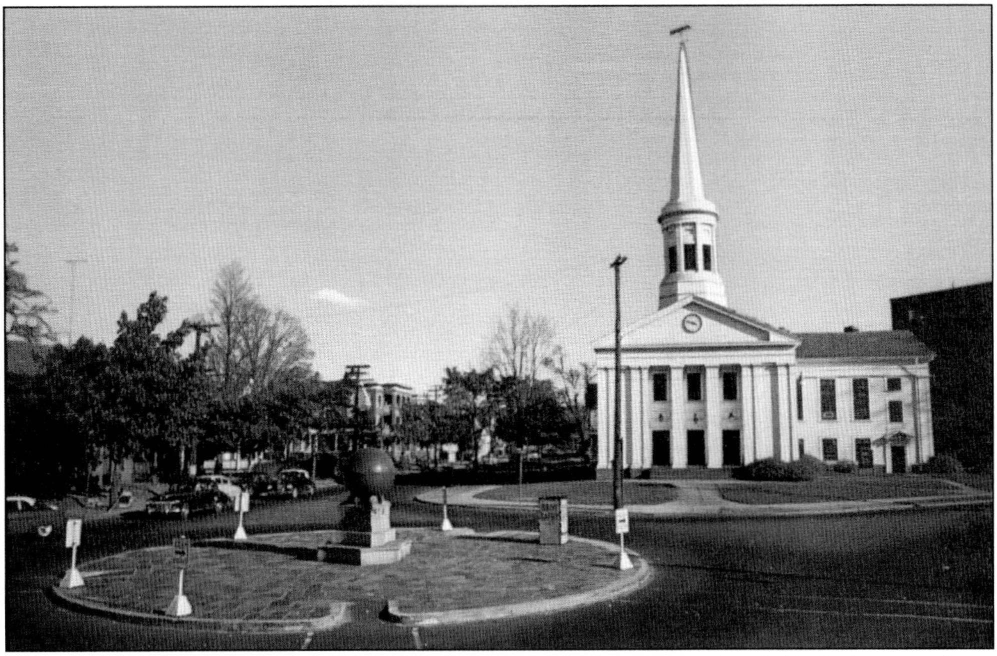

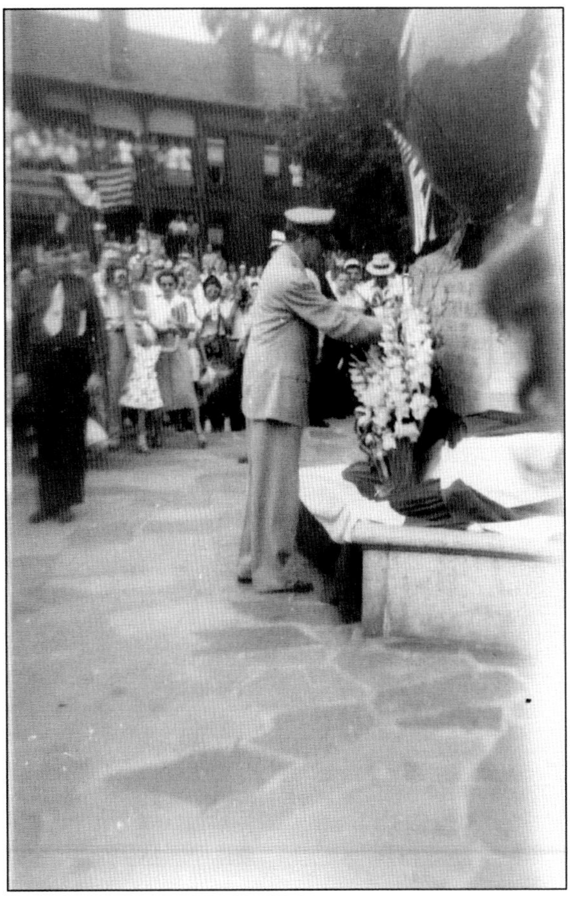

On September 7, 1942, the city of Chicopee dedicated a memorial in honor of Lt. Gen. Arthur MacArthur, the "Boy Colonel of the Civil War." An invitation to the dedication ceremonies was sent to Gen. Douglas MacArthur in Australia. He declined the invitation, but in typical fashion vowed, "I shall return to my father's home."

True to his word, Gen. Douglas MacArthur, relieved of command in Korea by Pres. Harry Truman and the center of a great national debate, made good on his promise to return to his father's home on July 26, 1951.

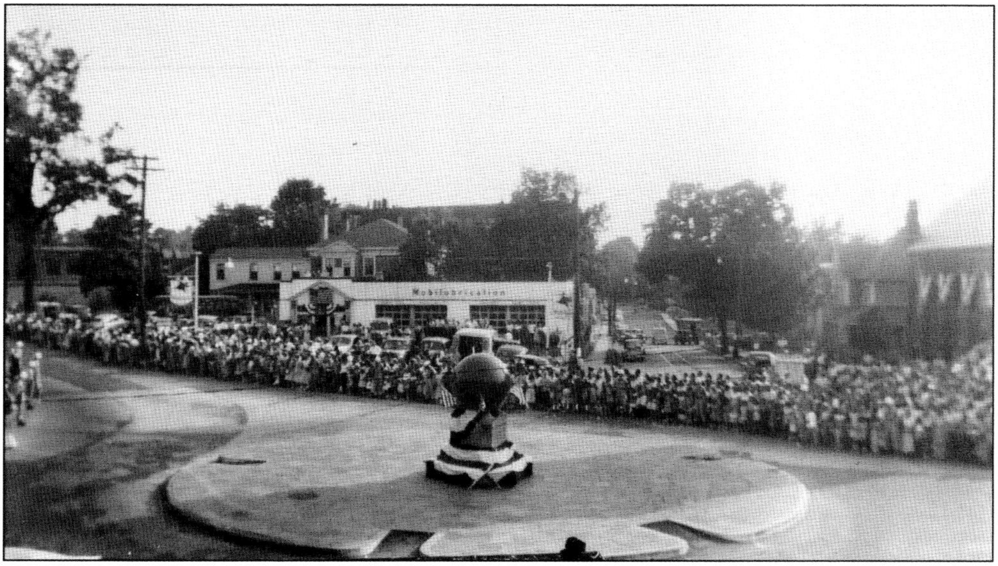

Gen. Douglas MacArthur arrived to the cheers of more than 80,000 people lining the route from Union Station in Springfield to the center of Chicopee Falls. The Springfield Union reported that more than 10,000 men, women, and children stood in reverend silence as the hero of the Pacific War addressed the assemblage.

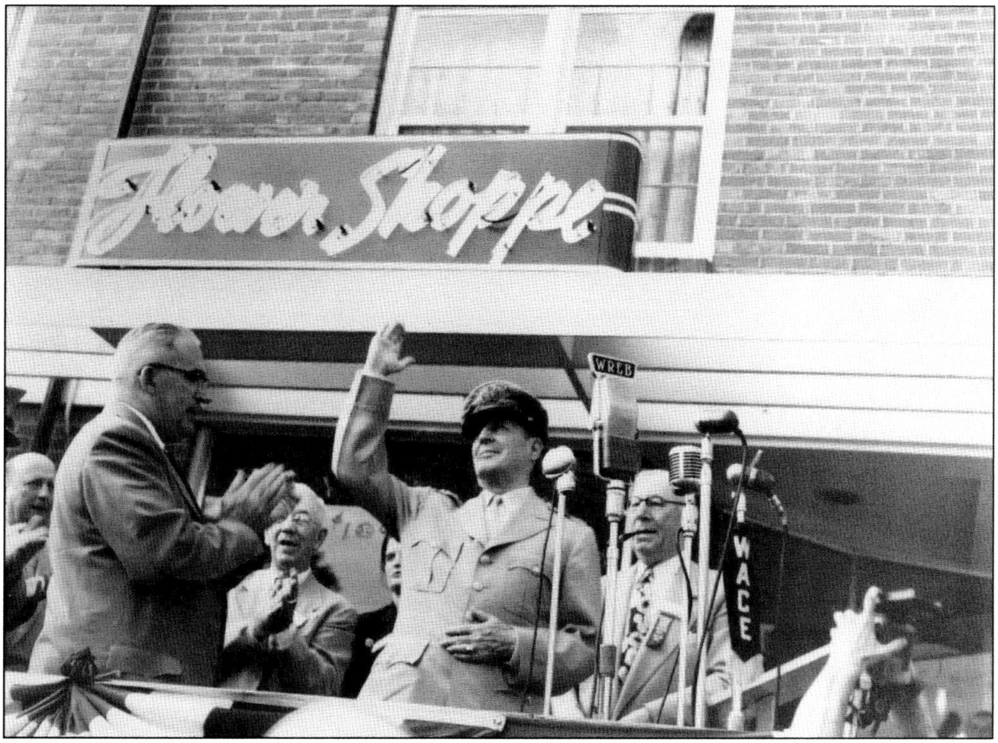

For Gen. Douglas MacArthur, a man who had lived in military posts all his life, the monument, the Belcher Homestead, and the visit to his grandmother's grave were a very special homecoming. The picture of the general responding to the cheering crowd was taken by Chicopee Falls resident Roland Coderre.

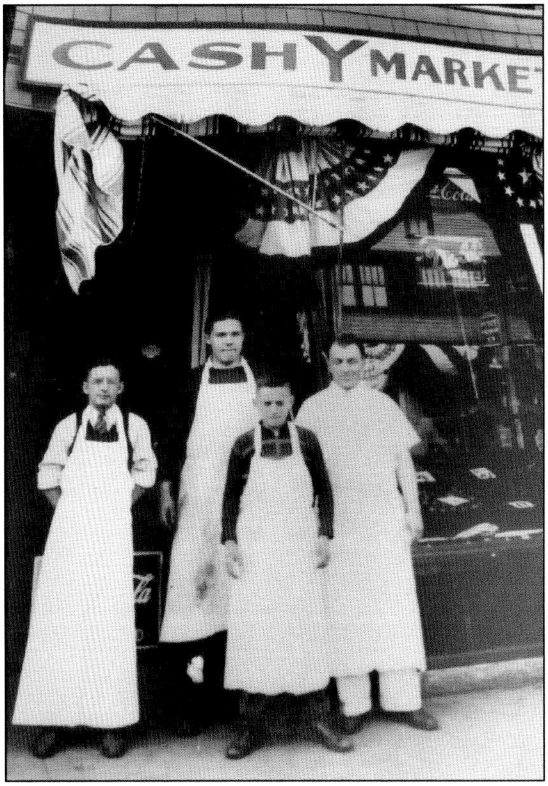

The Big Y story began in the Willimansett section of Chicopee. The company takes its name from the crossroads of Chicopee and Meadow Streets in the center of the little community. With less than $10,000 in family savings and a small bank loan, Paul D'Amour (right) bought the 900-square-foot market in 1936. Paul and his staff are pictured in front of the Big Y Cash Market in 1939.

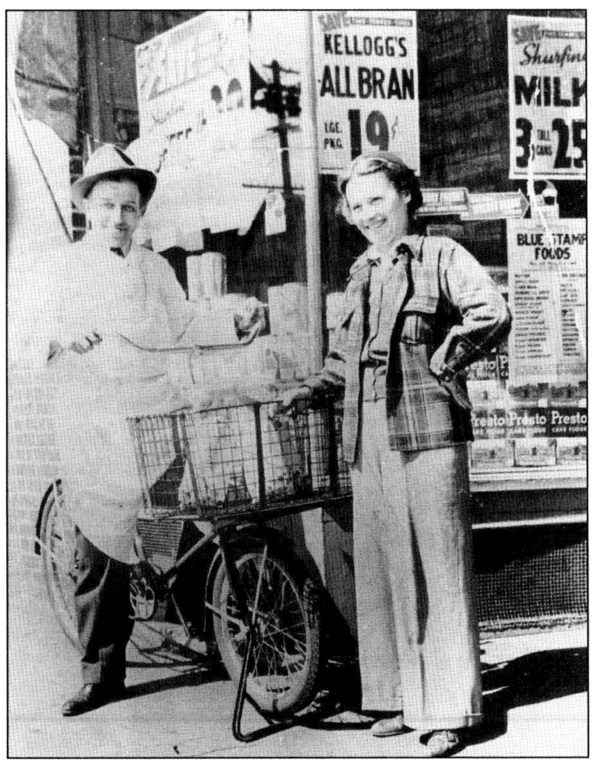

Paul D'Amour and his wife, Yvette, prepare a bike for grocery delivery. When Paul's brother Gerald returned after four years in the Army Air Corps, he joined the company as an equal partner, and they opened a second Y Cash Market on Grattan Street in the Aldenville section of the city. In this picture, Paul and Yvette D'Amour prepare a wartime delivery.

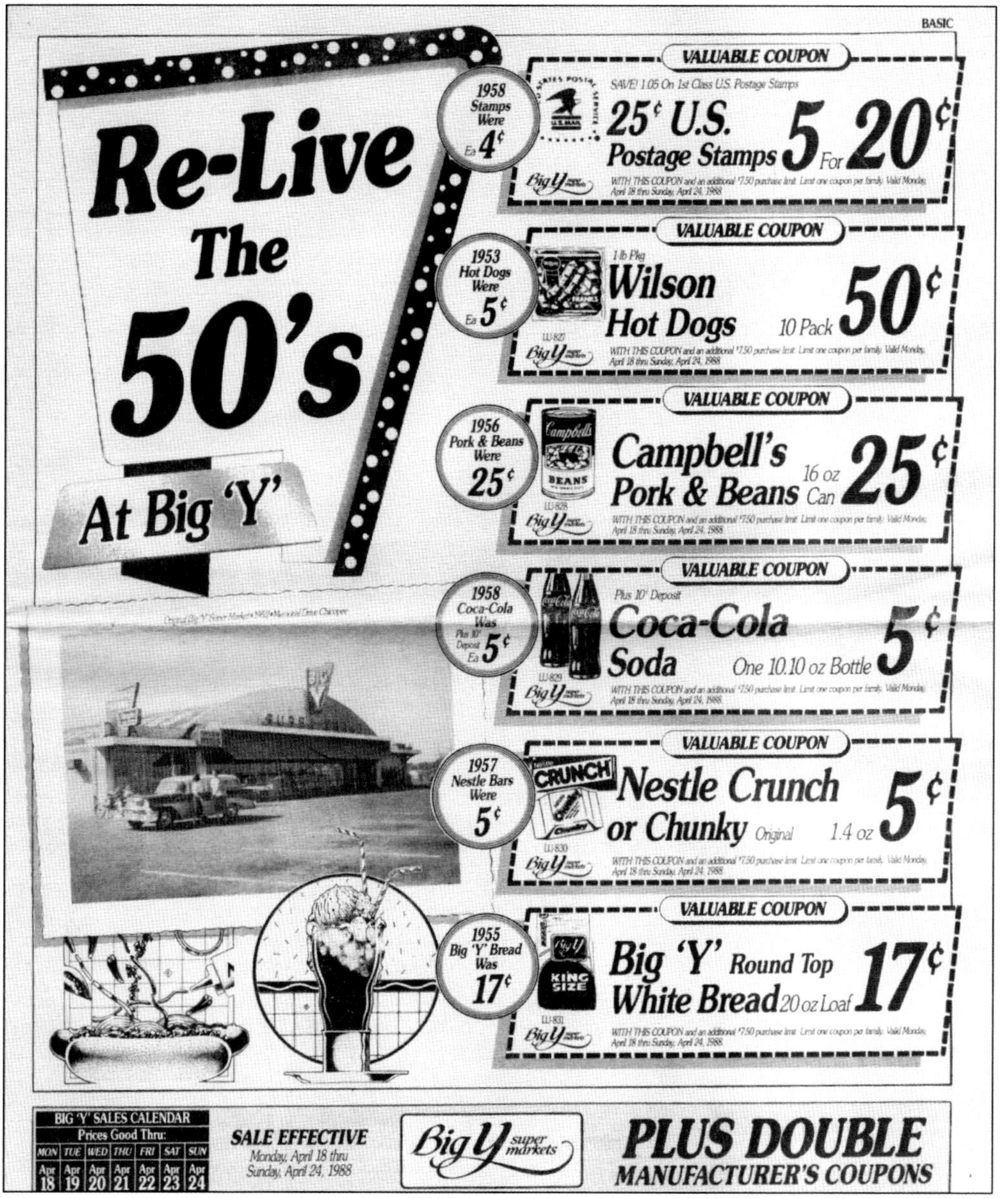

In 1988, the Big Y weekly circular featured sale prices from the 1950s. Pictured in the advertisement is the area's first supermarket, which the D'Amours opened on Memorial Drive in 1952. The D'Amours understood the fast-moving life changes taking place in the 1950s. The grocery business was changing rapidly. Gone forever were the days of full service, customer credit, five-cent bread, and after-school delivery boys. It was the beginning of high-powered media advertising, competitive pricing, and a huge selection in a giant store. Paul and Gerry had moved their operation to a huge Quonset hut with the first branch bank of the Chicopee Saving next door. They were in the super-store business. The bold move was the beginning of a great American success story. Today, Big Y Foods, Inc., is the seventh-largest privately held company in Massachusetts with $1.4 billion in revenue. In New England, the D'Amour family operates 60 stores, employs nearly 4,000 workers, and is the only locally owned supermarket chain in the region.

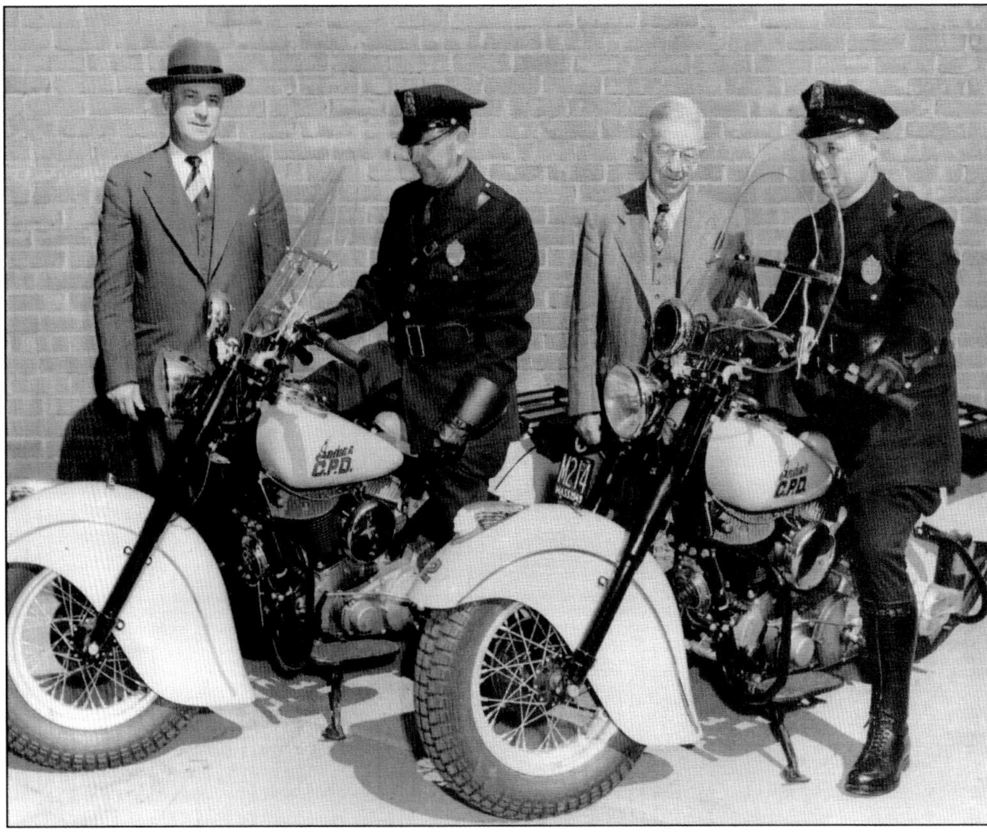

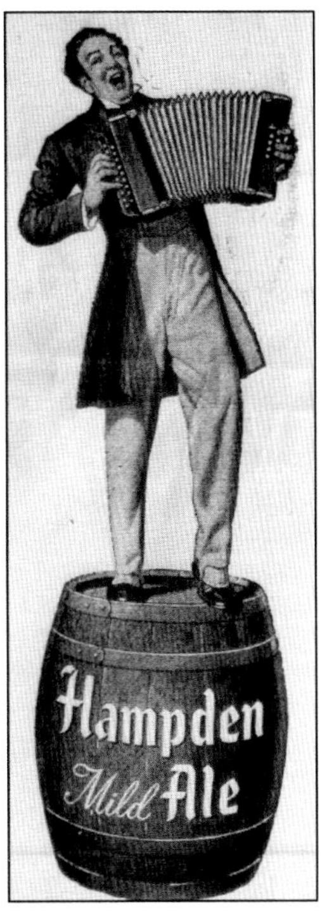

In 1950, Chicopee's new police chief, Theodore A. Fisher, convinced Mayor Edward Bourbeau to bring back the department's motorcycle patrol. The new machines were purchased from the Indian Motorcycle factory in Springfield, Massachusetts. From left to right are Chief Fisher, an unidentified officer, Mayor Bourbeau, and officer Joseph Orszak; the officers are sitting on their new Indian Scout motorcycles. (Courtesy of David Orszak.)

Facing the Willimansett Bridge in the 1950s was a giant billboard featuring a young, dark-haired man attired in a 19th-century waistcoat astride a giant keg of beer. He was playing an accordion. In 1937, Hampden Brewing built a modern bottling plant adjacent to the old brew house. In 20 years, the company had 300 employees and was considered the best place to work in the city.

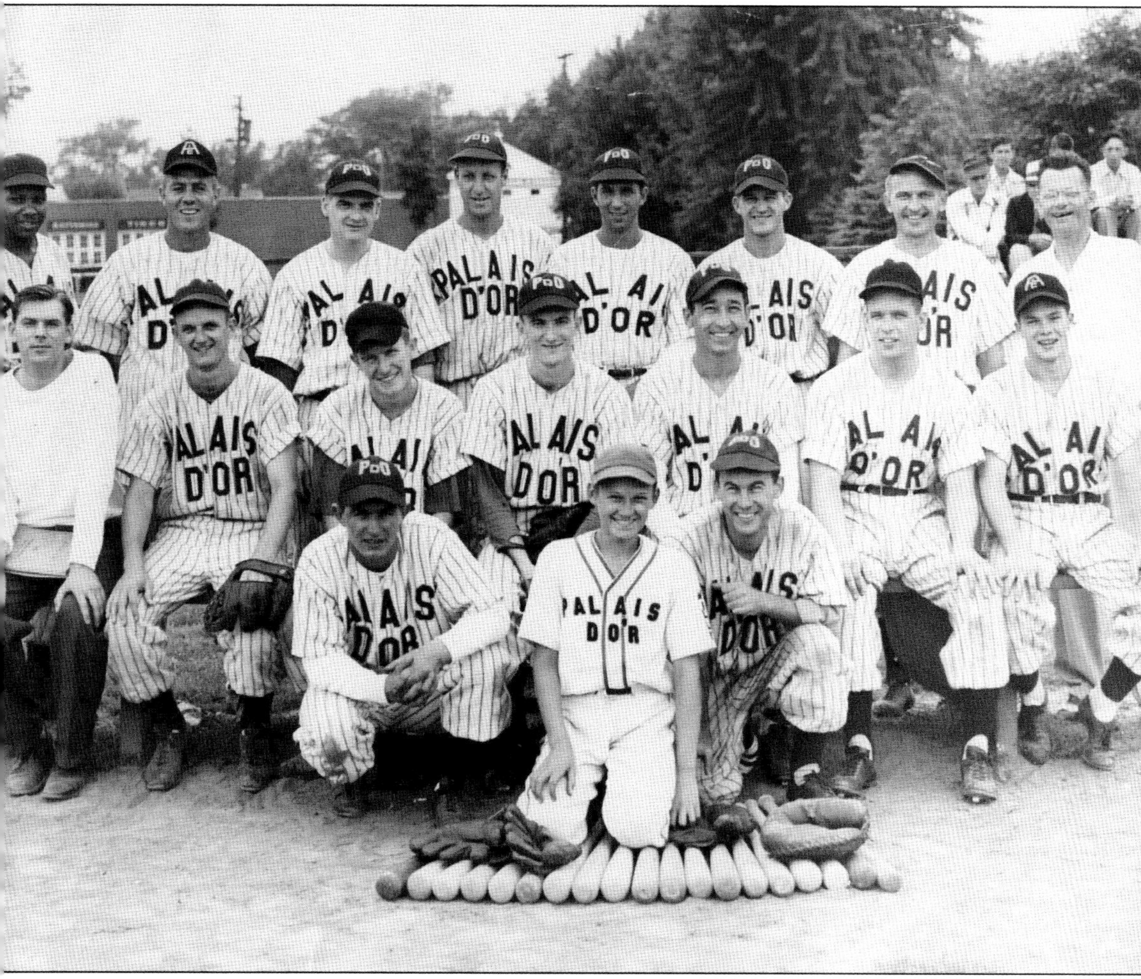

In 1952, semiprofessional baseball was still drawing large crowds on weekends. In western Massachusetts, televised major league games on a regular basis were still a few years into the future. Some of the prewar old-timers were still suiting up, but they were being replaced by young, far more talented athletes from nearby colleges and universities. Before World War II, factories offered employment to the best young players in the region. They played on the company teams in the highly competitive industrial leagues. Team sponsorships ended in the 1950s, and the leagues folded. Local sportsman Willie Nieckarz Sr. sponsored his Palais D'or team in both city and tricounty leagues. He recruited an all-star unit, which dominated both leagues at the beginning of the decade. Willie Nieckarz Jr., the team's batboy never played the game. Instead, he went on to MIT and Carnegie Tech, earning a doctorate in nuclear engineering.

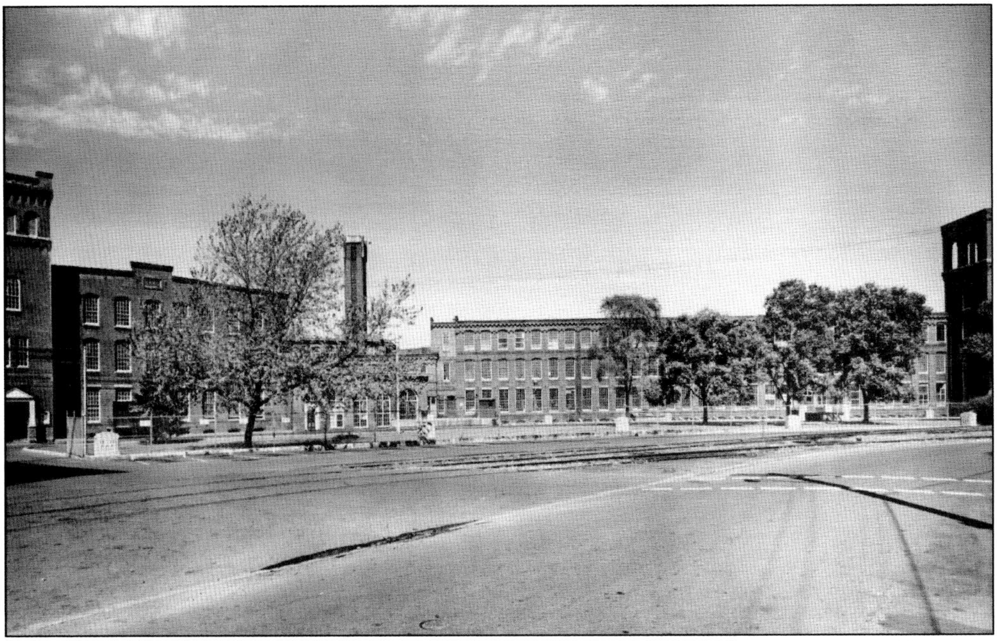

In 1822, Jonathan Dwight purchased a large track of land and the water privilege in Chicopee Falls. By 1827, the company had two four-story brick factories containing 7,000 spindles and 240 looms. Pictured in the 1950s, the Chicopee Manufacturing Company is a thriving textile facility at this time.

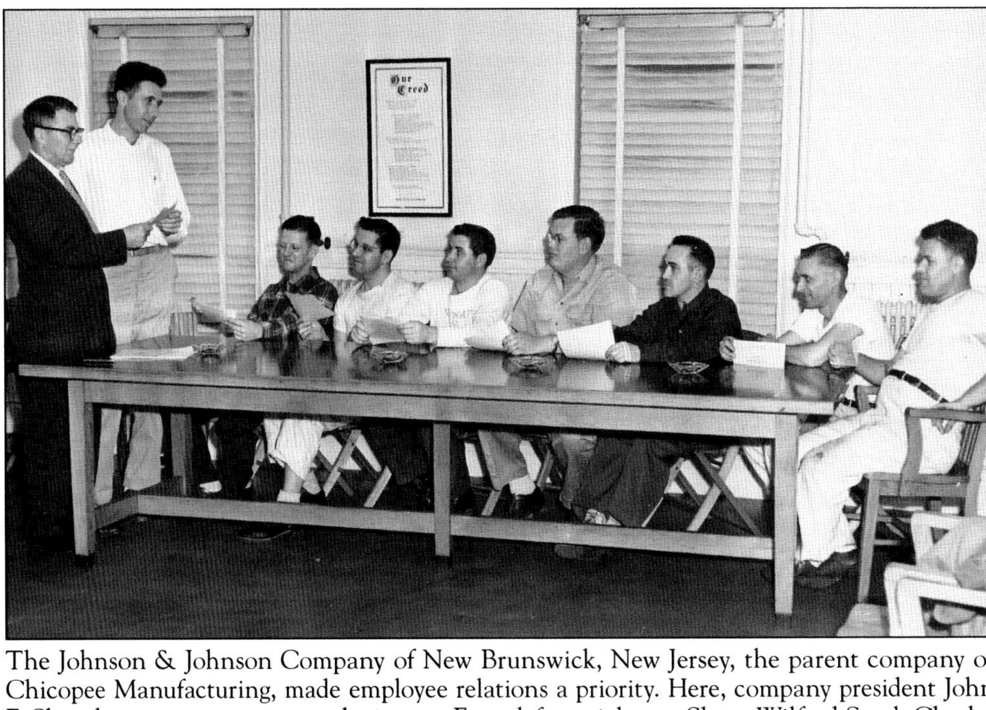

The Johnson & Johnson Company of New Brunswick, New Jersey, the parent company of Chicopee Manufacturing, made employee relations a priority. Here, company president John F. Shaw honors suggestion award winners. From left to right are Shaw, Wilfred Sorel, Charles Starzyk, Max Lentowski, Clifford Chisholm, Bill Tyndall, Stanley Supinski, Walter Zajaczkowski, and Anthony Crochiere.

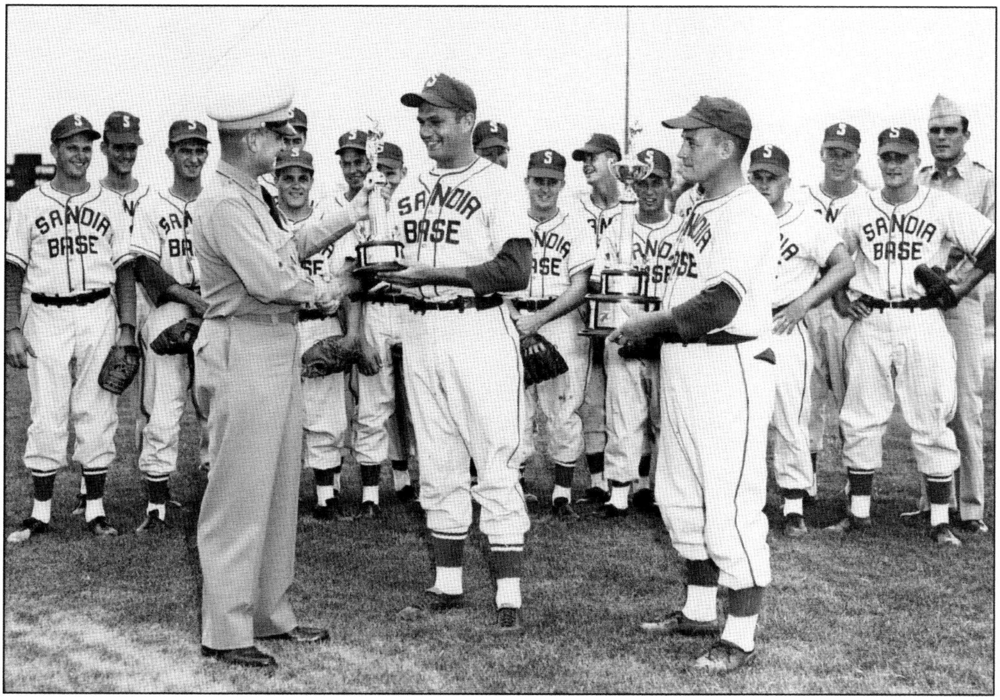

Clarence "Clarky" Wojtowicz was Chicopee's version of *The Natural.* After his graduation from Suffield Academy, he signed with the New York Yankees in June 1949. Before and after time lost to military service, Wojtowicz advanced to the Yankee's triple-A team, the Kansas City Blues, but never got a shot at the big leagues. He is pictured at center on his service team as he receives the most valuable player trophy.

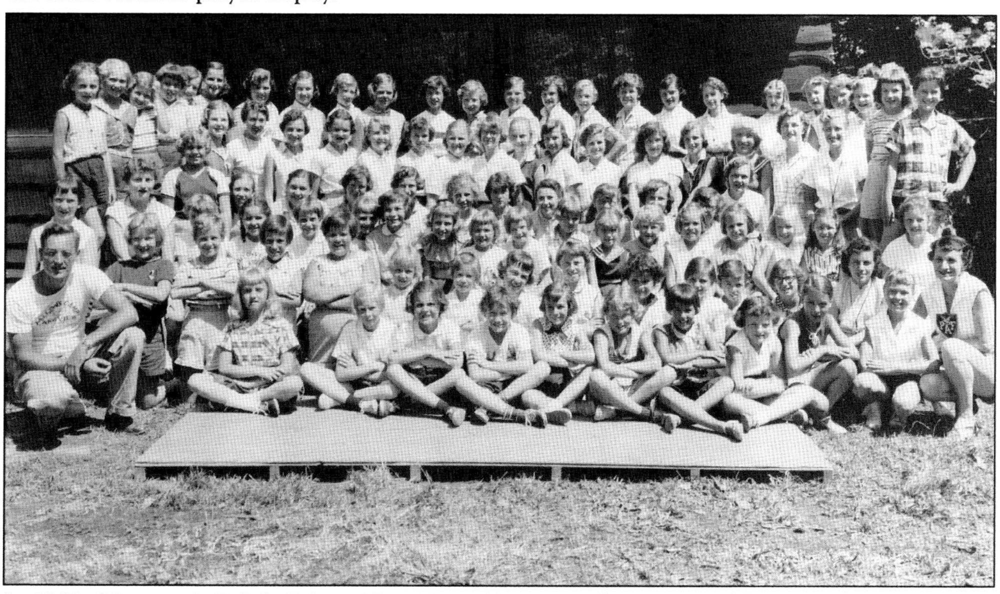

In 1952, Chicopee's Polish Falcon Nest No. 855 was nearly 50 years old. Originally founded for first-generation Polish Americans, the organization was now serving their children. The motto, "A Healthy Spirit in a Healthy Body" is clearly evident in this group of Chicopee youngsters attending Falcon Youth Camp in Connecticut.

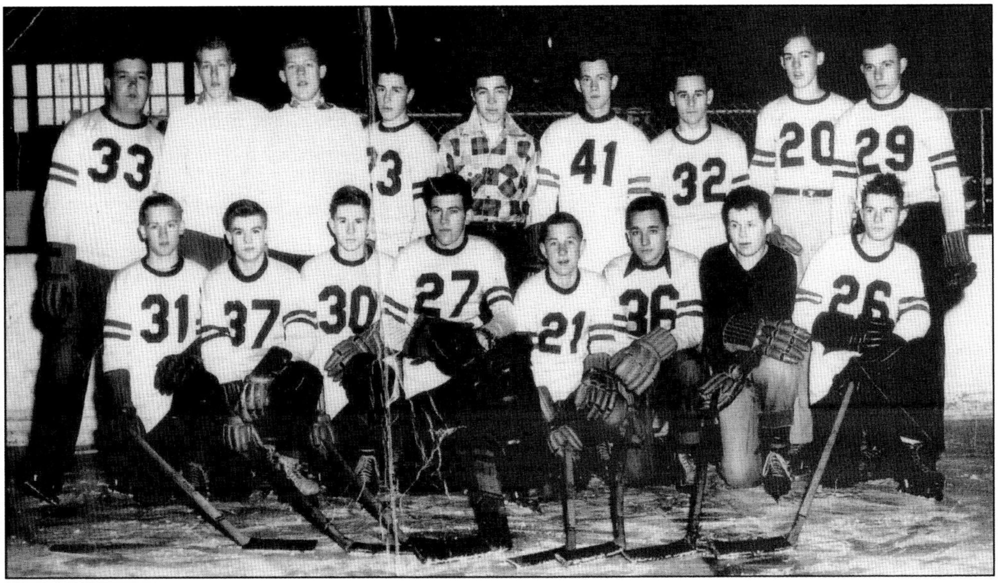

The Chicopee Falls Braves won the 14–16 age division of the Springfield Junior Amateur Hockey League. In 1953, six members of the team would be the core of Chicopee High School's first varsity hockey team. They were Bill Plummer, Stan Piantek, Joe Trela, Ed Gwodz, Roland Bibeau, and Stan and Walt Strycharz.

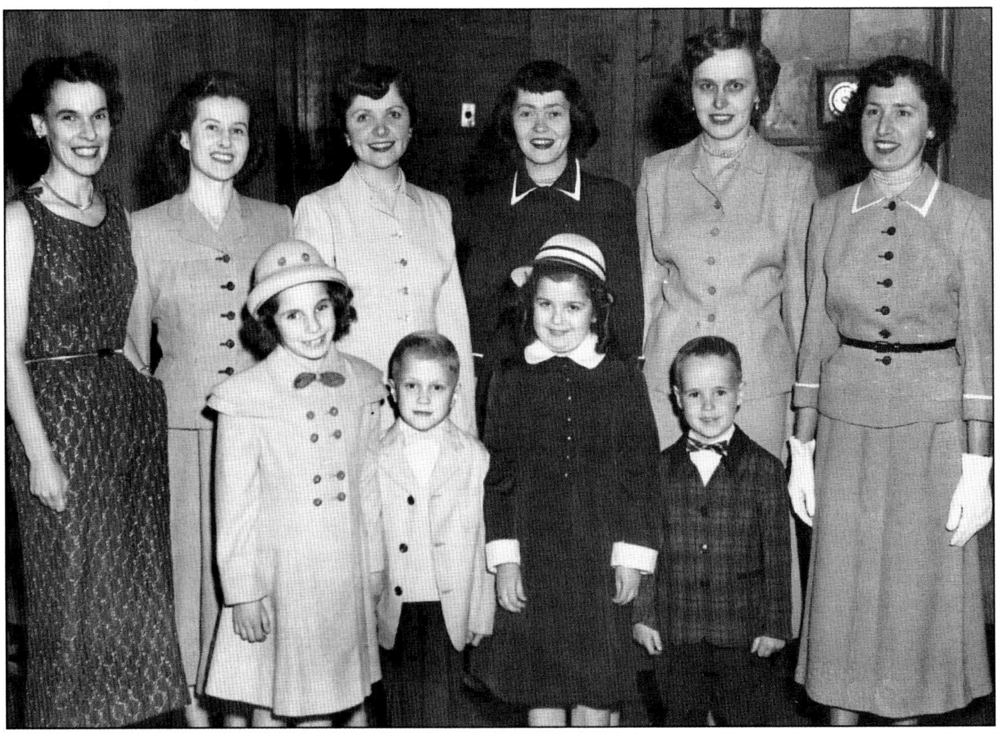

The postwar growth of parent-teacher associations expanded rapidly in the 1950s as school administrators encouraged parents to become involved in neighborhood public schools. Fashion shows and card parties were popular fundraisers. Pictured in 1952, parents, teachers, and students participate in a fashion show at the Kirby School in the Willimansett section of the city.

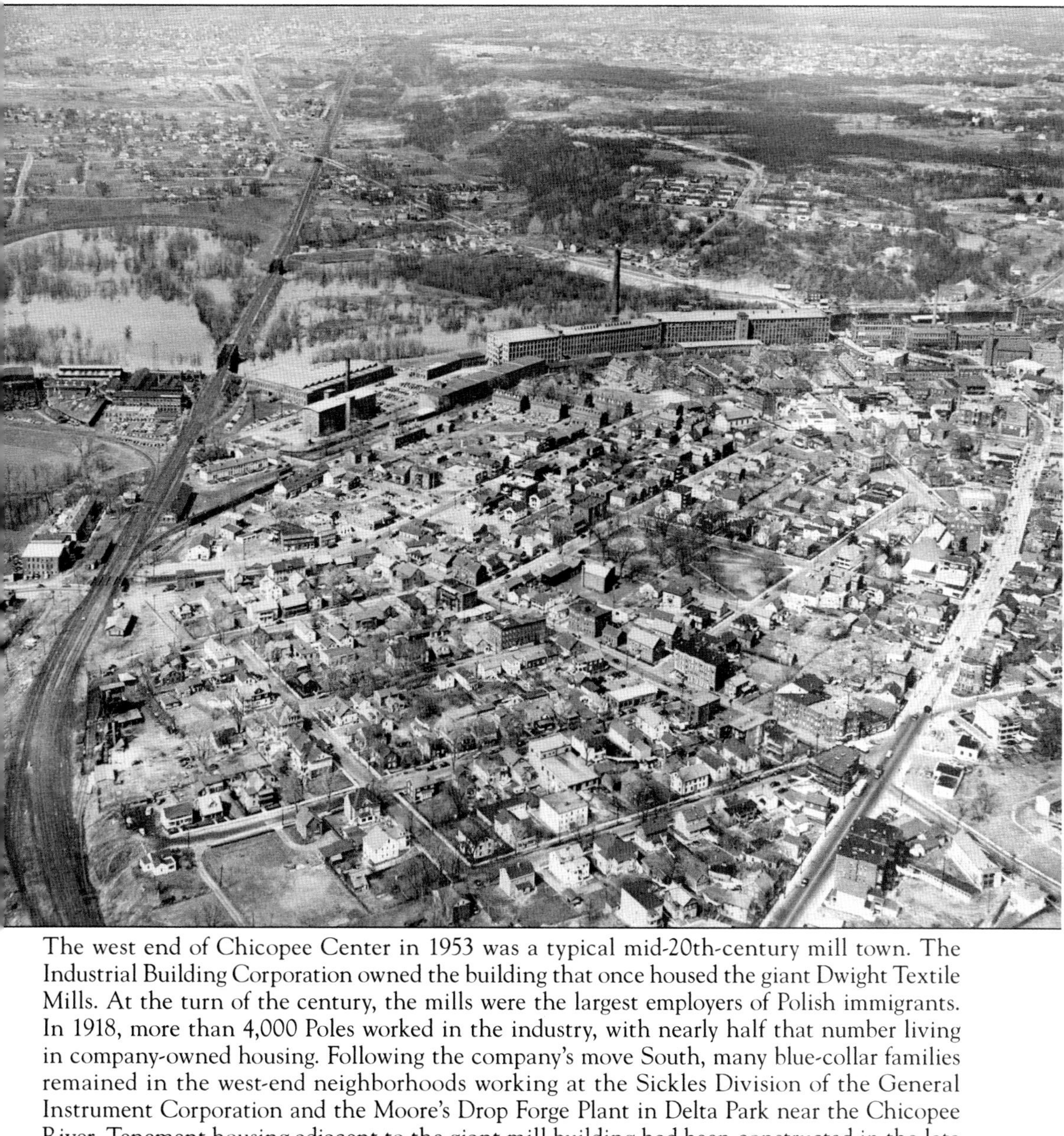

The west end of Chicopee Center in 1953 was a typical mid-20th-century mill town. The Industrial Building Corporation owned the building that once housed the giant Dwight Textile Mills. At the turn of the century, the mills were the largest employers of Polish immigrants. In 1918, more than 4,000 Poles worked in the industry, with nearly half that number living in company-owned housing. Following the company's move South, many blue-collar families remained in the west-end neighborhoods working at the Sickles Division of the General Instrument Corporation and the Moore's Drop Forge Plant in Delta Park near the Chicopee River. Tenement housing adjacent to the giant mill building had been constructed in the late 19th century. The area featured two-, three-, and six-family dwellings. All were constructed in easy walking distance of the place of employment.

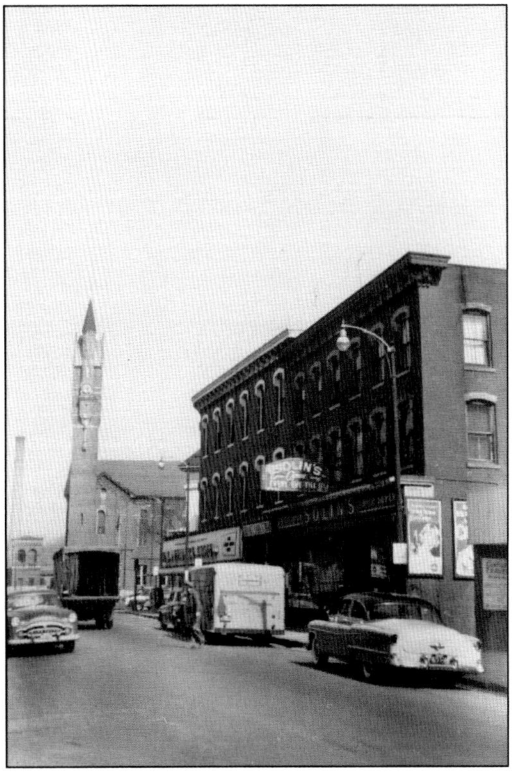

On September 21, 1953, in Chicopee's Market Square, people were going about their daily tasks. The highway department was cordoning off the downtown area. Residents were peering skyward hoping to get a glimpse of the *Columbine* (the official name of the president's Lockheed Constellation). Pres. Dwight D. Eisenhower would be the first president to visit the area by air. (Courtesy of Chet Kobierski.)

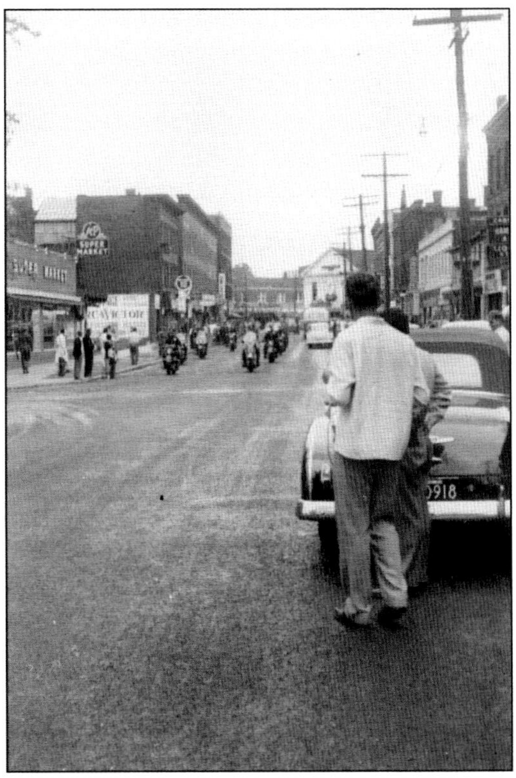

The presidential motorcade would proceed via Granby Road and Chicopee Center. The president encountered the largest crowd on the steps of Chicopee's city hall. There were only a small number of youngsters in the gathering because the schools were not closed. Pictured here, the motorcade turns onto Exchange Street. (Courtesy of Chet Kobierski.)

President Eisenhower acknowledged well-wishers as the presidential limousine sped down Exchange Street to the bridge. The new president was making his first visit to the region and was to be the guest of honor at a special New England governor's reception in the Massachusetts Building at the Eastern States Exposition in West Springfield, Massachusetts. (Courtesy of Chet Kobierski.)

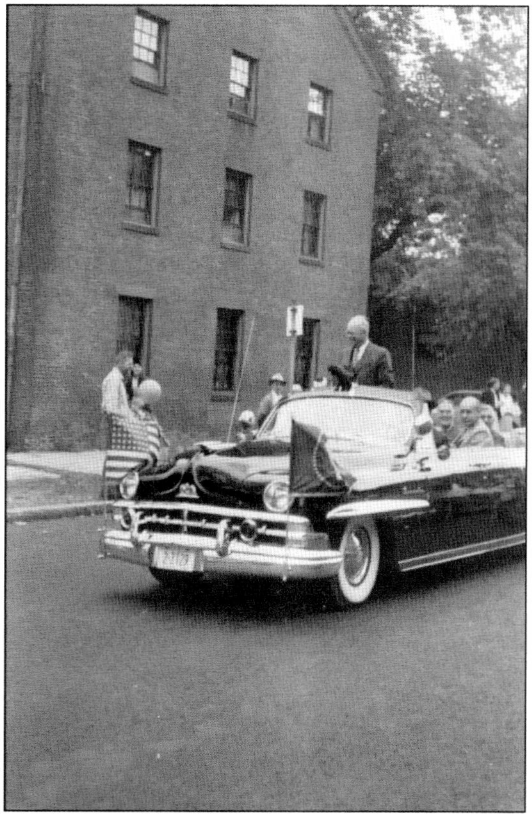

In 1953, Edwin Jasinski was home for the weekend on Gilmore Street in Chicopee. He is sitting on the boot of a Cadillac convertible signing autographs for the neighborhood children. Jasinski played the role of Clarabell the Clown on television's *Howdy Doody* program. (Courtesy of the Jasinski family.)

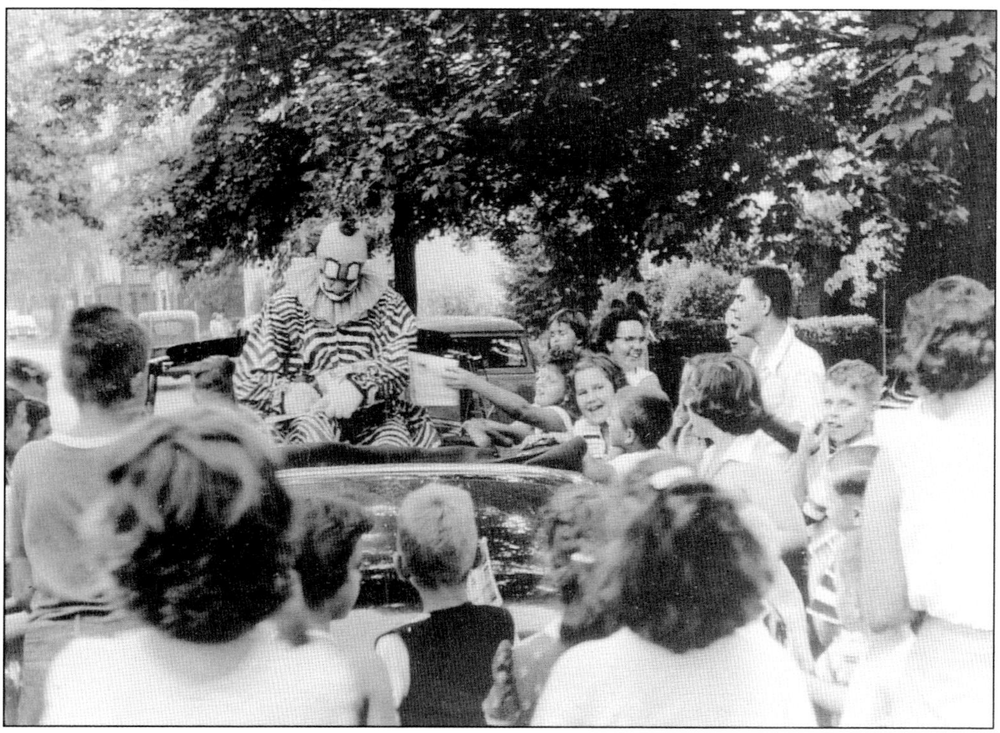

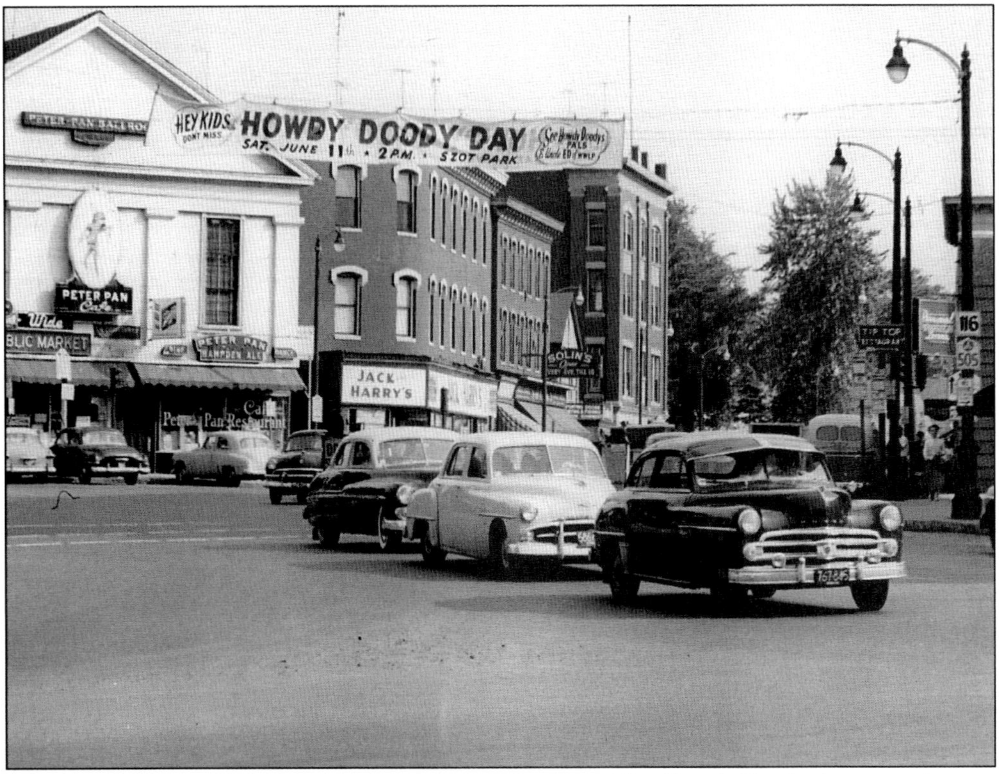

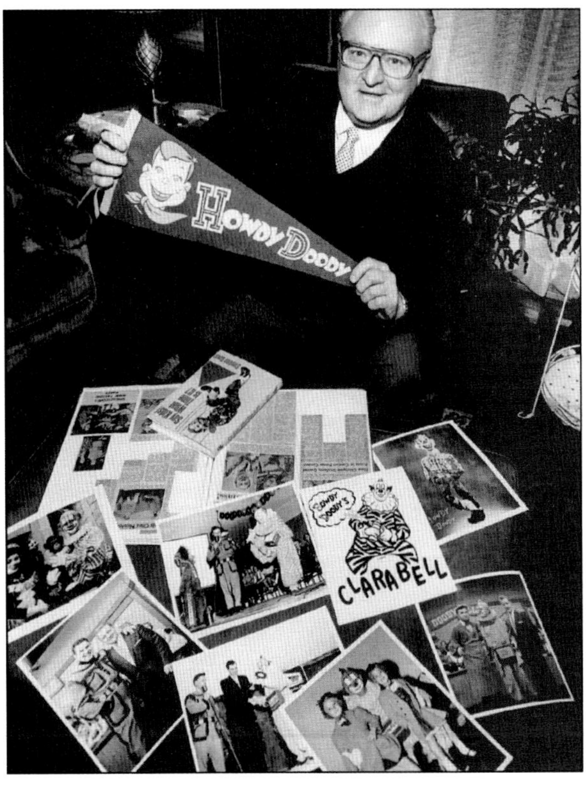

The *Howdy Doody* show was the nation's most popular children's program. In his clown costume, the Chicopee native ran around the stage dousing the show's star Buffalo Bob Smith with seltzer water. A banner across Chicopee's Market Square welcomed the local celebrity, who headlined a special children's show at Szot Park. (Courtesy of the Jasinski Family.)

Edwin Jasinski returned to Chicopee after a brief stint as the mute clown on the landmark, multimillion-dollar television show. His performing career ended when he established a successful advertising agency in Springfield and Chicopee. Here, he reviews his collection of *Howdy Doody* memorabilia.

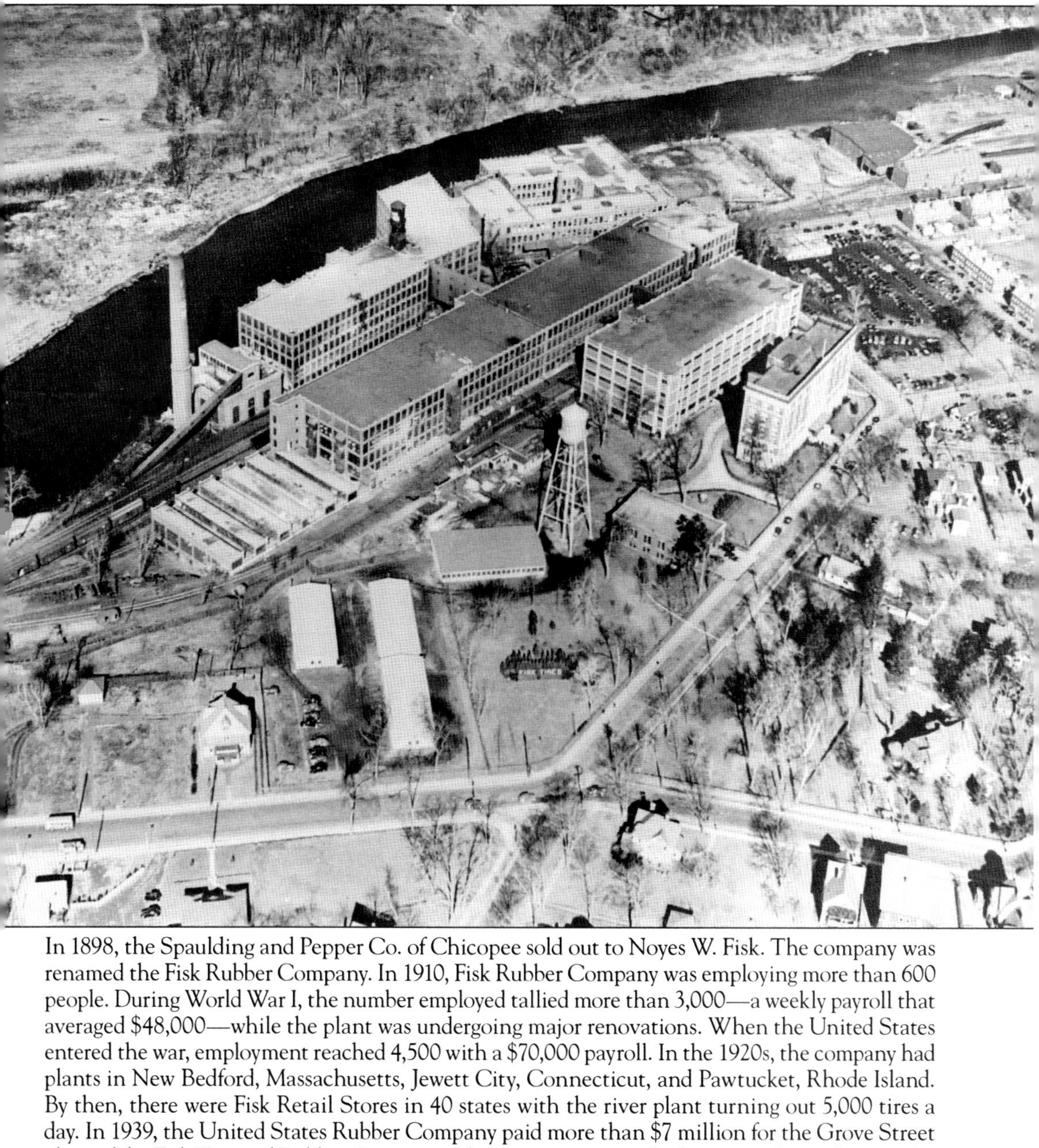

In 1898, the Spaulding and Pepper Co. of Chicopee sold out to Noyes W. Fisk. The company was renamed the Fisk Rubber Company. In 1910, Fisk Rubber Company was employing more than 600 people. During World War I, the number employed tallied more than 3,000—a weekly payroll that averaged $48,000—while the plant was undergoing major renovations. When the United States entered the war, employment reached 4,500 with a $70,000 payroll. In the 1920s, the company had plants in New Bedford, Massachusetts, Jewett City, Connecticut, and Pawtucket, Rhode Island. By then, there were Fisk Retail Stores in 40 states with the river plant turning out 5,000 tires a day. In 1939, the United States Rubber Company paid more than $7 million for the Grove Street plant of the Fisk Tire and Rubber Company. The transaction was the biggest such purchase in the history of the rubber industry. In 1953, the Fisk tire plant of the United States Rubber Company was Chicopee's largest employer with a manufacturing and office staff of 4,100.

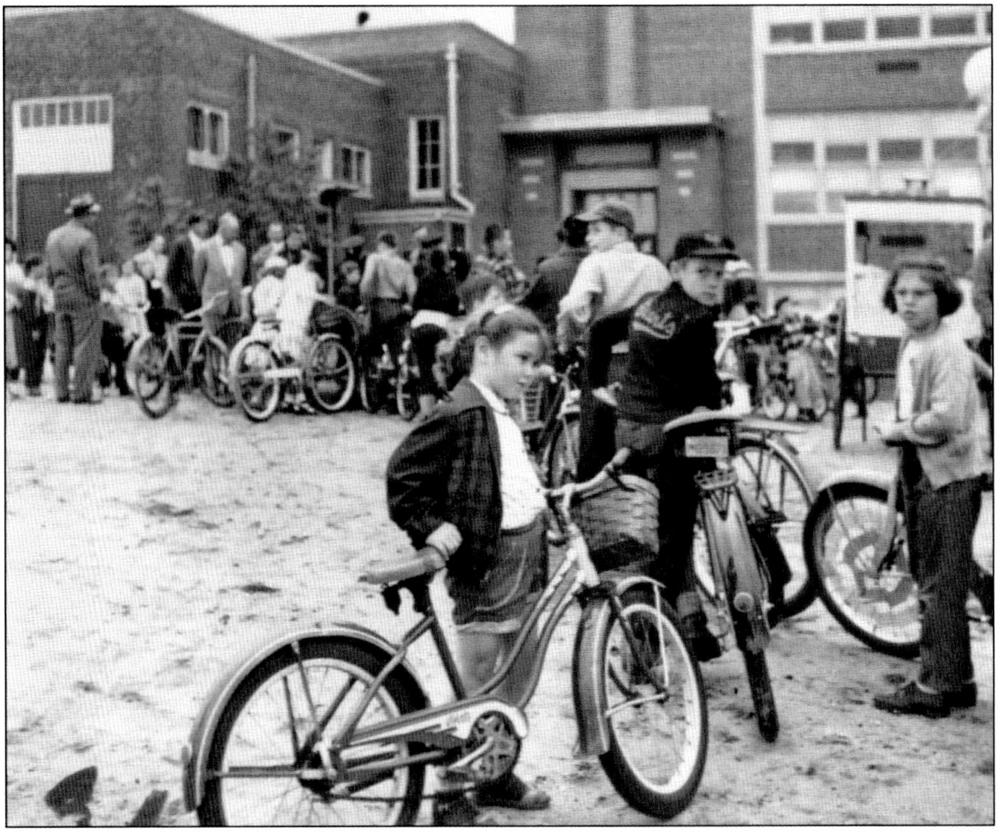

Russ Campbell was in the production department at the Fisk Rubber Company and a director of the Fairview Boy's Club. Campbell was a community leader in the Fairview section of Chicopee; he organized a bicycle field day at Vaillancourt Memorial Park near the Fairview Memorial School. Youngsters arrived to register for the seven events.

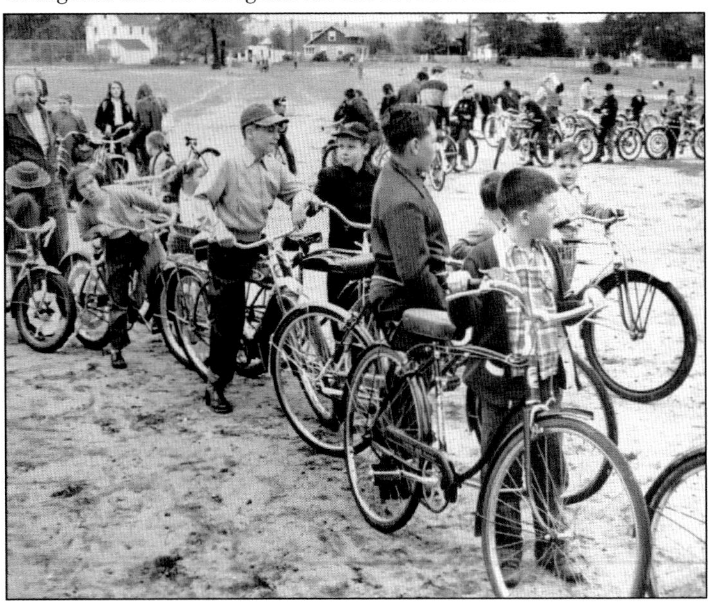

In 1954, a total of 2.5 million bicycles were sold in the United States. In Chicopee, Massachusetts, the police decided to license them all as part of a local bike safety program. Prior to World War II, Fairview was the least-populated section of the city. The growth of the nearby Westover Field and the new home construction swelled the local population. In spite of inclement weather, there was a very large turnout.

Police lieutenant. George Haggerty turned to the Teenities, a local club for boys and girls sponsored by the Fairview Boys Club, to coordinate the event. Here, the officer tags one of the popular new imported English racing bicycles.

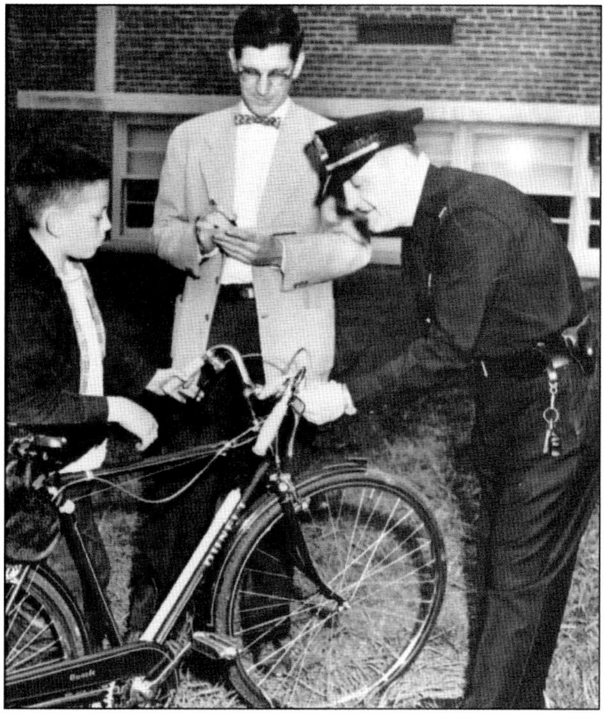

The most popular bicycles at community field days were built at the Columbia Manufacturing Company in nearby Westfield, Massachusetts. Here, Fairview Boys Club director Russell Campbell checks out a youngster's brand-new Columbia bike.

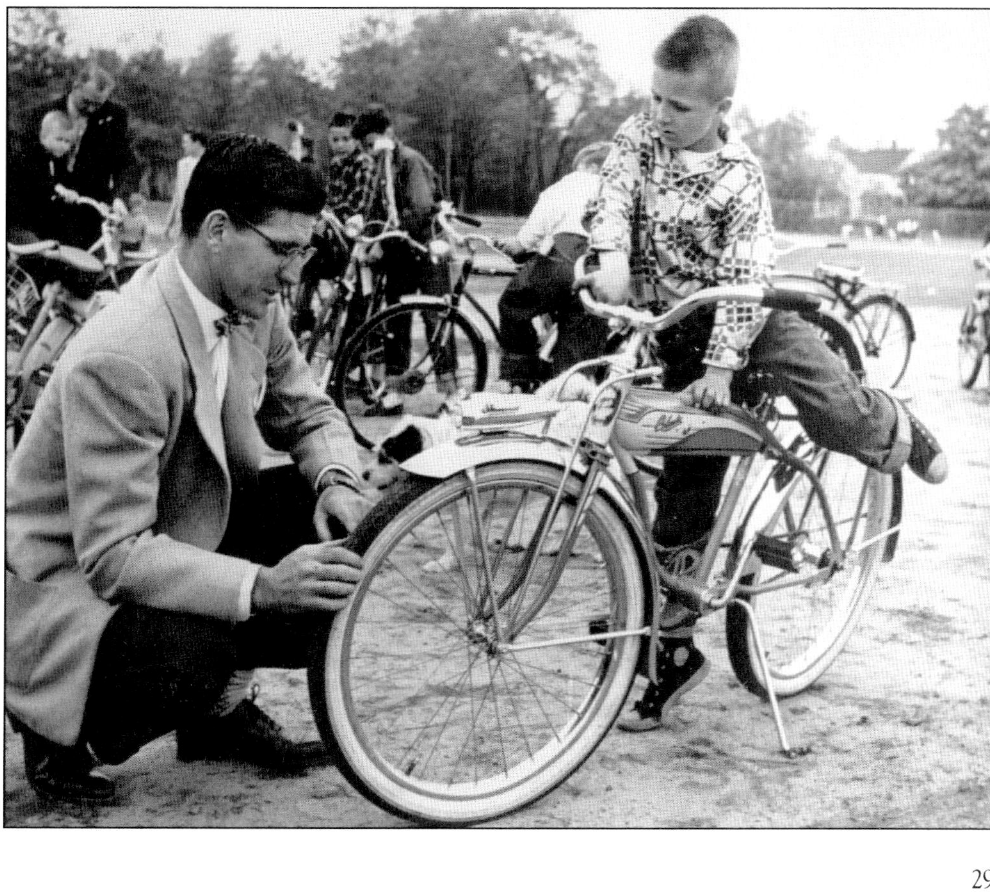

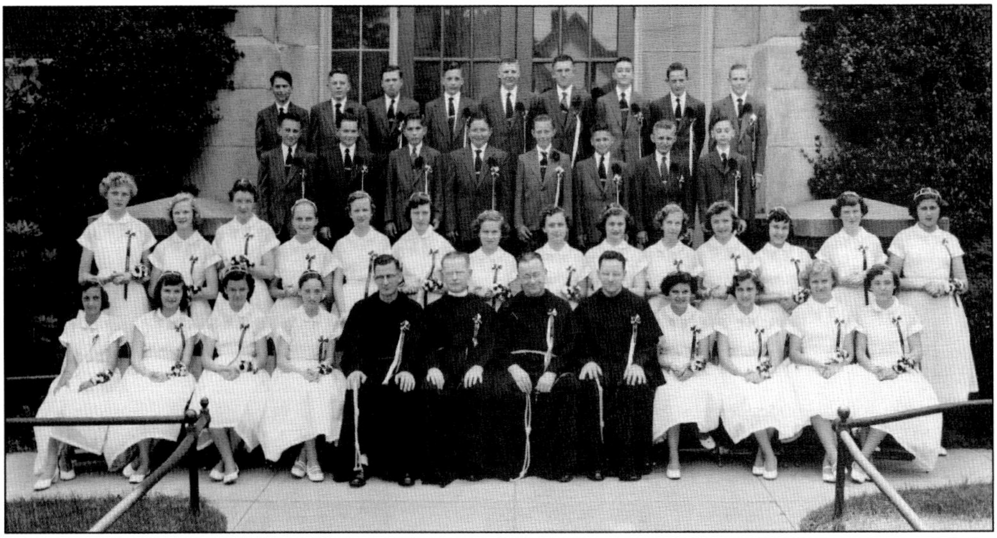

Pictured on the steps of the St. Stanislaus School on Front Street are the 39 graduates of the Class of 1954. Only one member of the graduating class would attend Cathedral High School in Springfield, and four young ladies would attend the Holy Name High School on South Street. The remaining 35 members would attend Chicopee High School.

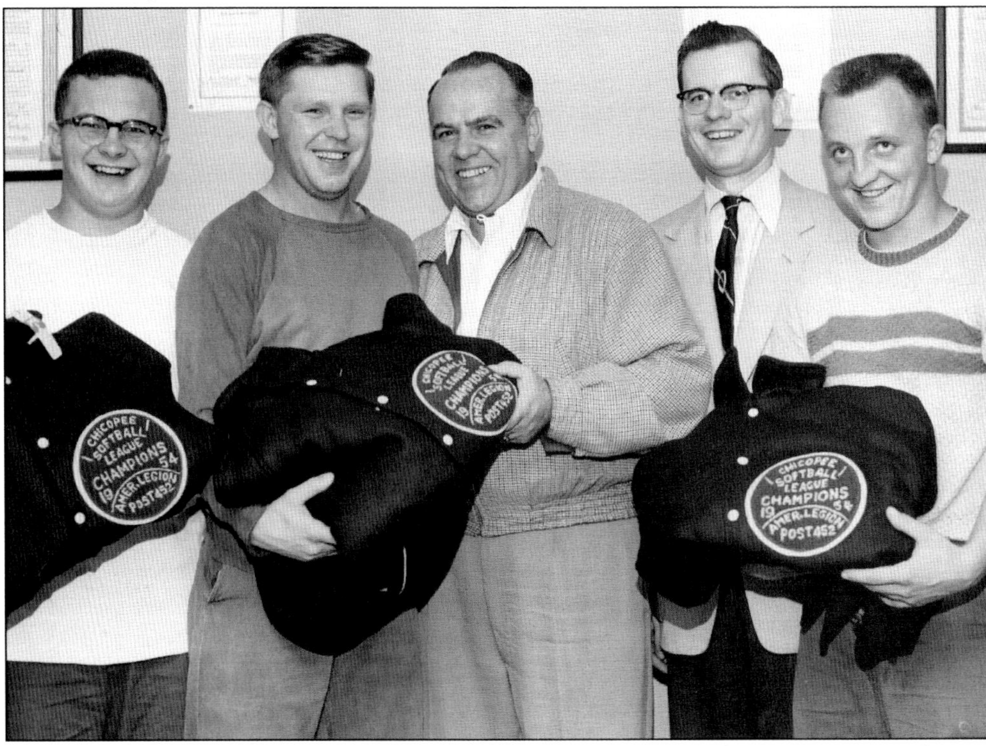

Chicopee Center American Legion Post 452 was founded by a group of Chicopee Center residents in 1950. The members met in the Chicopee House near the train depot at the foot of Exchange Street. Within a short time, the fledging organization was a major sponsor of community sports programs. Here in 1954, state representative Joseph "Bucky" Wisinowski (center) presents championship jackets to the post's softball team.

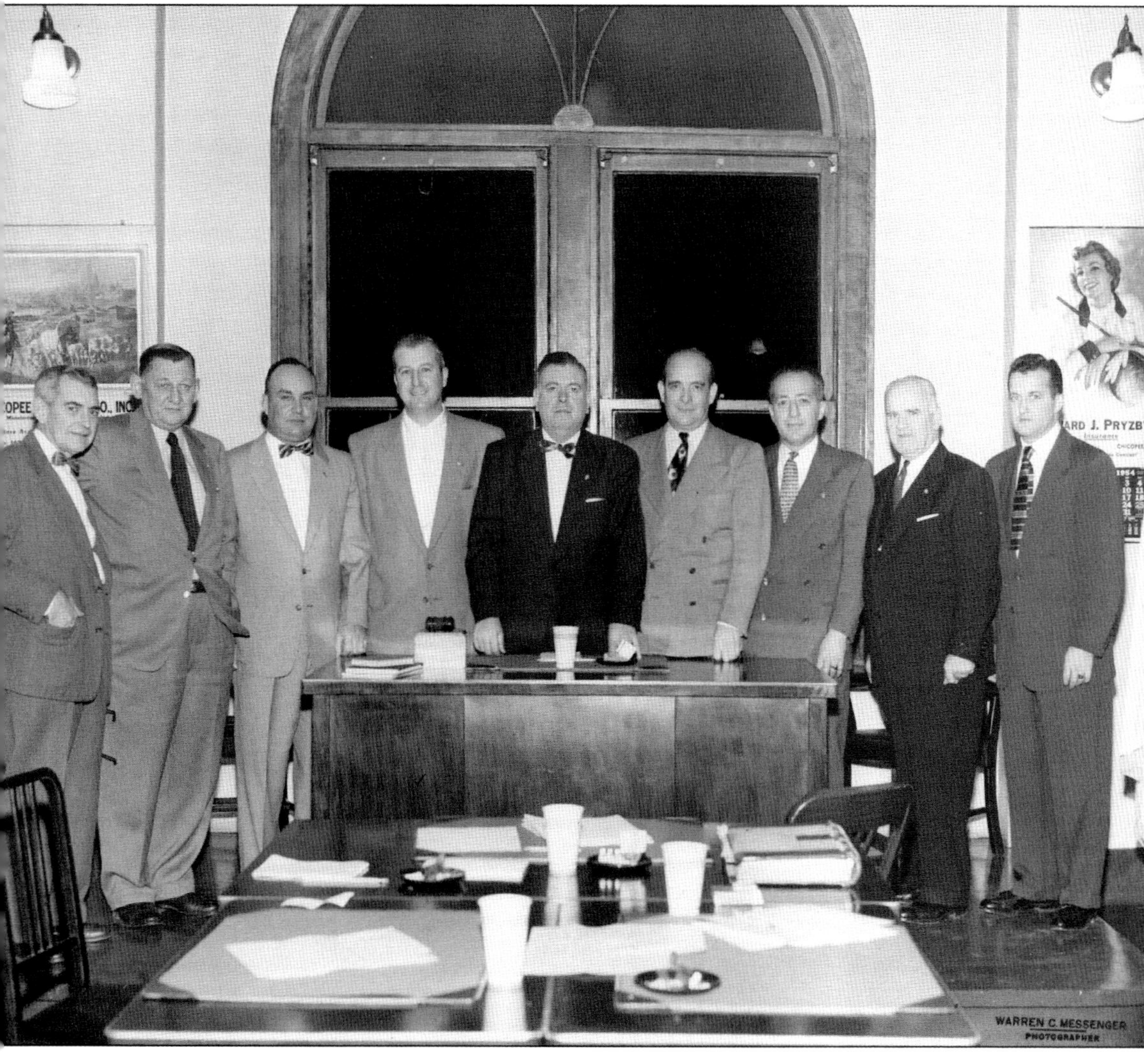

Members of the Chicopee Board of Aldermen pose in the aldermanic chambers of the city hall annex. When Chicopee became a city in 1890, the legislative body was called the common council. Today, the community's legislative body is called the city council. To this day, local elections remain nonpartisan (they have no party designation). In the 1950s, the last remnants of ethnic politics still gave life to the Polish and French Canadian ethnic voting blocs. Ward representation geared to dominant ethnic neighborhoods frequently were the base of a candidate's support and provided the manpower for a run for higher office. In 1954, a seat of the board was a stepping stone to the mayor's office. Longtime aldermen Walter Grocki (second from the right) would successfully challenge Mayor Trybulski in the 1955 municipal election.

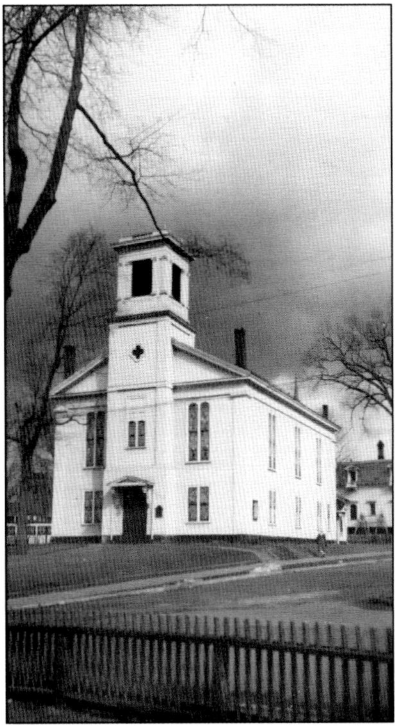

In 1955, the Second Congregational Church of Chicopee Falls was celebrating its 125th anniversary. A Springfield minister conducted Sunday afternoon services at the Belcher Homestead in 1822 for the first time. In 1830, it became the First Congregational Church of Factory Village (the original name of Chicopee Falls). In 1833, the name was changed to the Second Congregational Church of Chicopee.

During the anniversary celebration, Chicopee civic leader N.P. Ames Carter was declared the oldest member of the parish. He is pictured with Bruce Dickie, the church's youngest parishioner. In 15 years, the church would be demolished as part of the Chicopee Falls Urban Renewal effort.

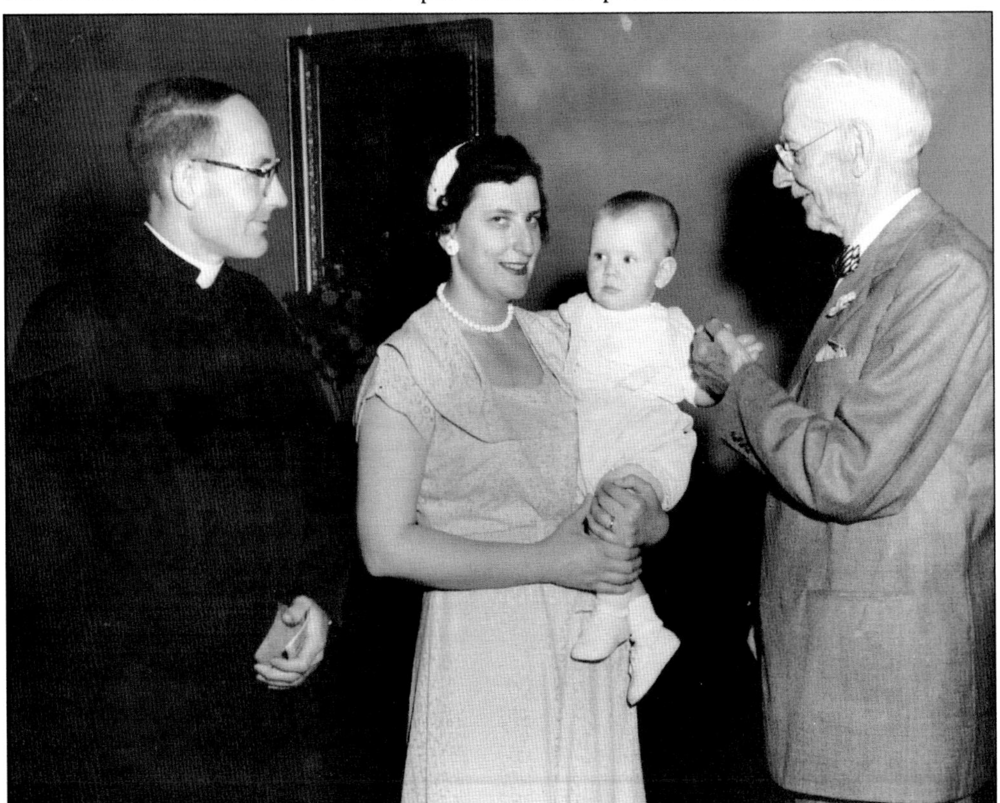

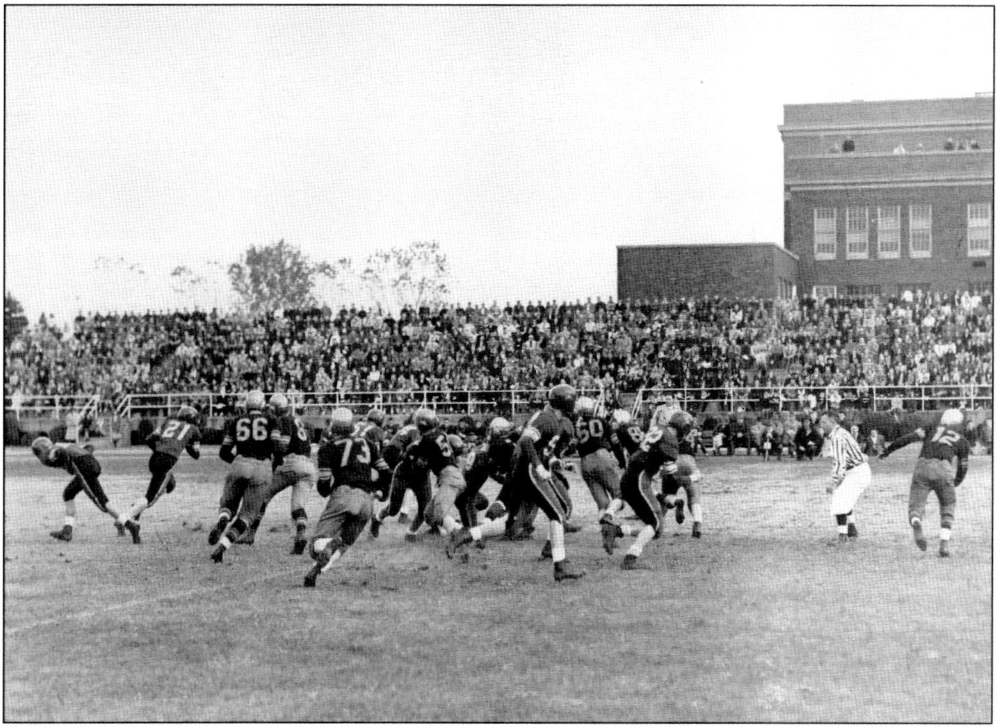

William Moge was the region's most successful three-sport high school coach. In 1950, his Westfield High School Bombers (pictured here before a huge crowd at Bullins Field) had completed a perfect undefeated season. Moge would accept a lucrative 25 percent raise in pay to take over the floundering athletic program at Chicopee High School. The citizenry wanted a team that could beat archrival Holyoke High School. The coach delivered—in the 1950s, the Pacers only lost to the Purple Knights once.

In 1955, Chicopee American Legion Post 452 established the Bronislaw J. Stepczyk Scholar Athlete Award. From left to right are first runner-up Clyde McCelland, cowinner Thomas Skypeck, Linda Stepczyk, cowinner Richard Kagan, and coach William Moge. All three young men were members of the Chicopee High School football team.

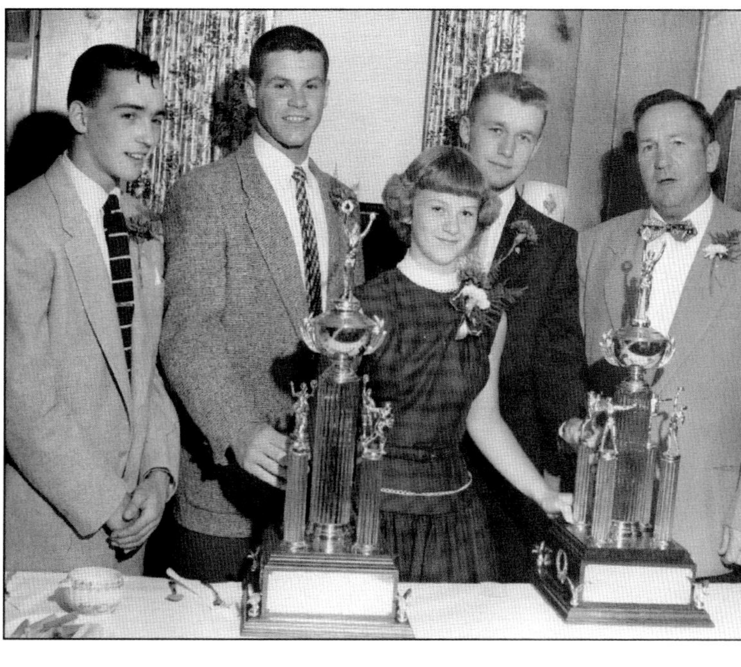

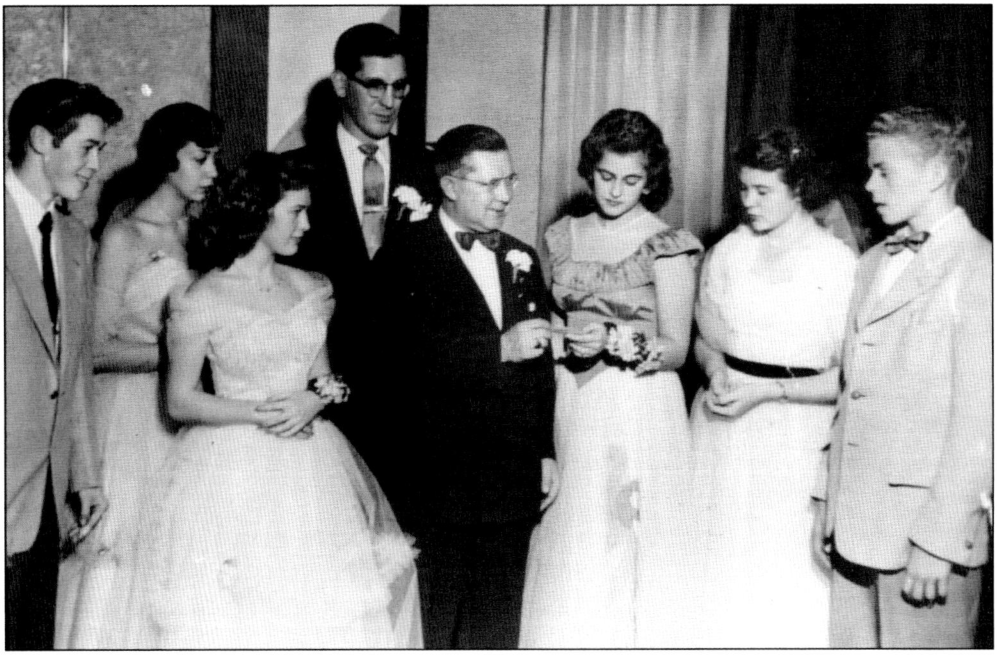

Mayor Walter J. Trybulski draws the winning raffle ticket at the Fairview Teenities Formal Dance. The group sponsored by the Fairview Boys Club was concerned about the condition of youth facilities in the city. The mayor outlined his plans for the recreational development of Bemis Pond and Szot Park.

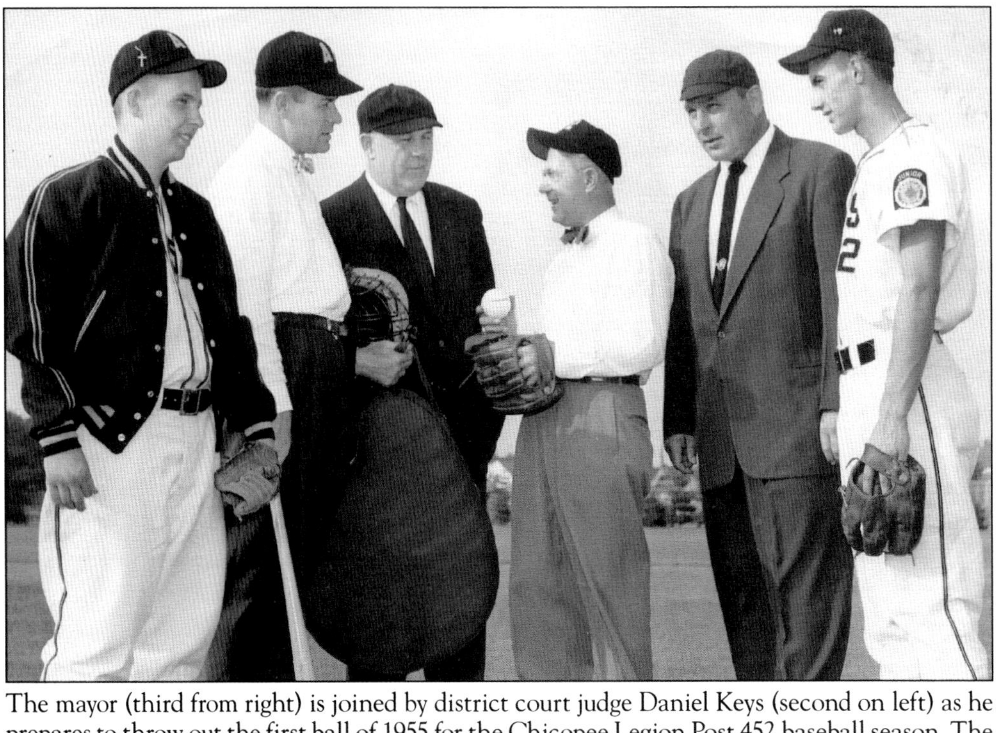

The mayor (third from right) is joined by district court judge Daniel Keys (second on left) as he prepares to throw out the first ball of 1955 for the Chicopee Legion Post 452 baseball season. The veteran's group was urging the mayor to install lighting for night baseball at Szot Park.

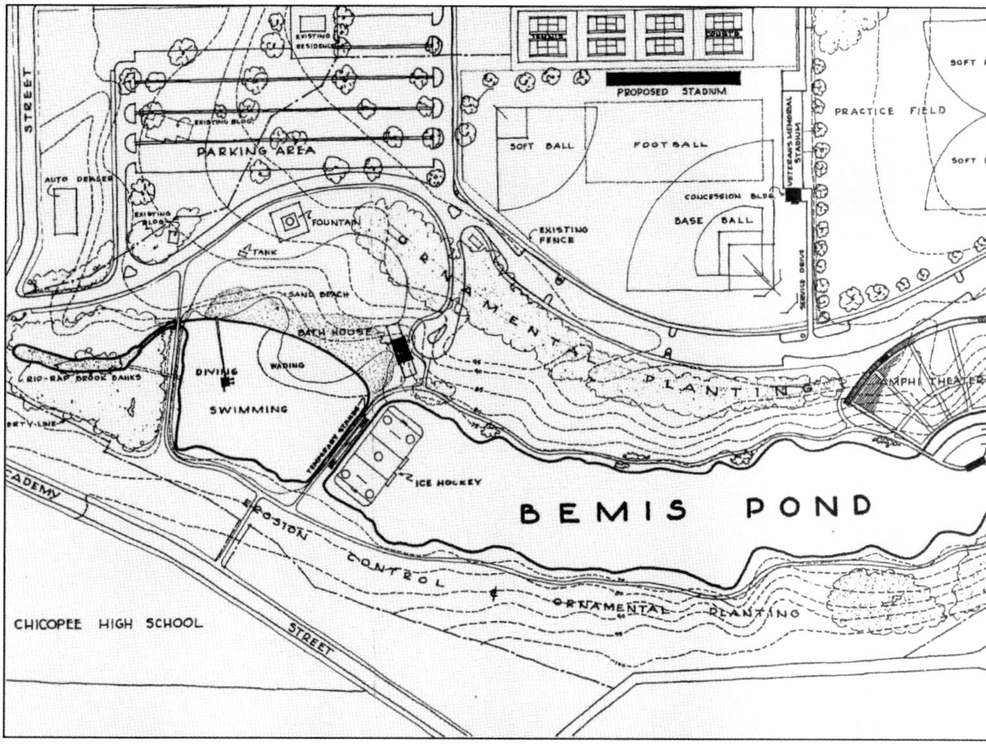

The Chicopee Park Commission hired a distinguished group of consultants to prepare extensive plans for the city's largest park. The ambitious plan ran into political trouble with the city's legislative body, and the mayor compromised. In 1954, the city had only one small outdoor swimming pool. Phase one of the project was approved. Work began on a bathing beach and skating facility for Bemis Pond.

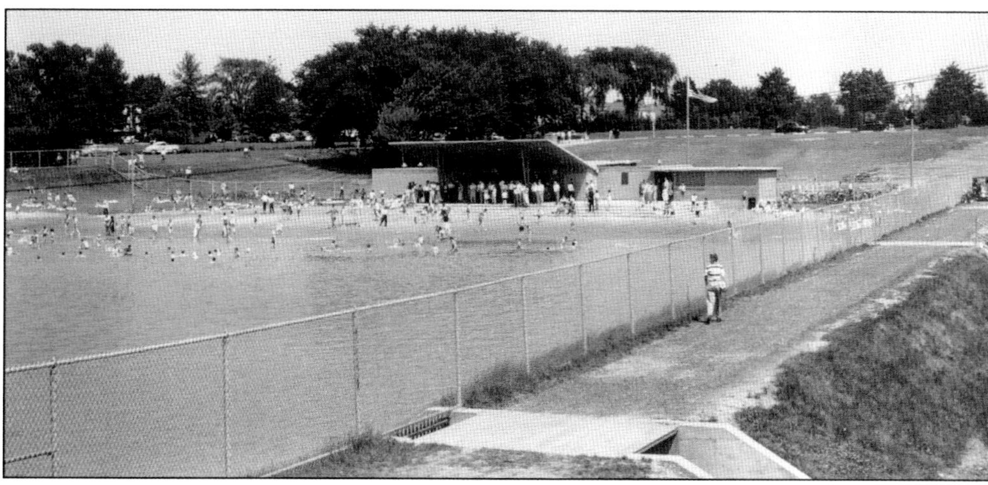

The project depended on the available technology of the 1950s and underestimated the environmental impact of new housing construction adjacent to springs and streams that fed the Bemis watershed. By damming the lake, the flow of water was controlled, and a chlorinator was installed at the dam to provide clean and protected water for the pool without the necessity for excessive chlorination in the large pond area. Water quality would quickly become a scientific and political issue. (Courtesy of Joanne Zaskey.)

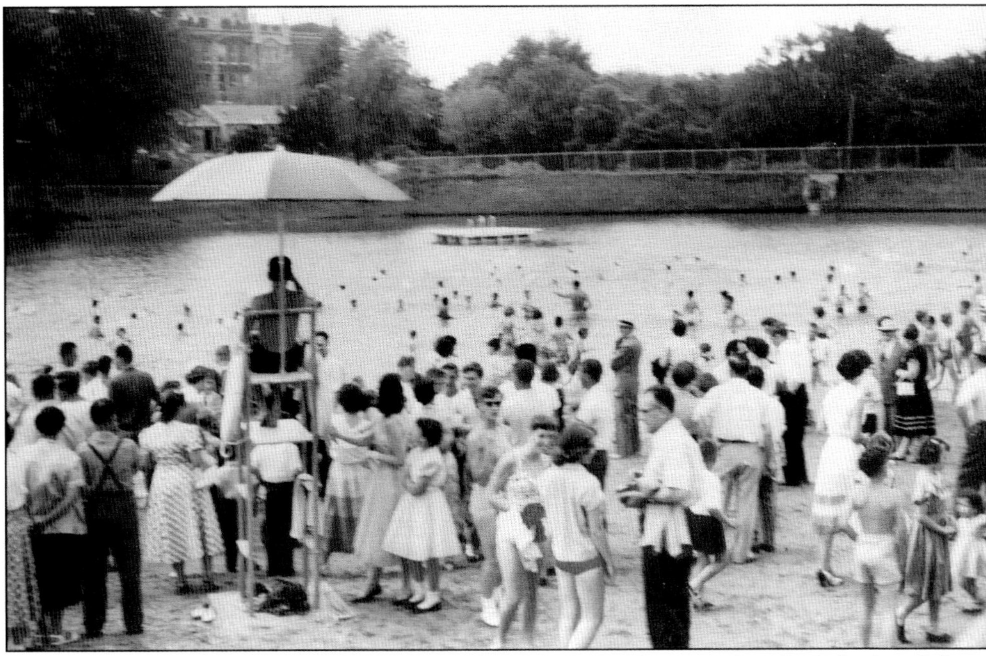

The early summer weather was ideal, and a huge opening-day crowd packed the beachfront. Newspaper stories trumpeted the opening day's activities. The event was planned and carried out by the park department with a considerable amount of hoopla, including radio and television coverage. (Courtesy of Joanne Zaskey.)

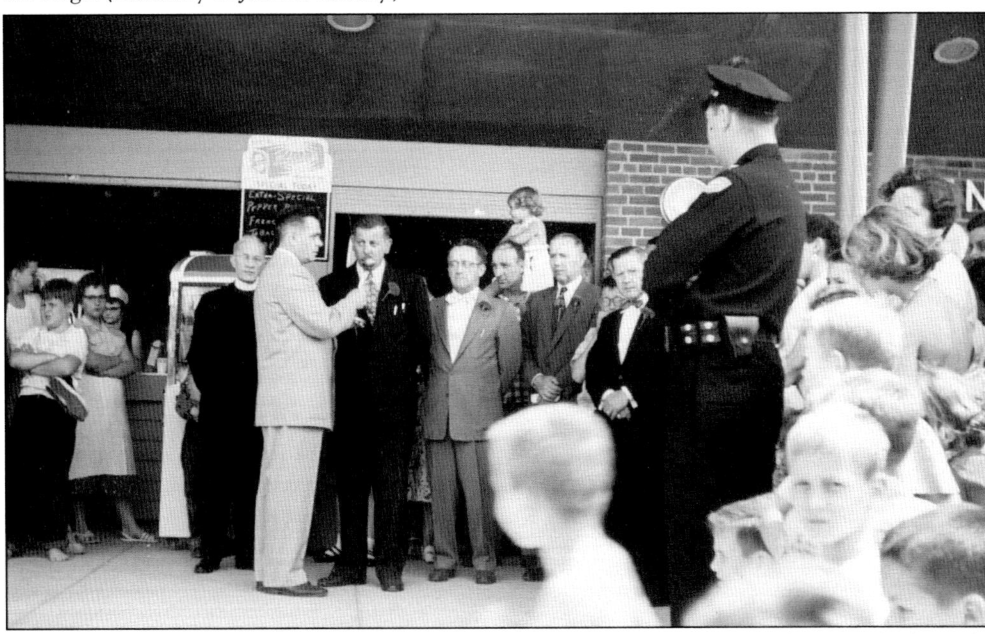

The mayor and park commissioners were very proud of their new facility. Unfortunately, from the outset, the young swimmers reported that the water was muddy. Comments by the mayor's political opponents began to appear in the letters-to-the-editor columns of local newspapers. In August, Bemis Pond would overflow its banks as torrential rains struck the area. Hurricane Diane was one of the greatest disasters ever to strike the New England states. (Courtesy of Joanne Zaskey.)

The flood of August 17–19, 1955, took its place in history along with the hurricane of 1938, the floods of 1936 and 1927, and the blizzard of 1888. All the dikes on the Connecticut River held. The flooding was caused by little streams and brooks swelling under the sheer volume of 15 inches of rain. In Massachusetts, damage was estimated at $12 million.

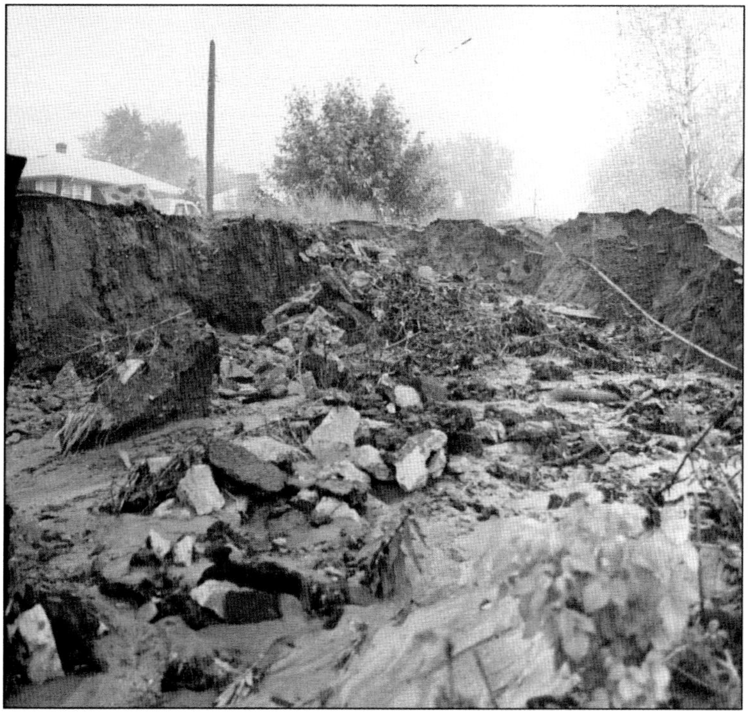

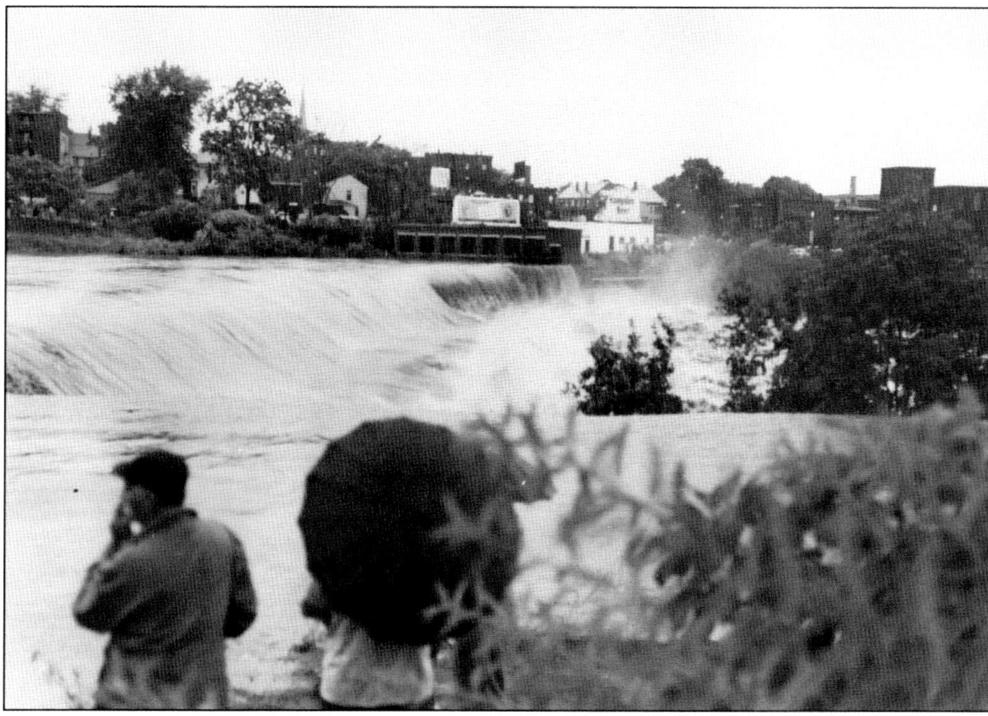

The Deady Bridge on the Chicopee River was closed to traffic. The US Army Corps of Engineers reported that the 150-year-old Chicopee Falls Dam was at risk. In 1955, there were no dikes on the Chicopee River. Below the dam, the river cut the bend and flowed right though the lower floors of the factory buildings.

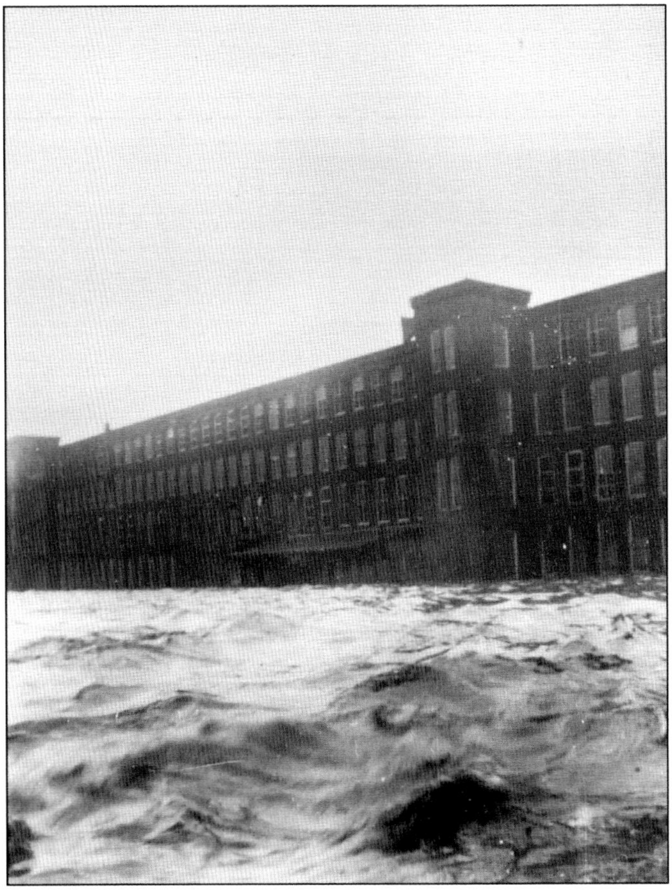

The Willimansett Brook inundated large sections of North Chicopee. A washout on Memorial Drive in Fairview was more than 60 feet deep as brooks and streams swept away backyards and driveways all over town. Pictured here, the Chicopee Manufacturing Company's entire lower floor is underwater.

The *Springfield Daily News* reported, "The waters of Bemis pond whipped a furious cataract by the conscienceless storm, charged across the highway, undermining the road. Only the concerted efforts of city employees and Westover Field Air Men prevented the dam from collapsing, sweeping the source of the city's electric power with it." The day after, on August 20, onlookers check out the damage.

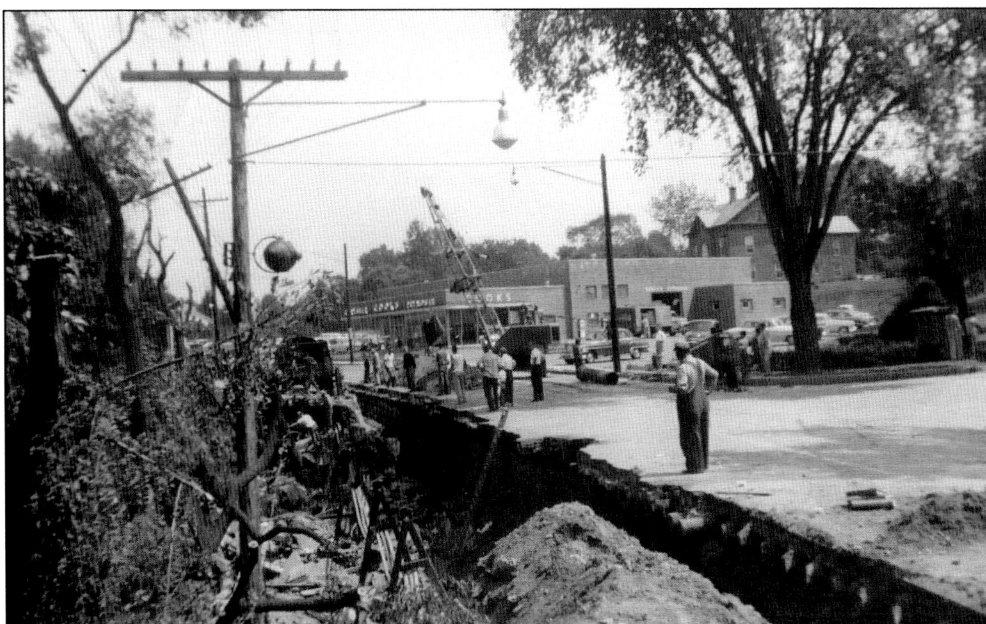

Two

High School Days 1957–1960

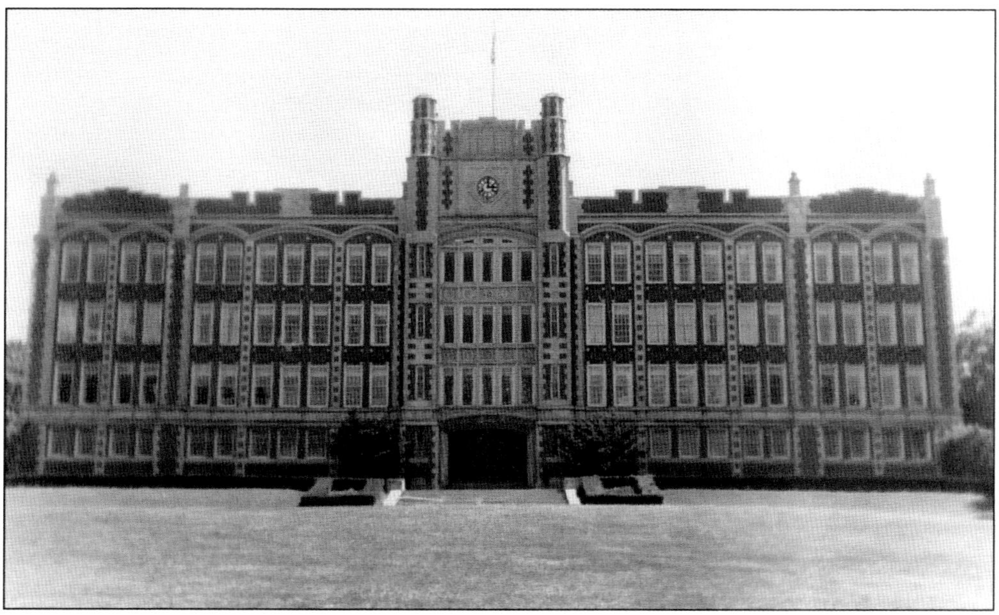

In 1956, Chicopee High School was 36 years old. America's teenagers, dubbed the "Silent Generation," were passively heading into the second half of the decade. On May 18, 1954, the US Supreme Court, in a unanimous decision, banned the practice of racial segregation in the public schools of the United States. The District of Columbia and 29 states were directed to prepare plans to desegregate their schools.

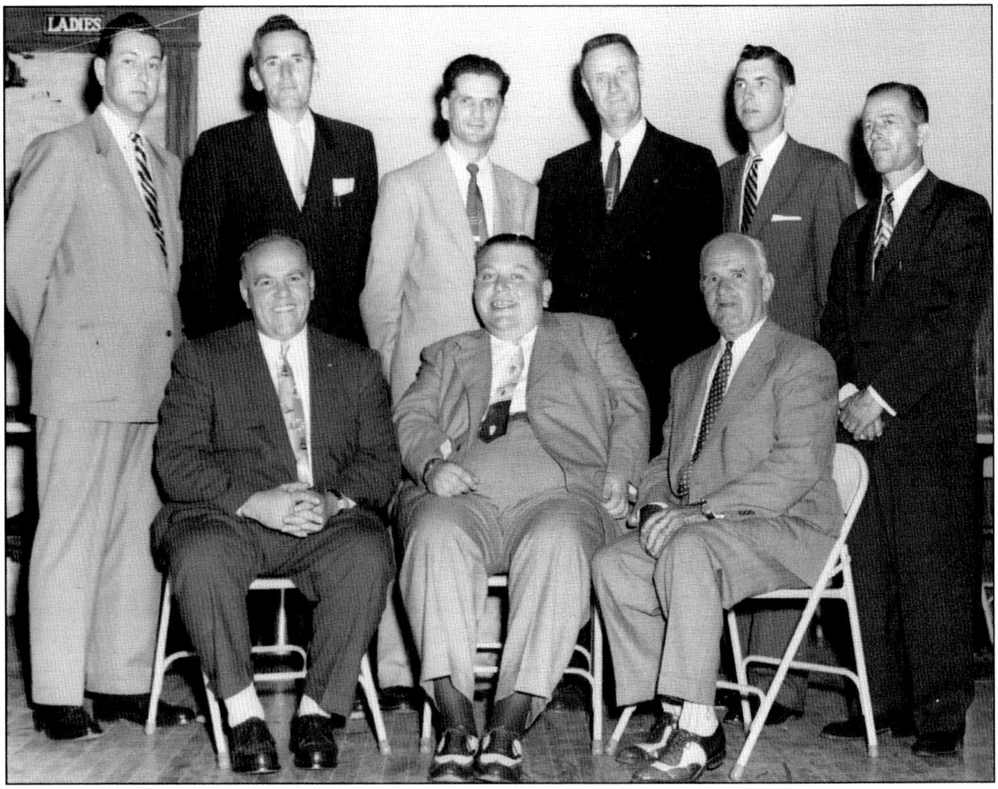

Chicopee's new mayor, former aldermen Walter Grocki, was an astute local politician who was eager for community support after a hard-fought election campaign. Pictured from left to right at the Colonels Club are (first row) Rep. Joseph "Bucky" Wisinowski, Ald. Thaddeus "Snapper" Drewniak, and Mayor Walter J. Grocki. The back row is unidentified.

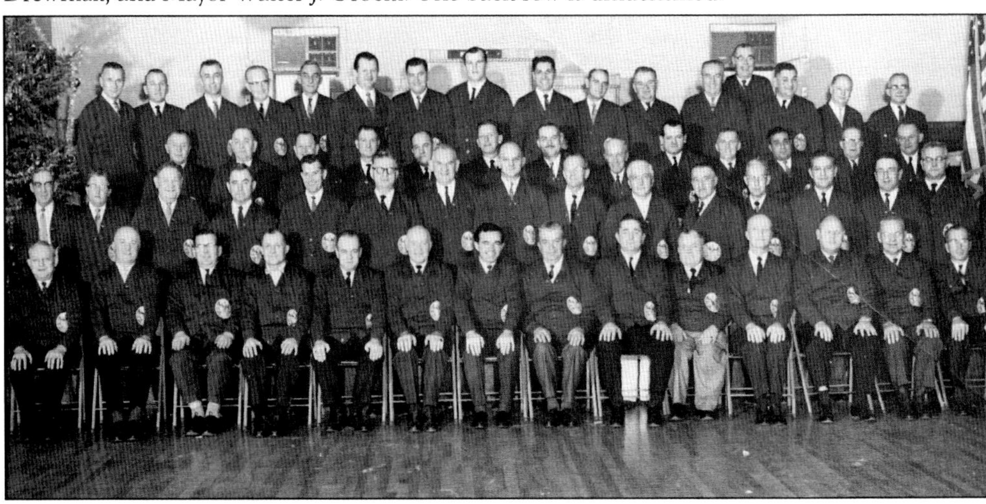

On January 30, 1955, the dedication of the Chicopee Lodge of Elks home on Granby Road signaled the beginning of the organization's 30-year reign as the community's most influential civic organization. The dynamics of the 1950s influenced the changes brought by the war years and the subsequent ideological fears of the Cold War. On May 1, 1956, the Elks were sponsoring a National Youth Day in the United States to counteract the Communist holiday.

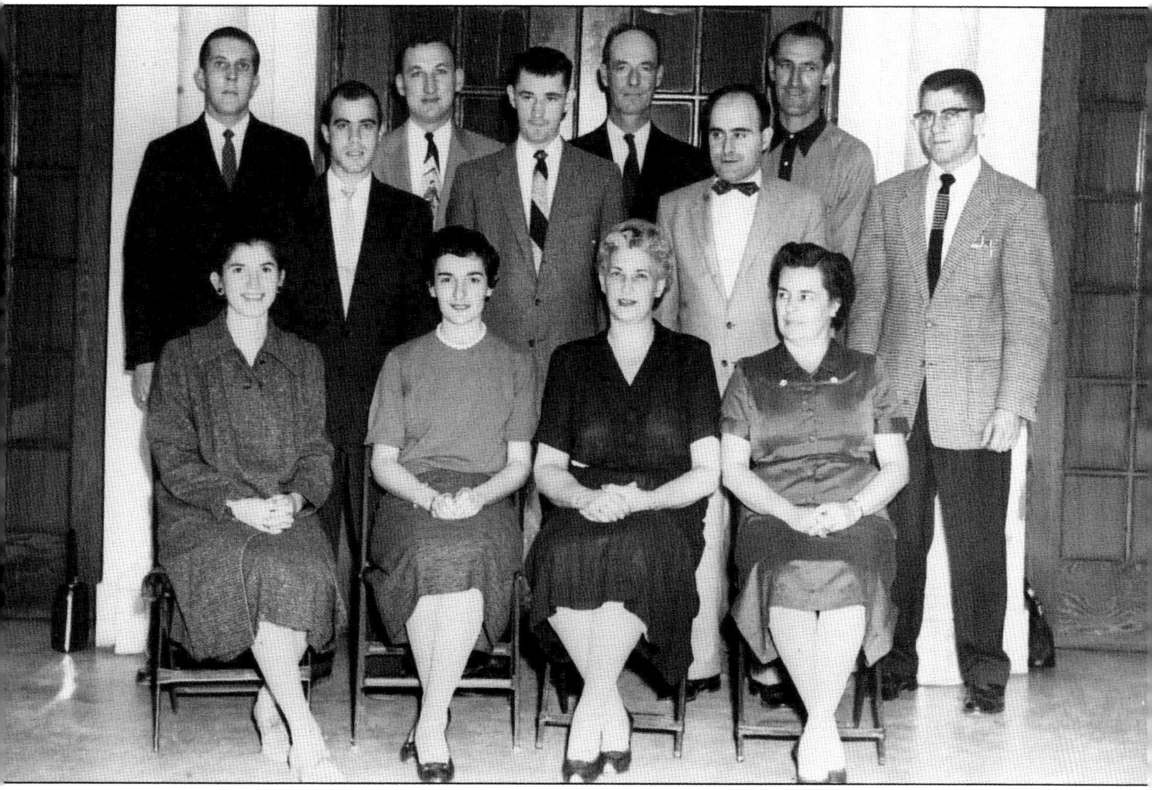

In the 1950s, all the schools were changing in the newly affluent America. At Chicopee High School, a combination of factors would accelerate the transformation. In five years, the school population would nearly double in size. In addition to the baby boomers, there was a substantial increase in high school–age students from families at Westover Air Force Base. The sons and daughters of Strategic Air Command personnel were an exotic addition to the small-town high school. At high school, the midpoint in the 1950s signaled a changing of the guard as postwar educators retired. This group of first-year teachers posing for their first yearbook picture are, from left to right, (first row) Betty Cassaro, Sally Ovian, Rachel Shumway, and Ruth Fuller; (second row) Dionysius G. Dulchinos, Thomas E. Hurst, and William J. Pappas; (third row) William Robinson, Edward Borucki, John Corridan, Charles Fox, and Edward Butova.

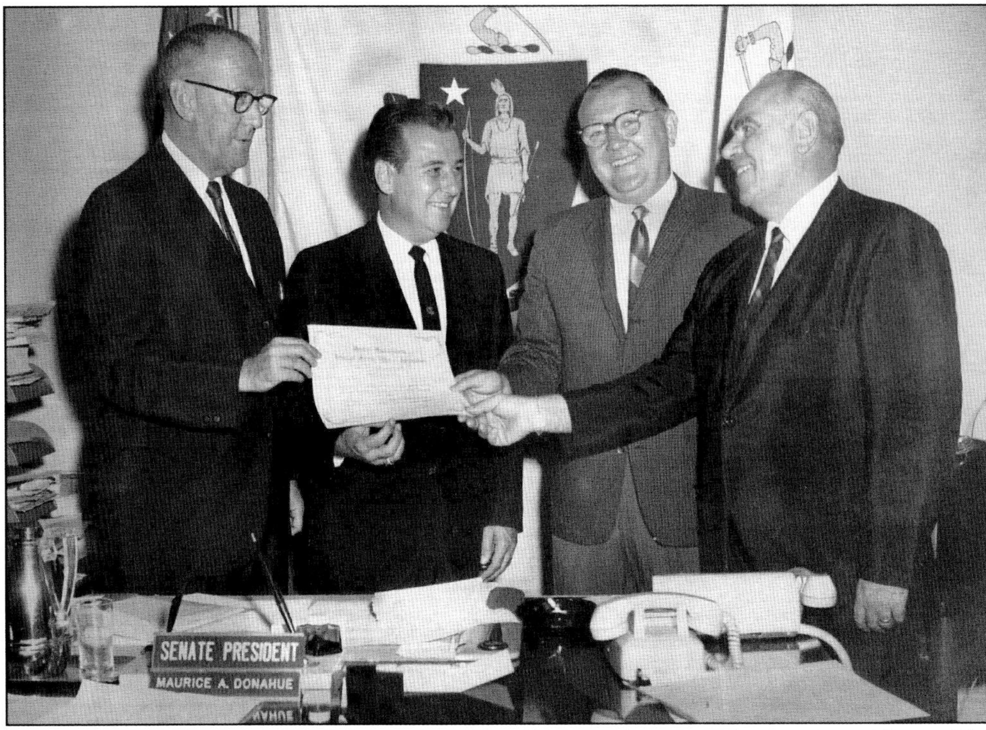

In 1956, Chicopee's legislative delegation was kept busy at the Massachusetts State House. The expansion of Westover Air Force Base, the construction of the Massachusetts Turnpike (with exits 5 and 6 in Chicopee), and a new industrial park made the city a key player. From left to right are Massachusetts Senate president Maurice A. Donahue (Holyoke), Sen. Roger Bernashe, Rep. Mitzi Kulig, and Rep. Joseph Wisinowski from Chicopee.

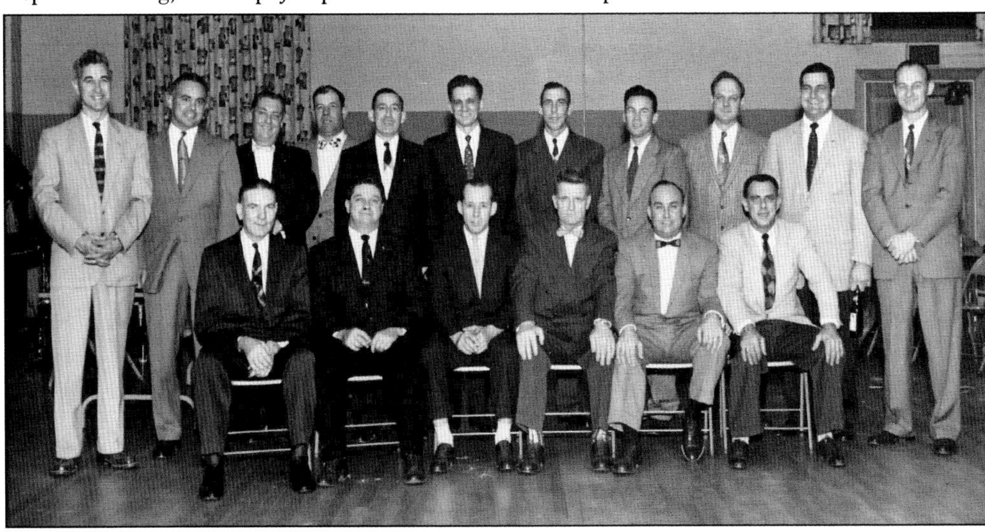

In 1956, members of the Aldenville Athletic Association held a very special 15th reunion. The last time they were all together was on the afternoon of December 7, 1941. The event was the organization's annual awards banquet. When the news of war reached the hall, all plans for the 1942 season were put on hold. At this event 15 years later, the aging athletes were talking about their children, the new generation of talented Chicopee baseball players.

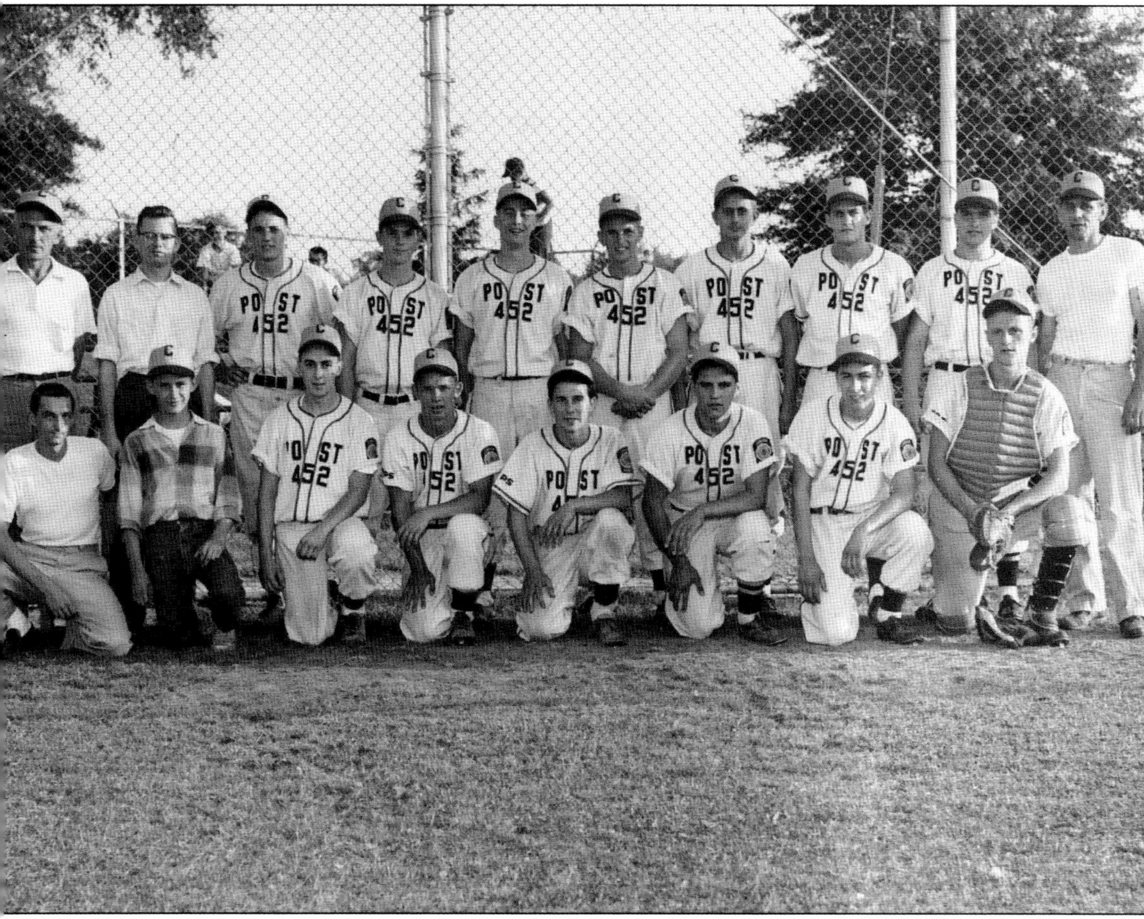

Chicopee American Legion Post 452 was headquartered at the site of the old Chicopee House Hotel near the railroad tracks at the foot of Exchange Street. The organization sponsored an array of adult and junior sports programs. In 1957, the jewel in the crown was the high school unit, which competed in the region's American Legion Junior Baseball League. On any given summer night, the fields in the old mill town were alive as large crowds of excited fans watched the peewee, sandlot, and tricounty adults softball games. Chicopee was five years away from night baseball at Szot Park. When the legion team was on the road, a cadre of loyal rooters accompanied them up and down the Pioneer Valley. In 1957, the city's talented young athletes represented a new level of achievement. Doing so, they raised the expectations of their fans and the entire community.

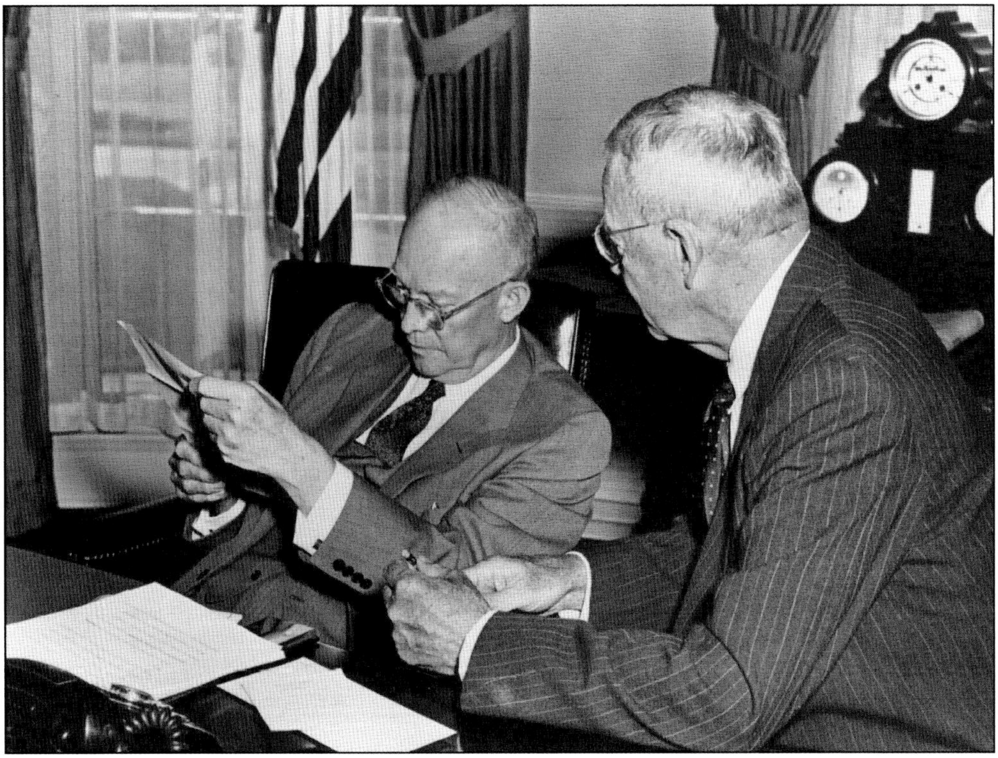

In 1952, the United States elected a retired five-star general to the oval office. The president and Secretary of State John Foster Dulles approved the establishment of the Strategic Air Command (SAC). The reorganization was part of an aggressive policy called New Look. That year, the US Air Force took delivery of the eight-engine B-52 jet bombers. (Courtesy of the Eisenhower Center, Abilene, Kansas.)

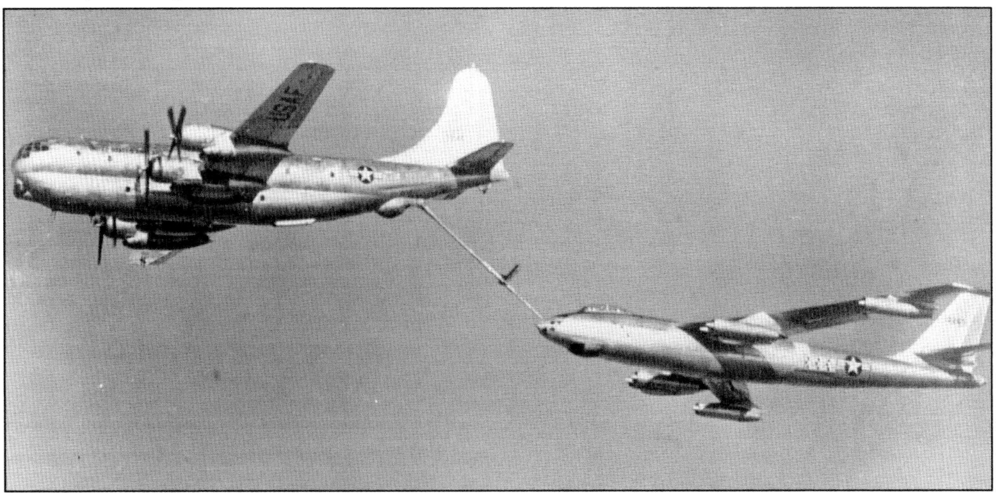

On April 1, 1955, the SAC assumed control of Westover Air Force Base. In June, the Eighth Air Force moved its headquarters from Carswell Air Force Base, Texas, to Westover. In September 1956, the 57th Air Division was reactivated, and the 4050th Air Refueling and the 99th Bombardment Wings were assigned to the 57th Air Force at Westover. (Defense Department photograph; courtesy of Ron Groleau.)

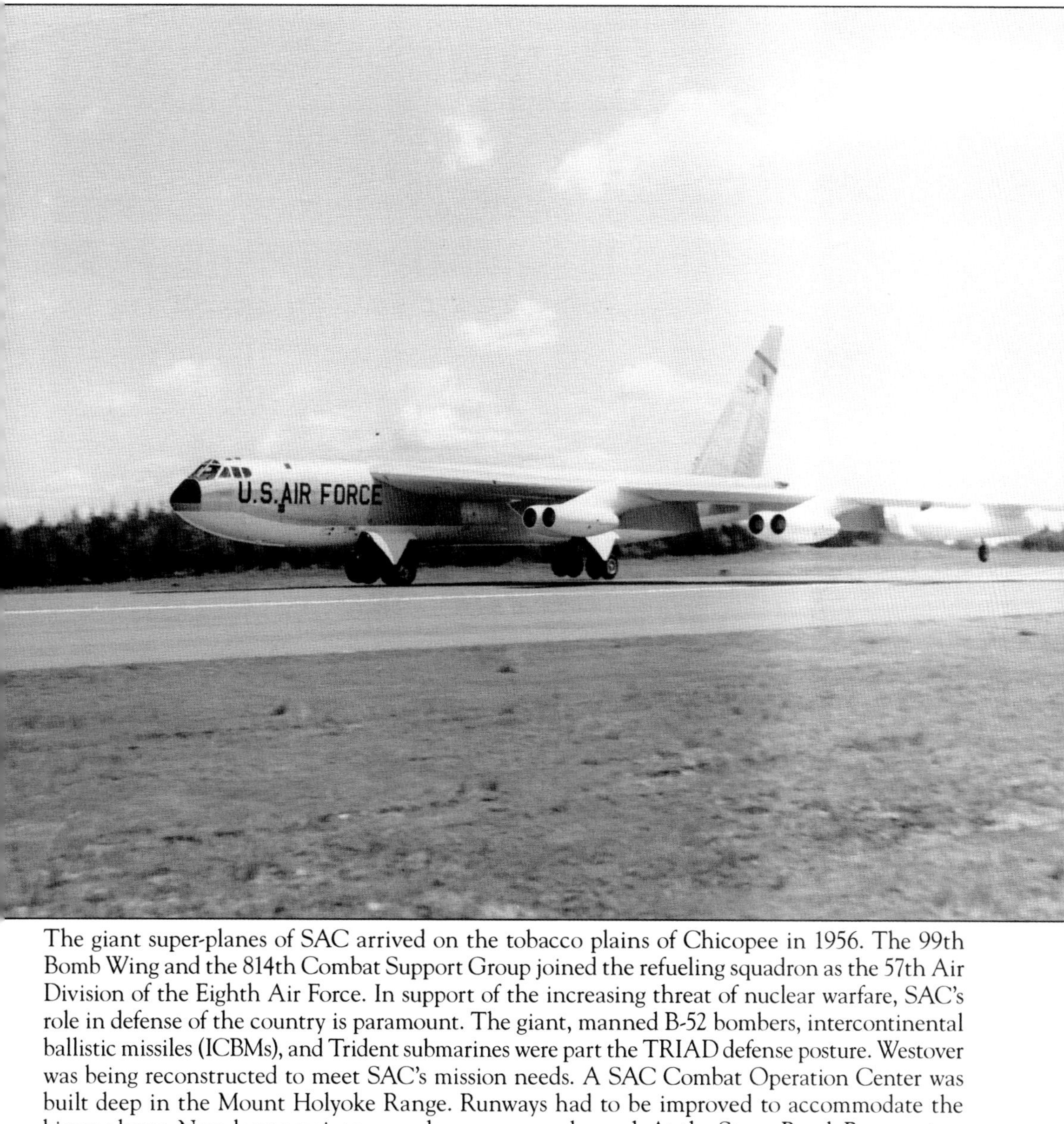

The giant super-planes of SAC arrived on the tobacco plains of Chicopee in 1956. The 99th Bomb Wing and the 814th Combat Support Group joined the refueling squadron as the 57th Air Division of the Eighth Air Force. In support of the increasing threat of nuclear warfare, SAC's role in defense of the country is paramount. The giant, manned B-52 bombers, intercontinental ballistic missiles (ICBMs), and Trident submarines were part the TRIAD defense posture. Westover was being reconstructed to meet SAC's mission needs. A SAC Combat Operation Center was built deep in the Mount Holyoke Range. Runways had to be improved to accommodate the bigger planes. New, larger maintenance hangers were planned. At the Stony Brook Reservation, armament bunkers were constructed to store nuclear bombs. (Defense Department photograph; courtesy of Ron Groleau.)

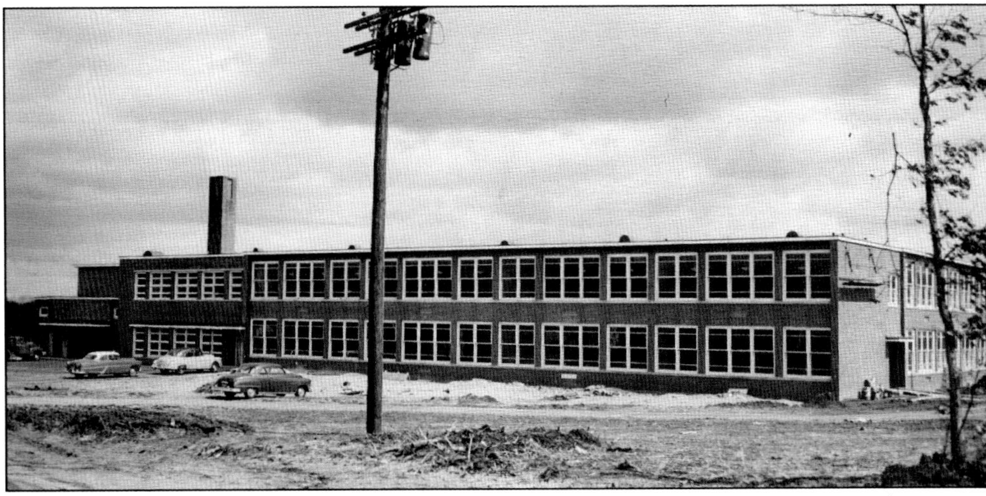

On December 5, 1956, community leaders gathered to dedicate the city's newest elementary school. The school was built to replace the old Aldenville School. The facility memorialized two young men from the neighborhood. Pfc. Joseph Lambert was killed in action with the 5th Cavalry Regiment in 1951. Lost the same year in the skies over North Korea was Lt. George Lambert, a World War II veteran recalled to active duty in the Korean War.

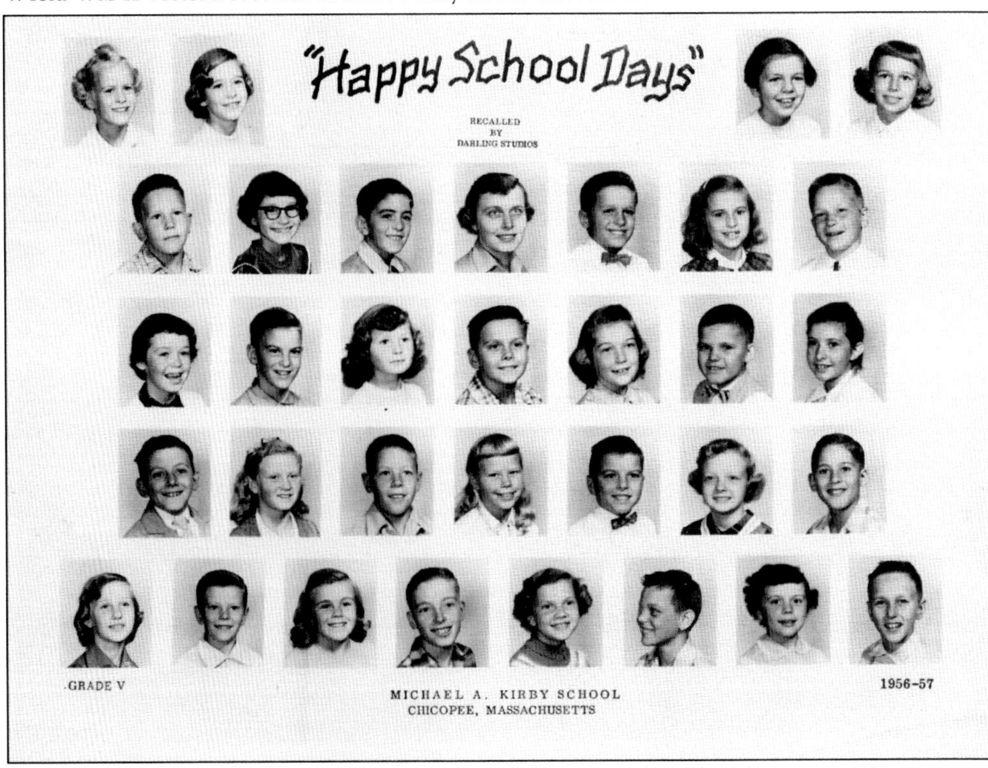

During the 1950s, the city would build a record five new schools and renovate the Fairview Memorial School. Supt. John L. Fitzpatrick reported to the school committee that the impact of the postwar baby boomers and the anticipated expansion of Westover made Chicopee the fastest-growing school system in the state. Pictured here is Miss Stella Ciszek's fifth-grade class of boomers at Kirby School.

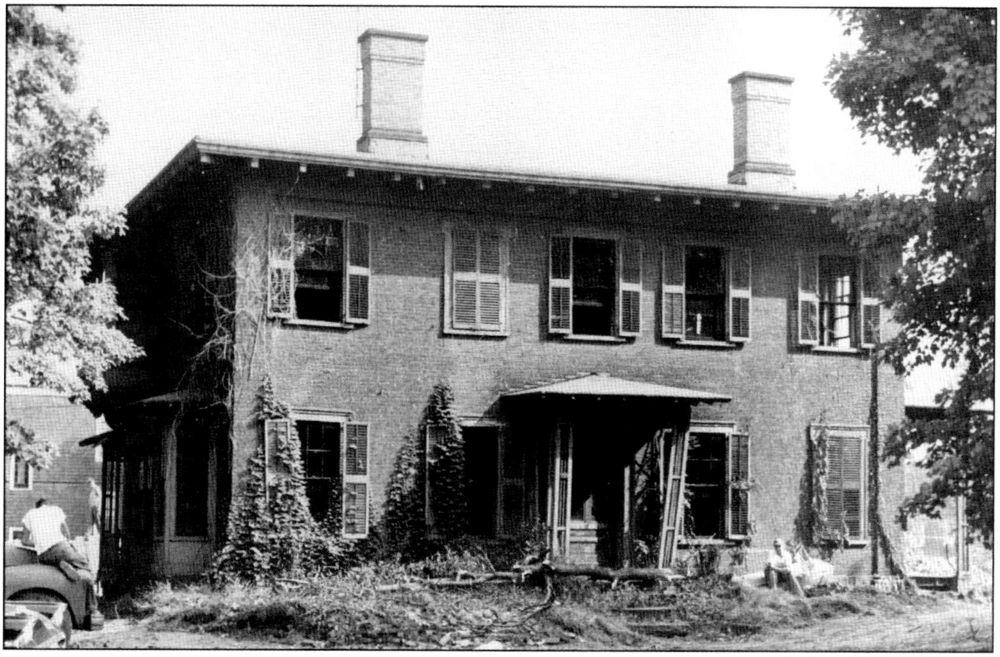

During the Civil War, the Ames Sword Company was a major supplier of cannons and swords for the Union army. For many years, the James Tyler Ames Homestead on the corner of Grape and Front Streets was a museum. In 1957, the building was demolished, and the Ames memorabilia collection was sold at auction in New York City.

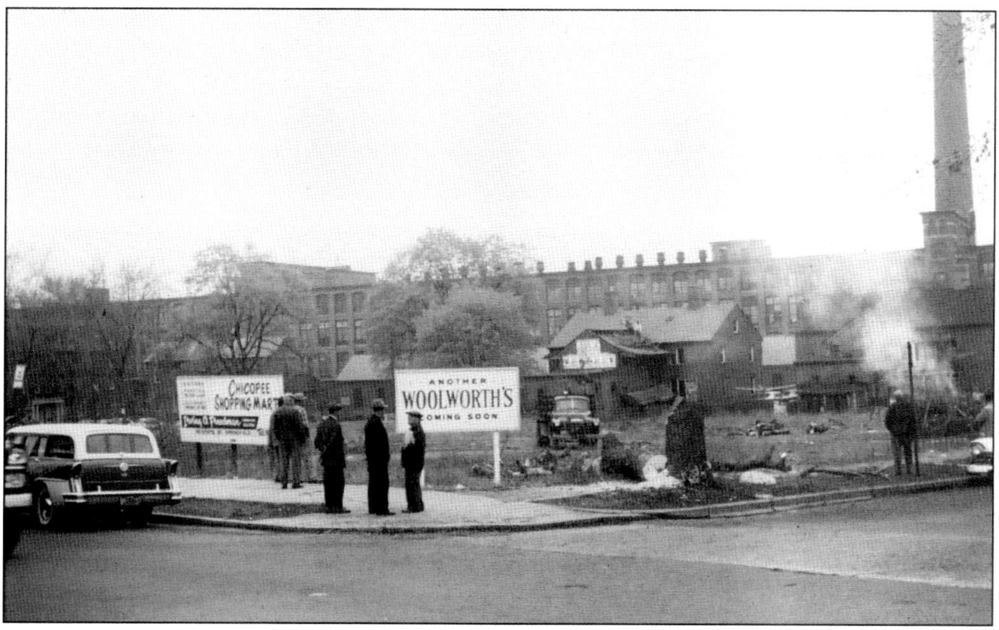

In 1830s, three textile mills were constructed in Chicopee Center. The Cabot Company, the Perkins Company, and the Dwight Mills shared the space. In 1856, the three merged under the Dwight name. The streets in the downtown area bearing the company names were undergoing major changes in 1957. The mill tenements were being demolished for a downtown shopping plaza. (Courtesy of Joanne Zaskey.)

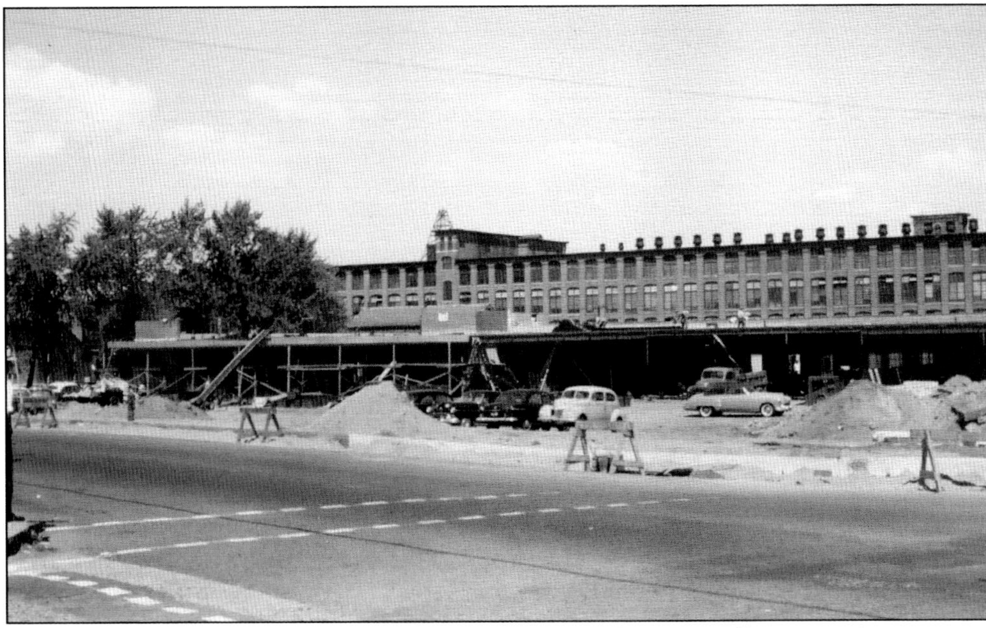

When the Dwight Manufacturing Company shuttered the Chicopee Mills in 1928, the tenements on Cabot, Perkins, and Dwight Streets were converted into private rental housing. Some of the units that were demolished in 1957 were nearly 100 years old. Each of the six units on Exchange Street (bordered by Cabot and Dwight Streets) was three stories high. An entire city block would provide ample parking for the new stores being constructed. (Courtesy of Joanne Zaskey.)

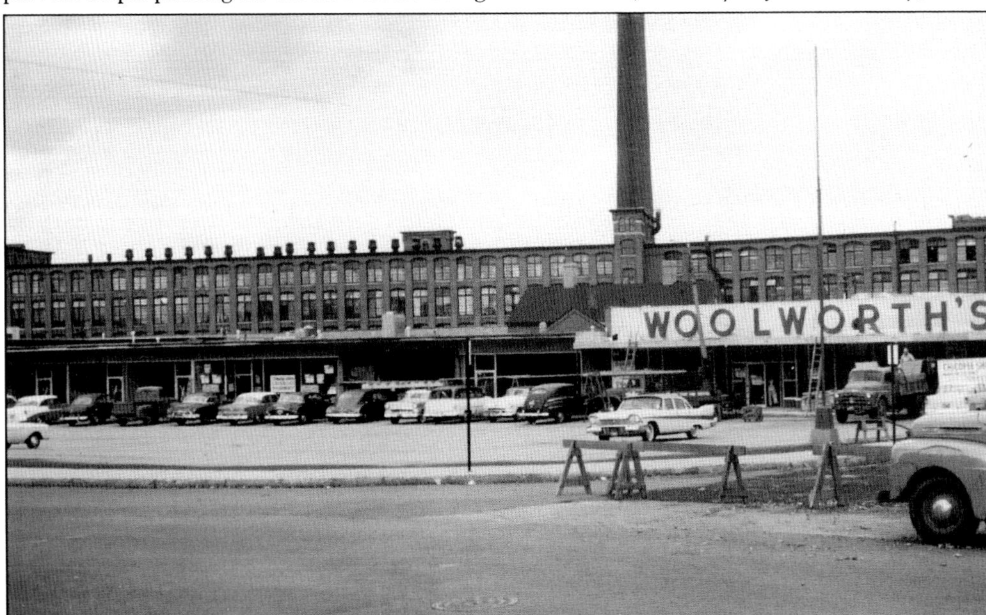

The developers of the Chicopee Plaza had as their main tenant a large new space for the Woolworth Store. The legendary chain store became the plaza's anchor joined by a Popular Super Market, a Friendly's Ice Cream Restaurant, and the relocation of the downtown Loiselle's Drugstore. For the next 40 years, Friendly's hamburger specials and "Awful-Awful" milk shakes were legendary local fare. (Courtesy of Joanne Zaskey.)

Industry in the northeastern part of the United States was being referred to as the "Rust Belt." Pictured here, workers at the Savage Firearms Company are assembling a line of Savage power lawn mowers. In 1960, the company would abandon the lawn mower business, moving from its firearms operation from the 60-year-old hill plant in Chicopee Falls to a smaller modern facility in Westfield, Massachusetts.

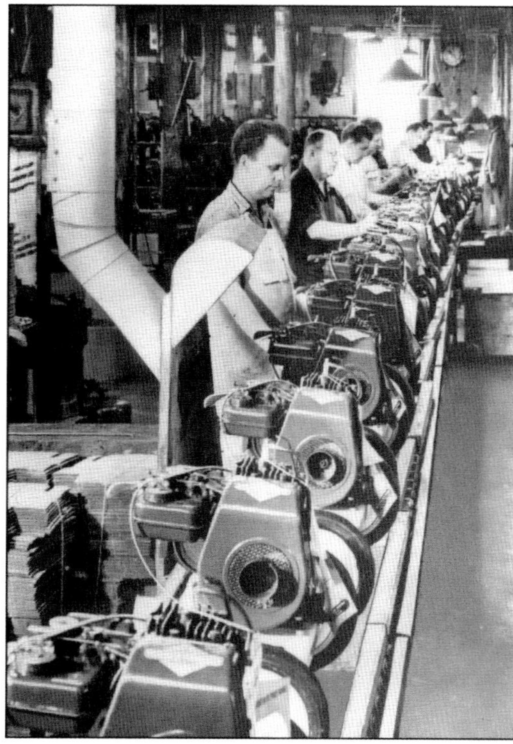

In the 1950s, the Johnson & Johnson Company had reduced its New England operations to one plant in Chicopee Falls, Massachusetts. Founded as one of America's first textile mills in 1829, the newest building in the Main Street complex of the Chicopee Manufacturing Company was nearly 70 years old. Company president John F. Shaw presents a 10-year service ink pen to Julia Drezek and a 25-year service ink pen to John Stec.

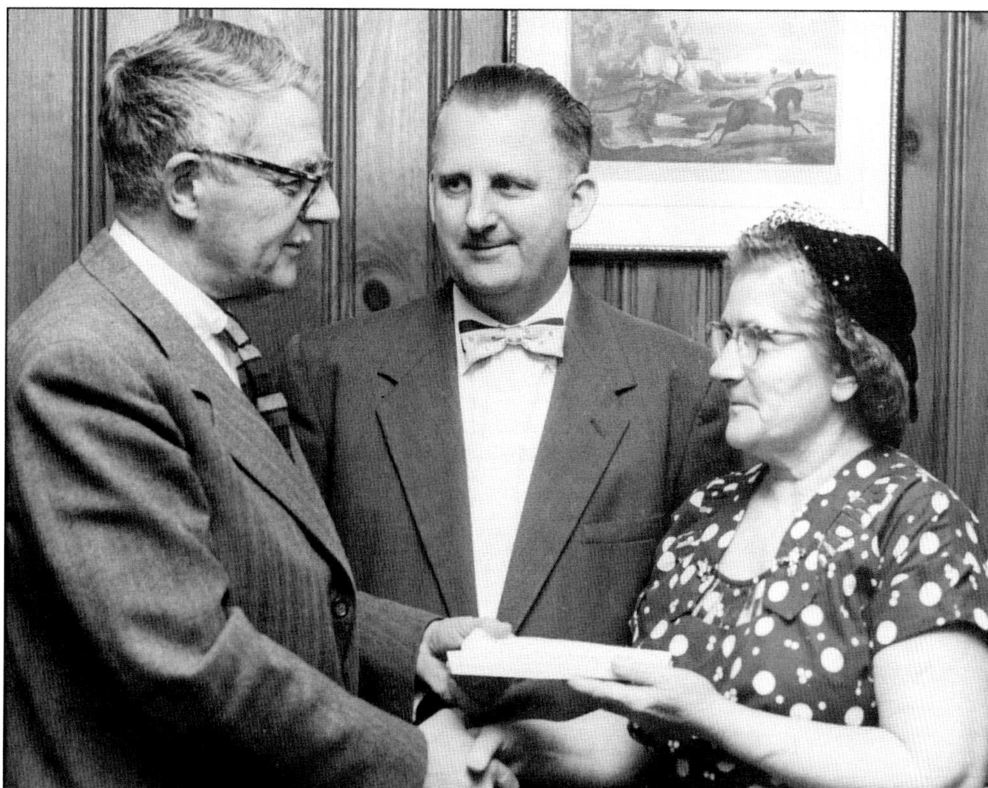

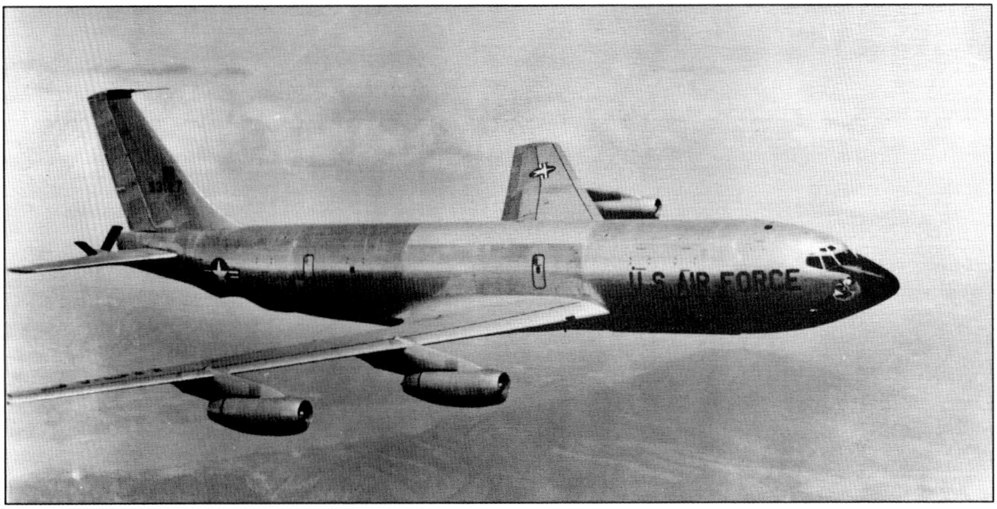

On November 15, 1957, Gen. Curtiss E. Lemay, Air Force vice chief of staff, and a seven-man crew set a nonrefueling, nonstop flight world record when they flew a KC-135 tanker from Westover to Buenos Aires, Argentina, in 13 hours and two minutes. The plane covered the distance at an average speed of 484 miles per hour. (Defense Department photograph; courtesy of Ron Groleau.)

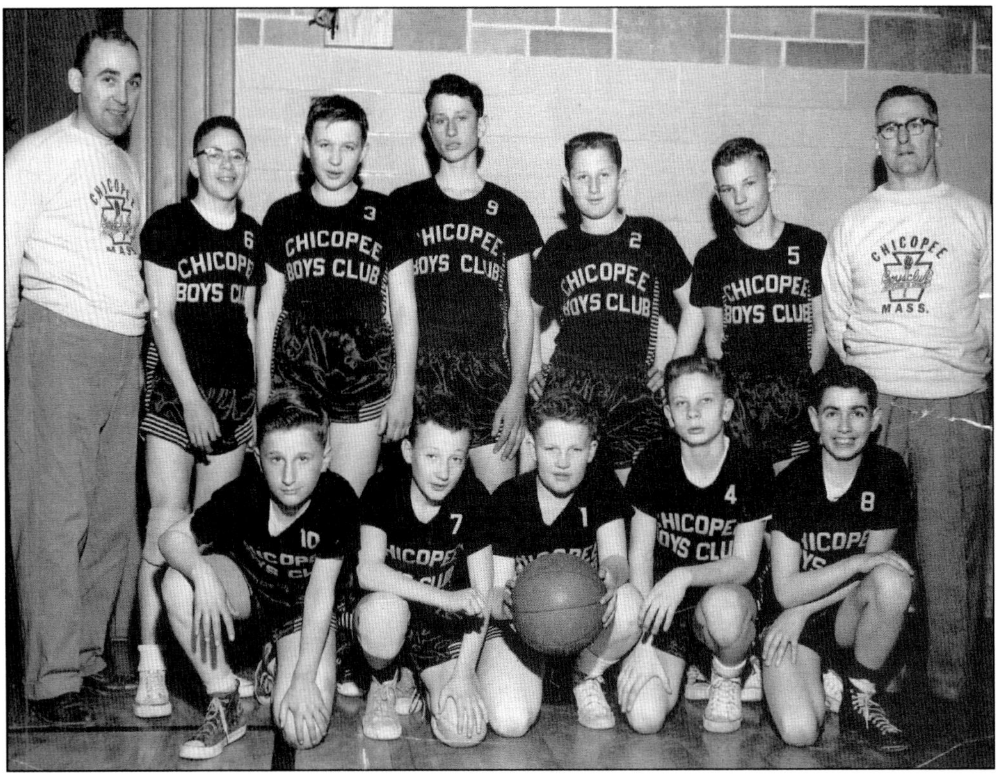

The 1955 basketball team in this photograph was a highly competitive squad coached by Hank Gonet and Dan Riordan. From left to right are (first row) Ray Lavigne, Chuck Dooley, Danny Riordan, Jim Kijak, and Tom Bucalo; (second row) Coach Gonet, Gerald Johnson, Bill Muldoon, Pete Mason, Walter Valego, Matt Zawidowski, and Coach Riordan.

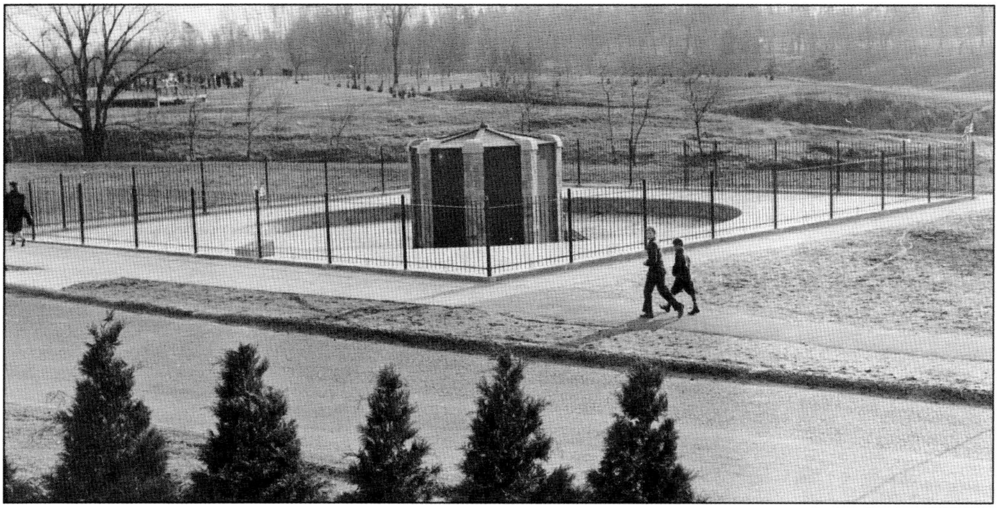

In 1957, Chicopee High School principal Henry B. Fay was dealing with an acute parking problem on Academy Street. The teenagers of the 1950s had part-time jobs and money to spend. The automobiles they owned were generally nearly 10 years old and in need of constant repair. The safest place to go parking with a favorite companion was near the Szot Park fountain. Everyone's friends were there, and the police arrived on the hour to chase the students out.

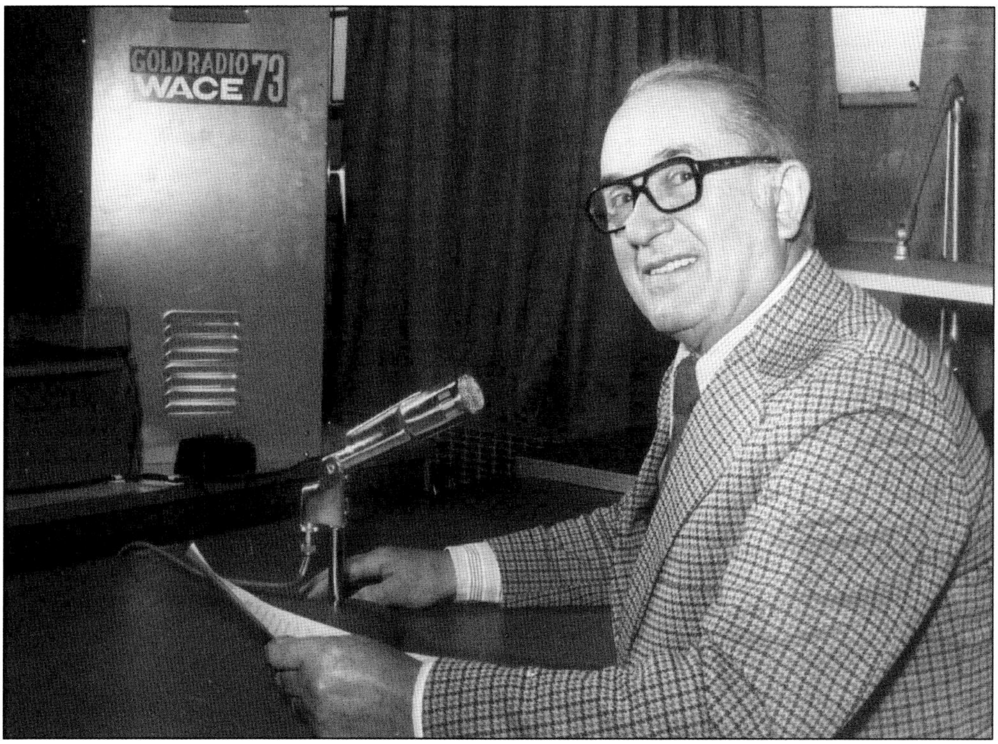

The number-one attraction of WACE, Chicopee's only radio station, was a Polish rhyming announcer named Andy Szuberla. He would write and produce his *Polish Melody Time* show for 36 years on the local station. Szuberla, pictured at the microphone, was one of three polka programs on WACE. Johnny Banas and his *Polka Time* program and Frank Skibinski's *Sunday Show* featured the best local polka bands.

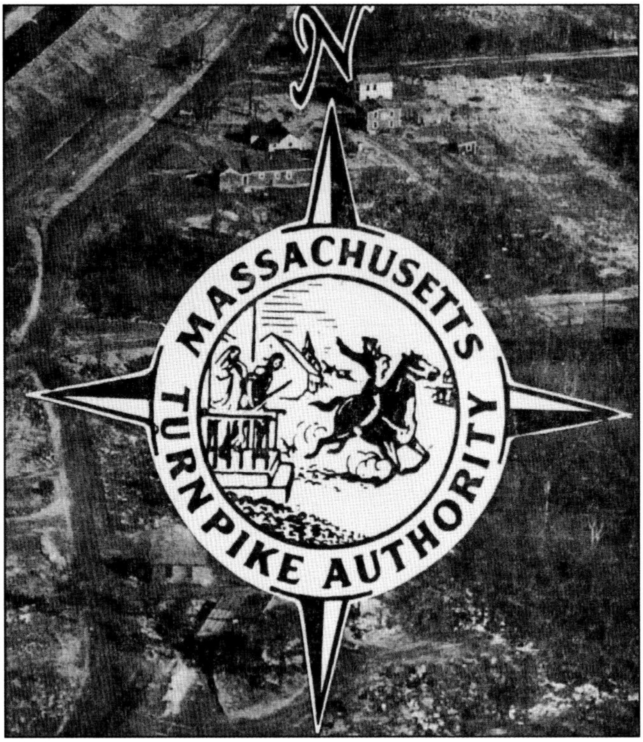

On June 29, 1956, Pres. Dwight Eisenhower signed the Federal Aid Highway Act. Ike is known as the "Father of the Interstate System." As commander of Allied forces in World War II, he admired Germany's countrywide autobahn highway network. Since then, the United States has spent $425 billion on Eisenhower's superhighway bill, forever changing how America travels. Even before federal funds became available, Massachusetts opened its own east-west superhighway: the Massachusetts Turnpike.

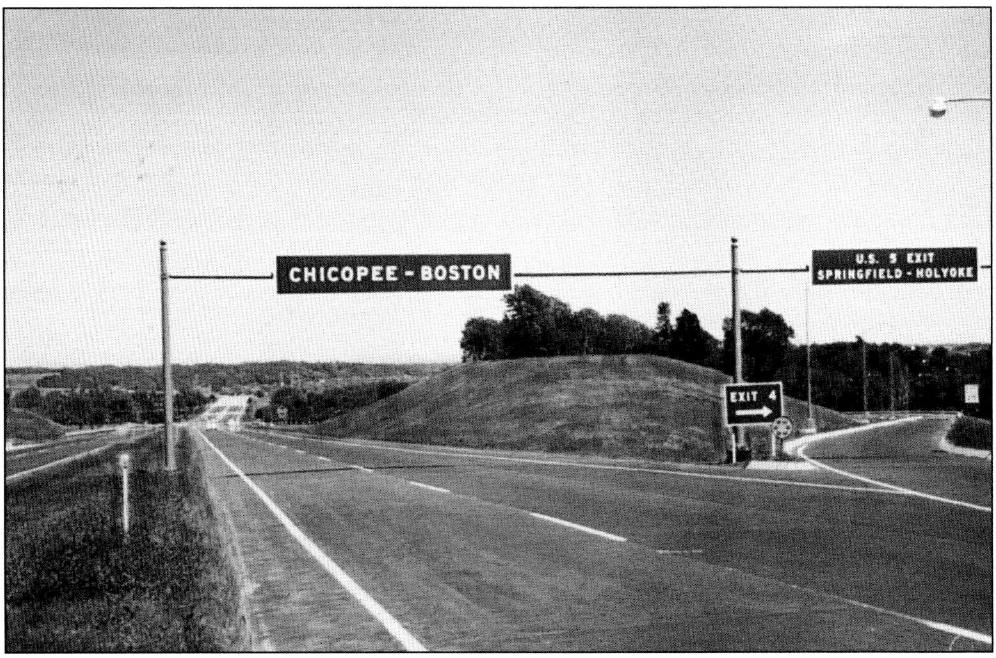

On Wednesday, May 15, 1957, Gov. Foster Furcolo officially opened the 123-mile expressway. The road was built for speed. It shortened the distance between Albany, New York, and Route 128 in Weston by nine miles. The savings in time was estimated at 122 minutes for automobiles and 129 minutes for trucks. The Massachusetts Turnpike design incorporates maximum curve radii, long-sight distance, and easy grades with long, vertical curves on summits of hills.

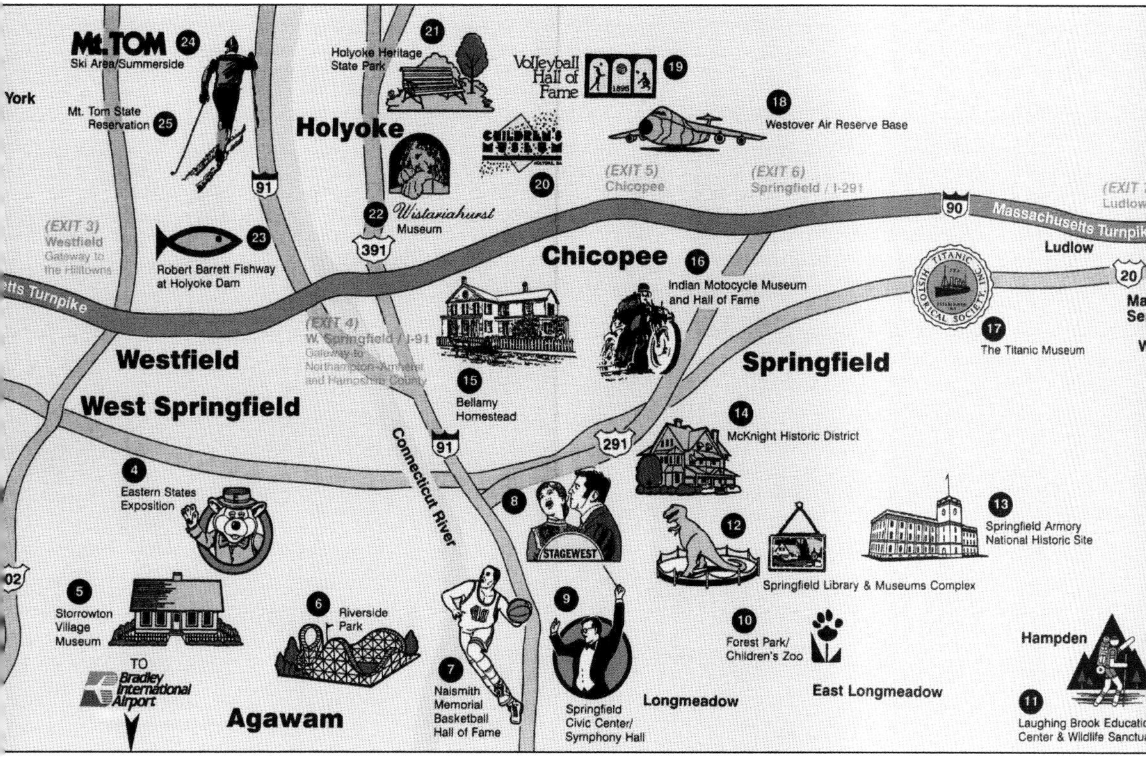

The turnpike's original plans had the Springfield exit 6 serving Chicopee and Springfield. The US Air Force stepped in, indicating that the base's huge runways blocked access to the base via exit 6. The modified plans added an immediate access to the SAC base from a new exit 5 on Massachusetts Route 33 in Chicopee. A Boston company with roots in the state's industrial past purchased a 128-acre tract of land already zoned for industry. The Cabot, Cabot & Forbes development was called the Massachusetts Industrial Park in Chicopee. The property was located at the northwest corner of the intersection of the Massachusetts Turnpike's Springfield exit 6. Because the tollgate was actually located in Chicopee, the city had two exits on the state's premiere toll road. In the 1960s, Chicopee mayor Edward Lysek erected billboards declaring his little city the fastest-growing urban community in the Commonwealth of Massachusetts. When anyone questioned the chief executive, he indicated that he had the statistics to prove it.

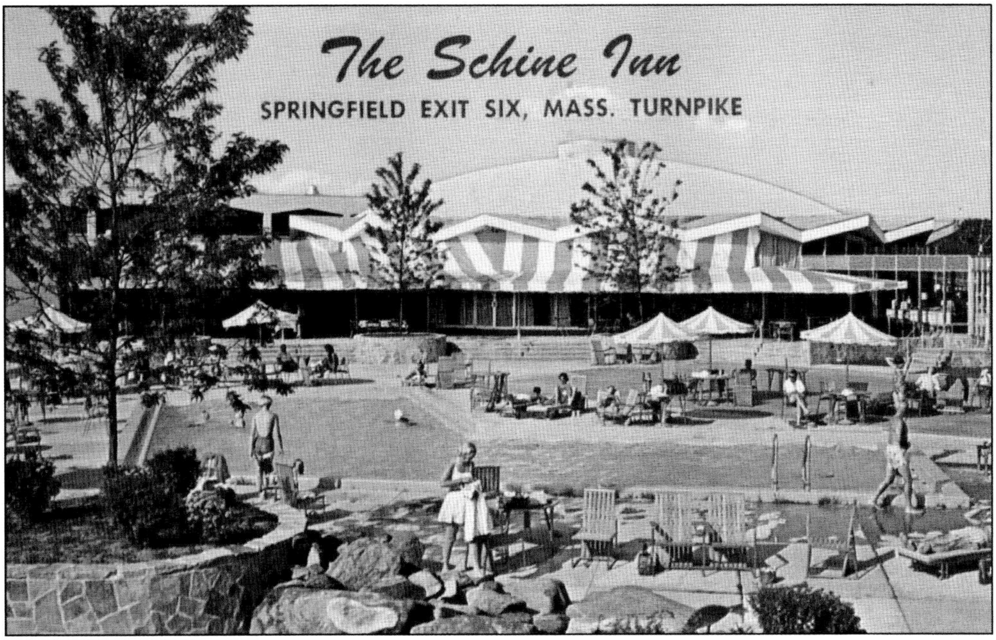

In 1957, the exits on the new turnpike were prime enterprise zones, and Chicopee's two exits were ripe for development. Westover was now headquarters for the fabled Eighth Air Force of the Strategic Air Command. The following year, on the junction of the turnpike at exit 6, a new world-class hotel was constructed by the Schine Hotel chain.

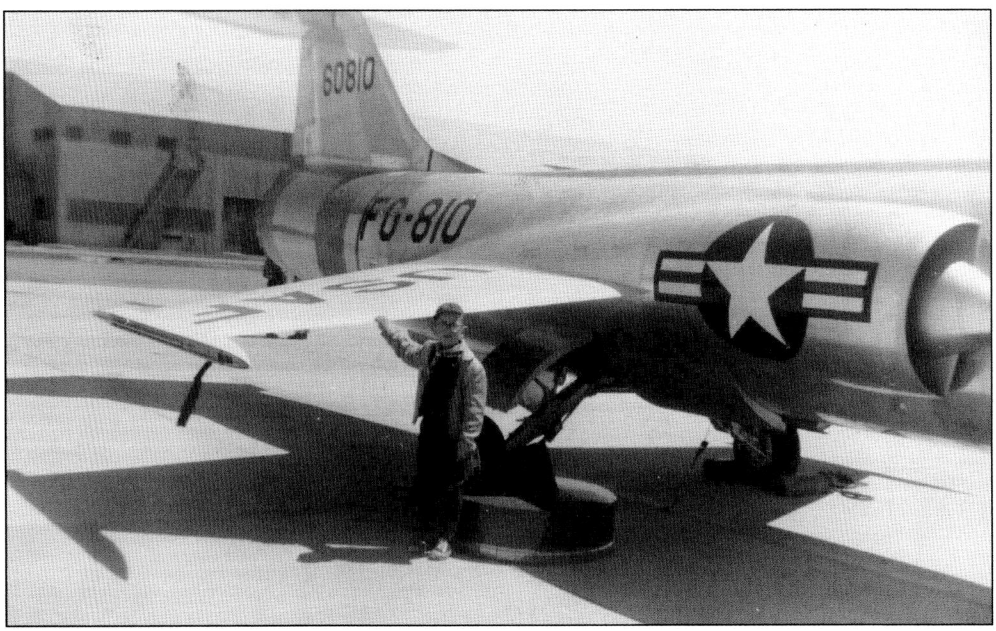

Chicopee Cub Scout John Moran poses with a US Air Force F-104. In 1958, the program was called an "open house." Westover Air Force Base was opened to the public for the day. Over the next 50 years, the program would expand to become the Great New England Air Show.

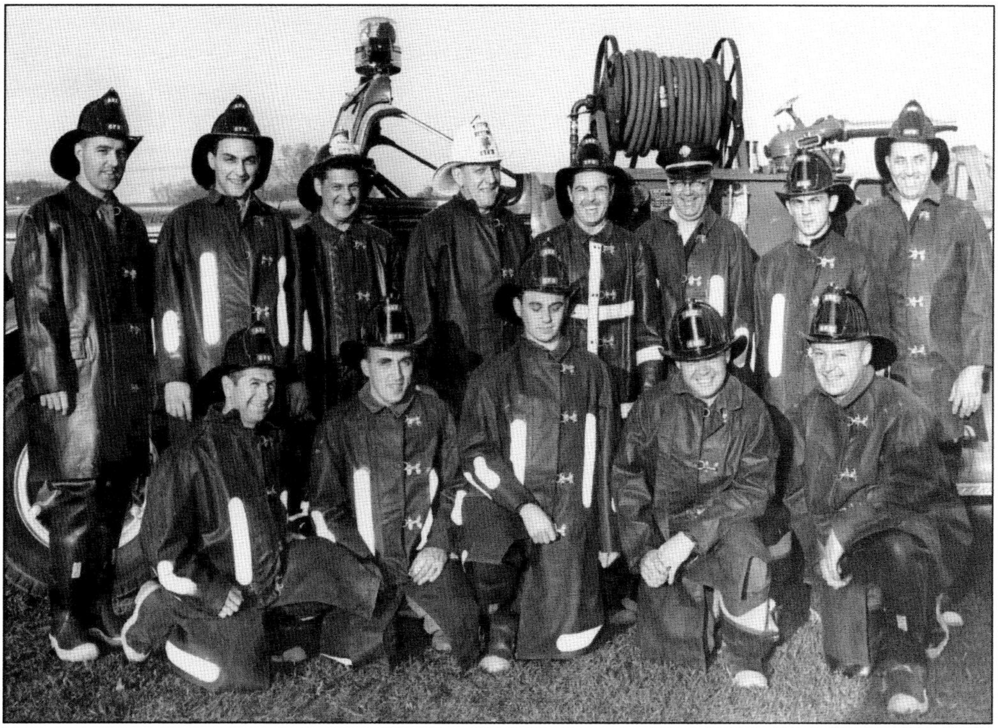

In the 1950s, communities across the nation responded to the dangers of nuclear war with a serious commitment to civilian defense. The city had a full-time local official who was assigned the task of coordinating volunteer efforts in the event of a national emergency. Pictured here, members of the auxiliary fire department were a well-trained and highly motivated group.

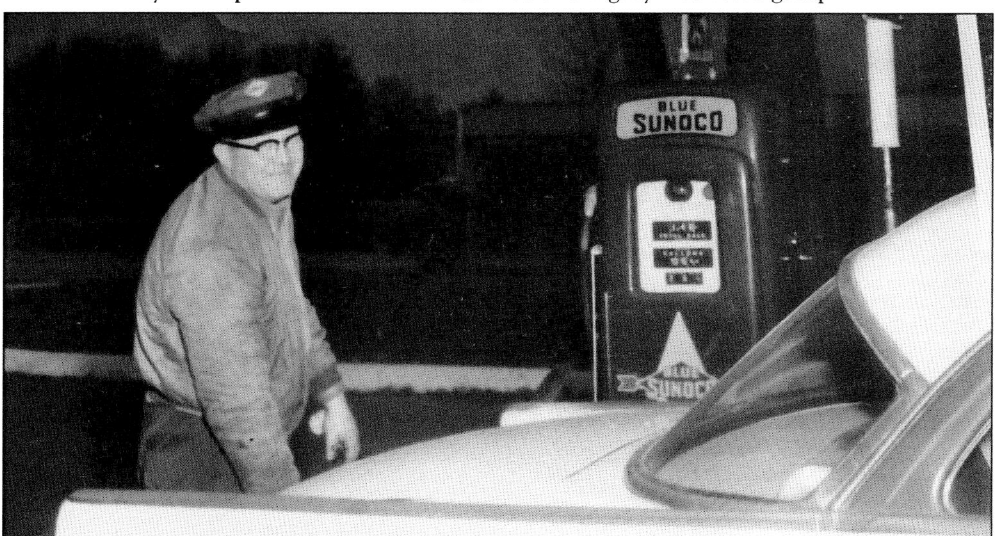

Tom Forgie Sr. was the owner of Tom & Tom (TNT) Sunoco across from the Airline Drive-in Theater on Route 33, the North and South Highway. Tom Forgie Jr. recalls 18-hour days, a 3¢-per-gallon profit, green stamps, and gas price wars. He reports that by 1963, there were 20 gas stations on Route 33.

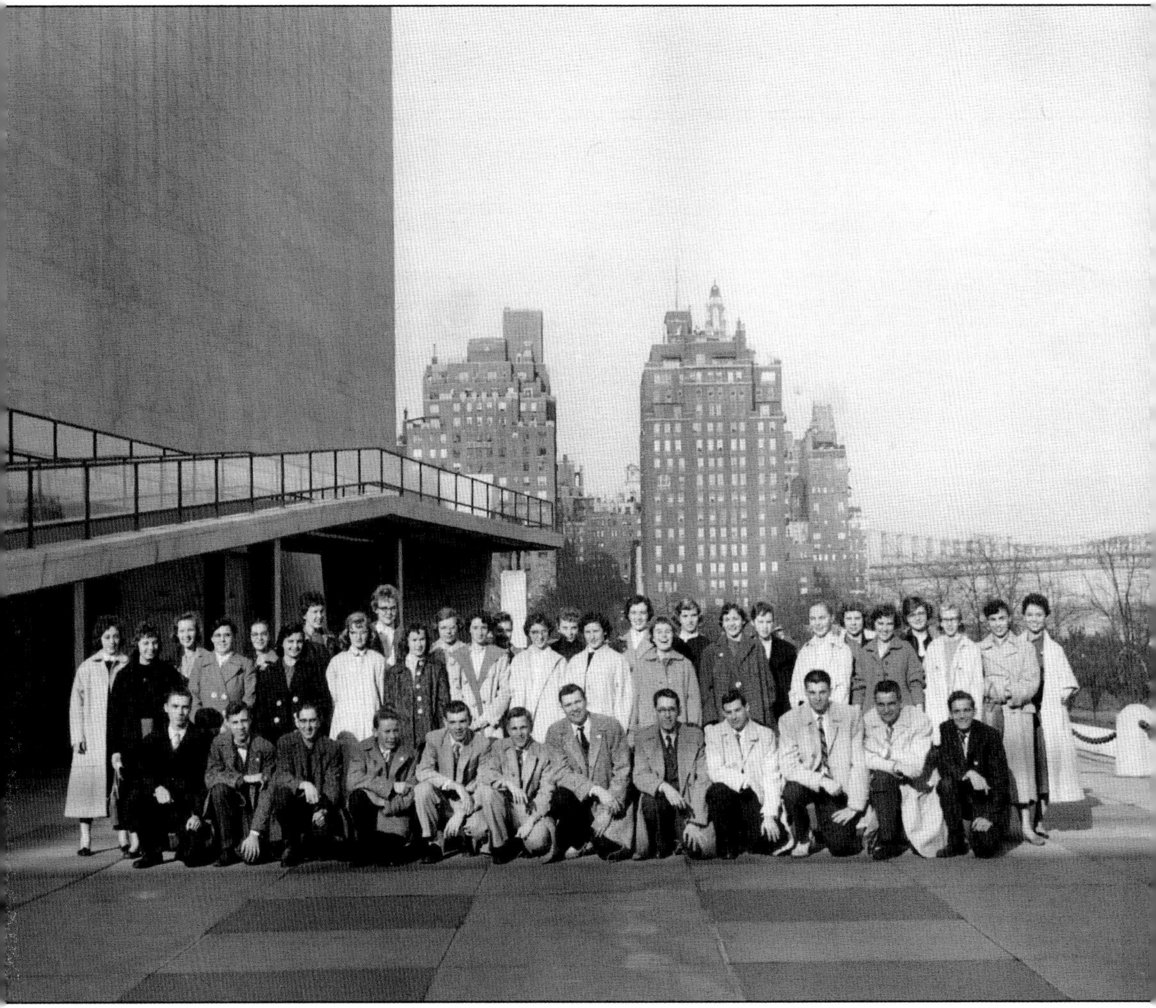

The new United Nations Building on the East River in New York City was a popular field trip destination. During the early days of the Cold War, the United States and the Soviet Union frequently faced off against each other during numerous debates in the United Nations Security Council. The US ambassador to the United Nations was former Massachusetts senator Henry Cabot Lodge, who proved an eloquent spokesman for the American position. In 1960, he was the Republican candidate for vice president. Photographed on East River Drive are members of Doris Harrison's problems of democracy classes. Chicopee High School students made the trip during rush hour by train from Springfield's Union Station to Pennsylvania Station in New York City. The students walked to the United Nations, staring up at the skyscrapers all the way.

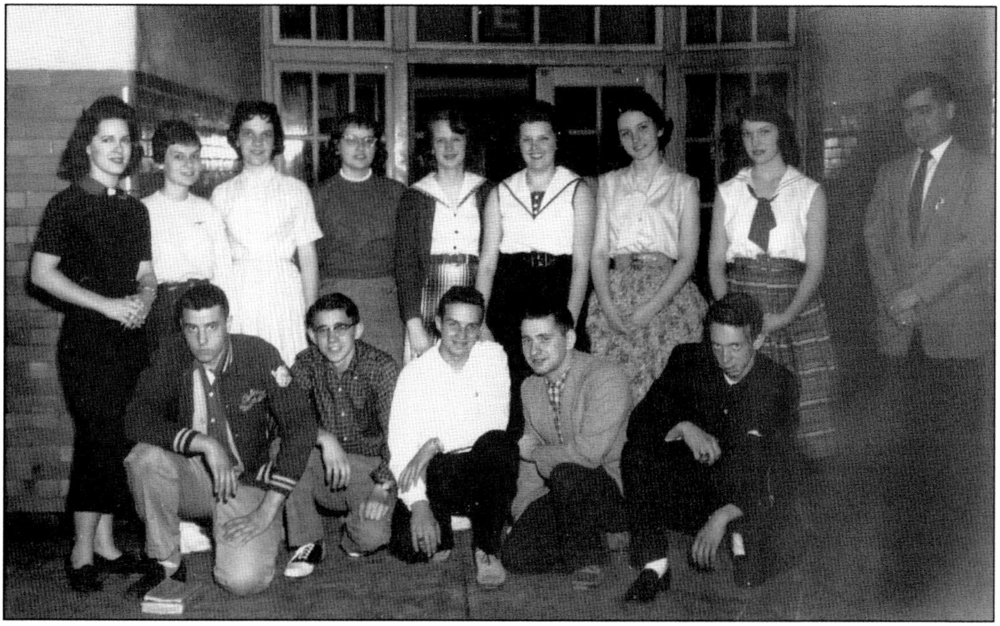

The Chicopee High School Drama Club's Class Advisor was a Joseph Plourde (far right). He was a member of the old school's revitalized English department. In the spring of 1958, the club presented three one-act plays to the delight of a full house in the high school auditorium. The club's president was Anne Sweeney (second row, far left), the daughter of Gen. Walter Sweeney, who was the commanding officer at Westover Air Force Base.

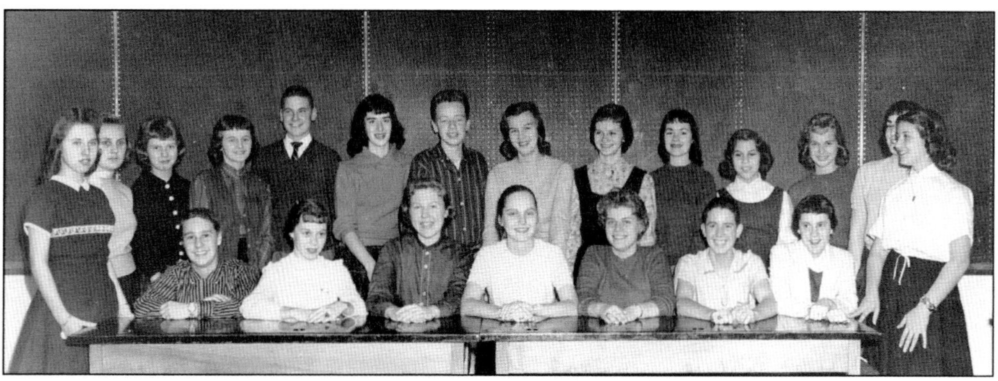

Pictured is the Chicopee High School student council in 1957. From left to right are (first row) John Dumont, Martha Johnson, Millie Trottier, student council president Barbara Ciszek, Marge Bozek, Darryl Osborne, and Nancy Schmidt; (second row) Pam Roy, Joyce Jochim, Carol Pieckarz, Judy Chaban, Mitch Stachowicz, Ethel Welch, Walter Ross, Pat Fugial, Bev Annis, Janet Gosselin, Carol Mason, Eileen Bragiel, unidentified, and Diane Bartlett.

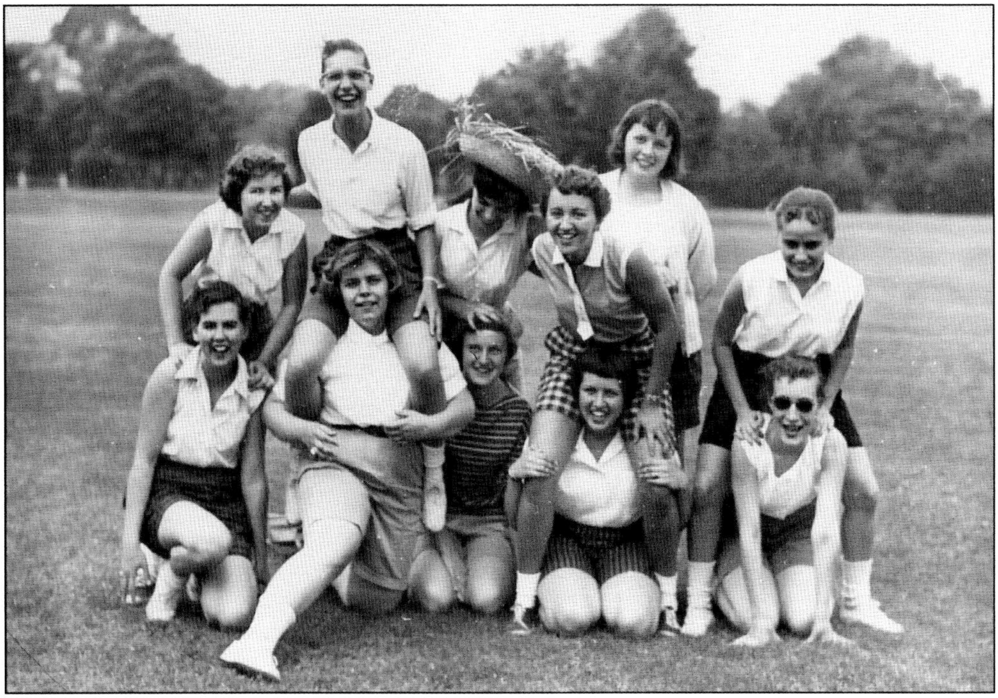

Young ladies take time out from Senior Class Field Day at Szot Park. From left to right are (first row) Patricia Murphy, Majorie Bozek, Janet Chapin, Carol Mitera, and Judy Ogrodnik; (second row) Heather Brough, Constance Blais, Adele Kochanek, Barbara Page, Kathleen McGinty, and Muriel Weissbrod.

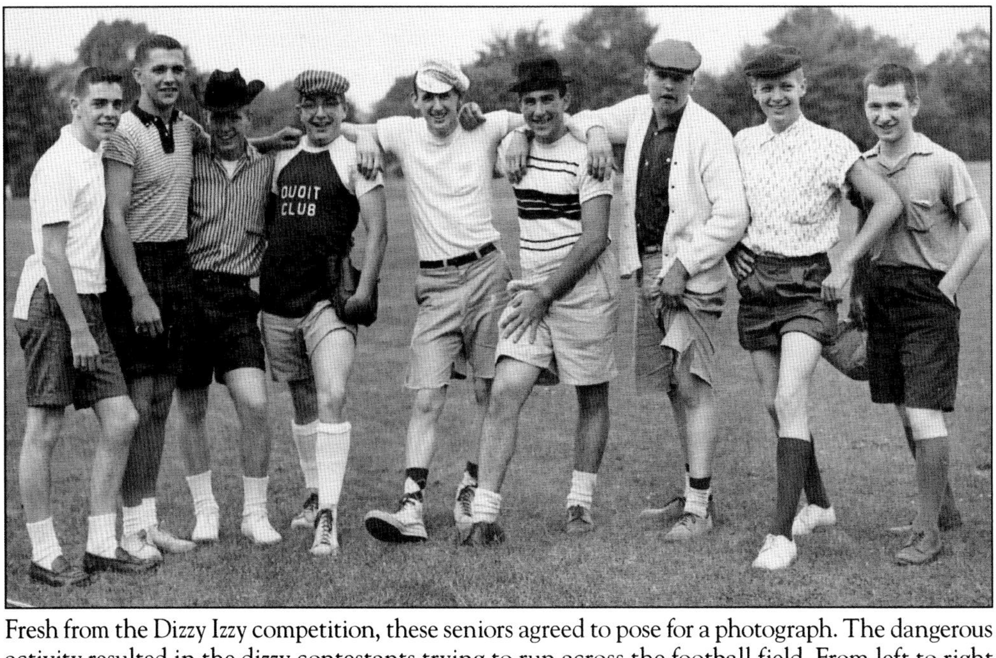

Fresh from the Dizzy Izzy competition, these seniors agreed to pose for a photograph. The dangerous activity resulted in the dizzy contestants trying to run across the football field. From left to right are Dick Sweeney, Tony Kumiega, Frank Plachta, Ed Connors, Jack Rochford, Tom Watson, Steve Jendrysik, David Korkosz, and Walter Tyminski.

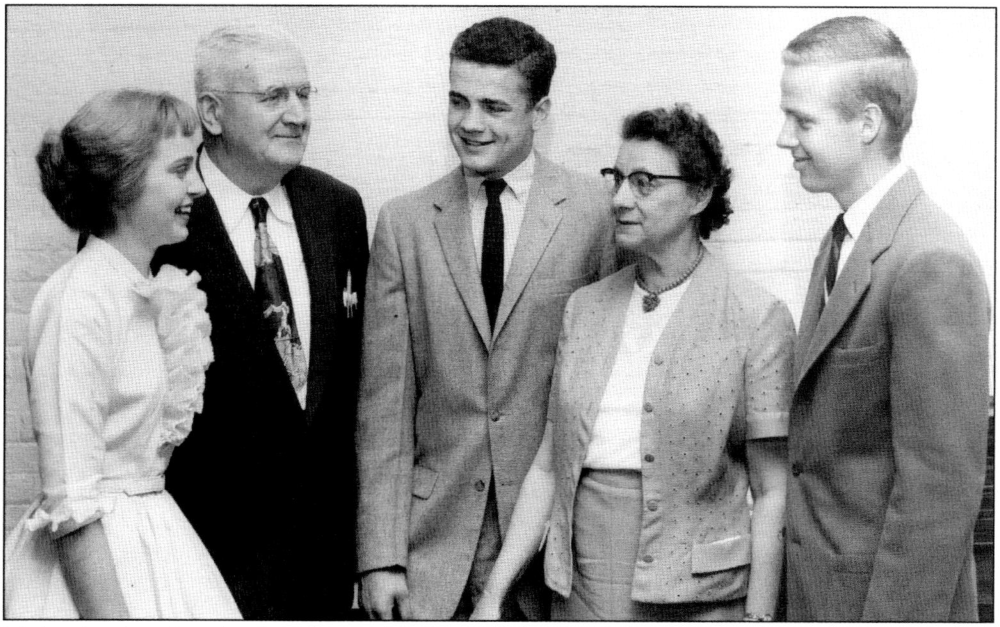

High school student leaders chat with retiring high school department heads. From left to right are Barbara Ciszek, student government president; John O'Connor, science department chairman; Thomas O'Connor, junior class president; Marion Snow, English department chairman; and David Korkosz, senior class president. Both educators had taught at Chicopee High School for 35 years.

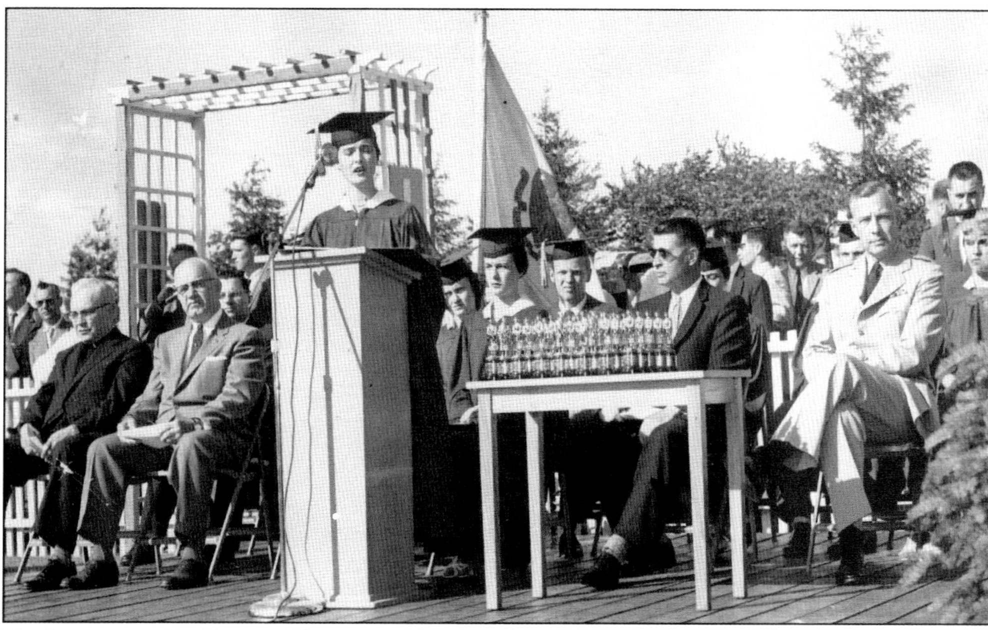

Graduation speaker Patricia Thompson addresses the graduating seniors of Chicopee High School's class of 1958. The gold statutes were presented by the Chicopee Lodge of Elks to graduating members of the National Honor Society. During the ceremonies at Szot Park, 299 students received their diplomas. In 1958, the freshman class was on double sessions. The school would operate a dual schedule until a new high school in the Aldenville section of the city opened in 1962.

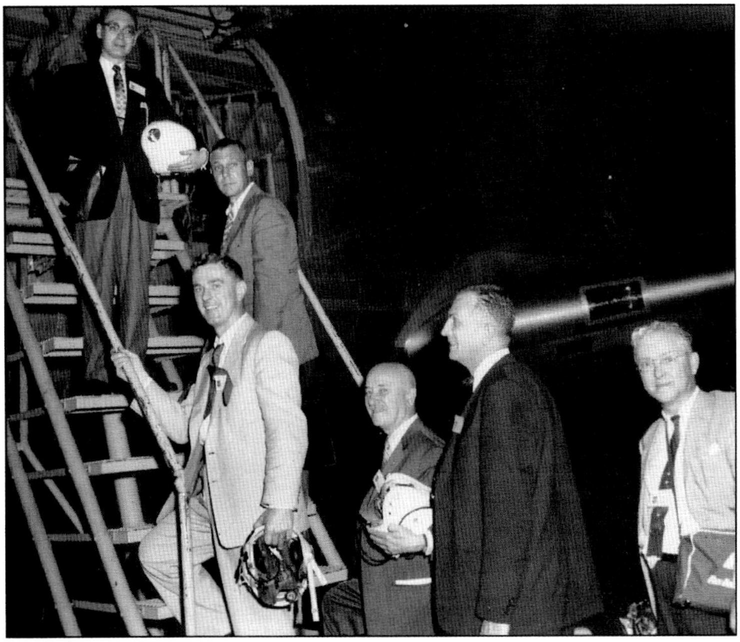

The newsmen are boarding the KC-135 tanker for the record-setting journey—six hours to London at the unheard of speed of 500 miles per hour. While two Westover jets would set a new transatlantic record to Brize Norton Air Base in London, England, the third plane (pictured) crashed on takeoff in a Chicopee cornfield. (Defense Department photograph; courtesy of Ron Groleau.)

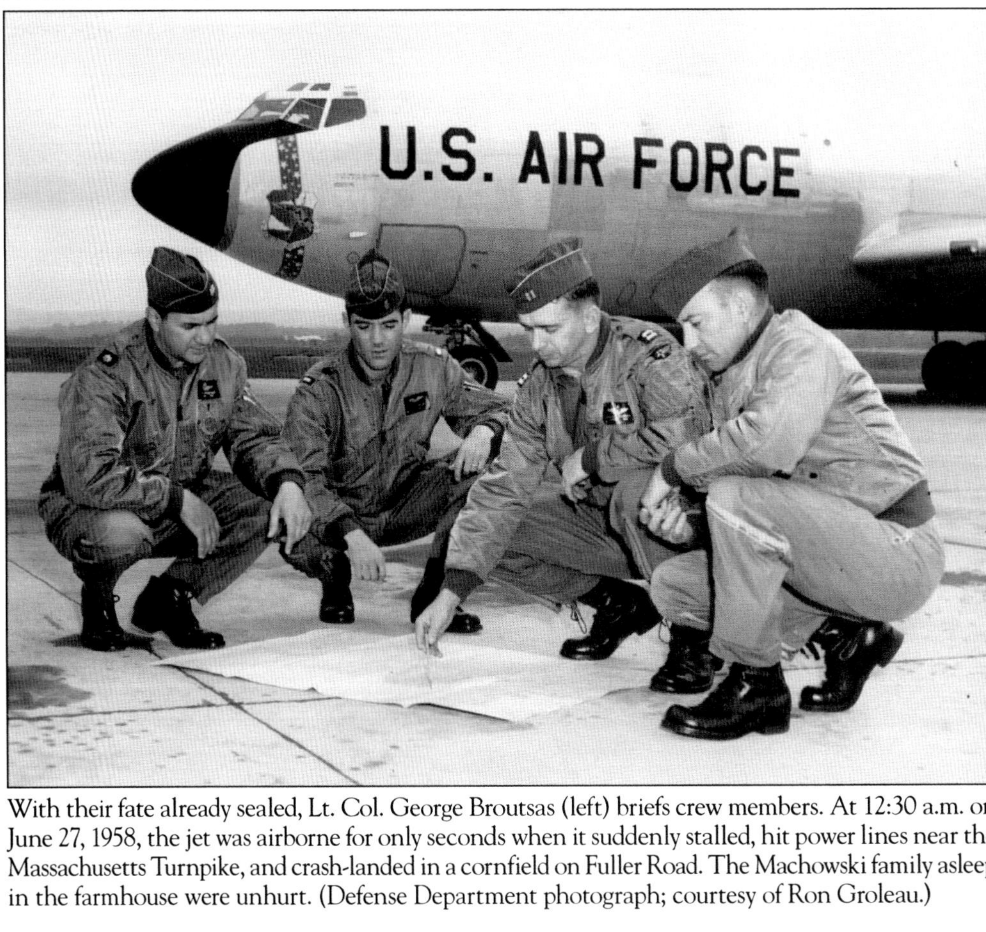

With their fate already sealed, Lt. Col. George Broutsas (left) briefs crew members. At 12:30 a.m. on June 27, 1958, the jet was airborne for only seconds when it suddenly stalled, hit power lines near the Massachusetts Turnpike, and crash-landed in a cornfield on Fuller Road. The Machowski family asleep in the farmhouse were unhurt. (Defense Department photograph; courtesy of Ron Groleau.)

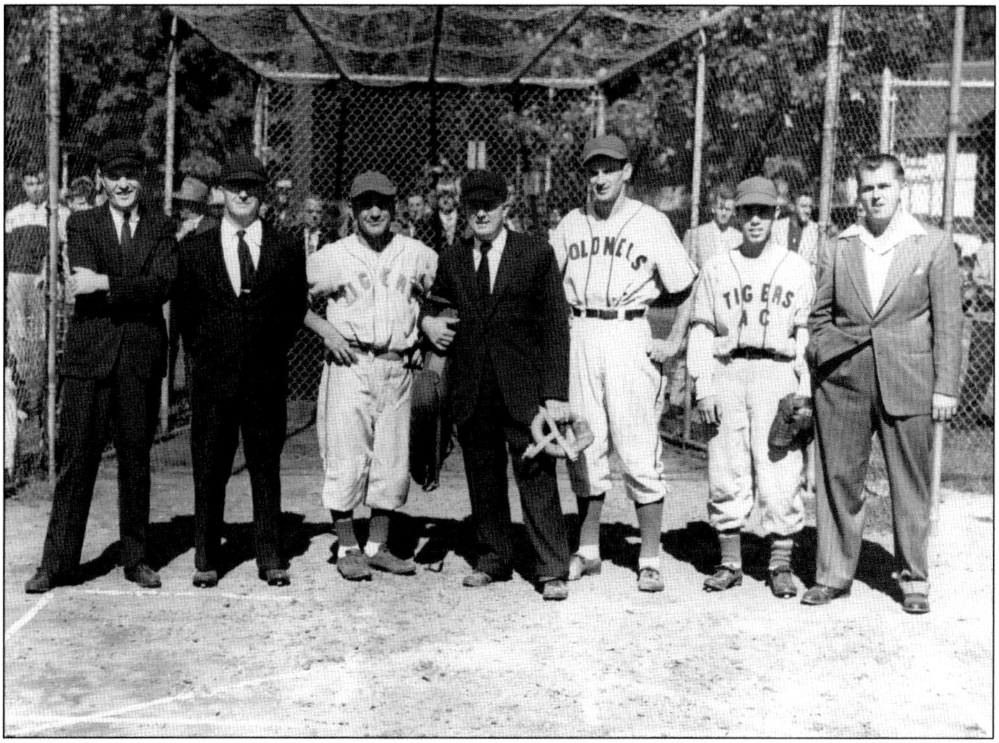

The original objective of Chicopee Falls Tigers Athletic Club when it was organized during the winter of 1936 was to promote and foster recreational, social, and educational activities in the city. When the Tri-County League was formed in 1949, the Tigers were there among the original entries. This vintage photograph at Lincoln Grove Park was taken at home plate on opening day, 1950.

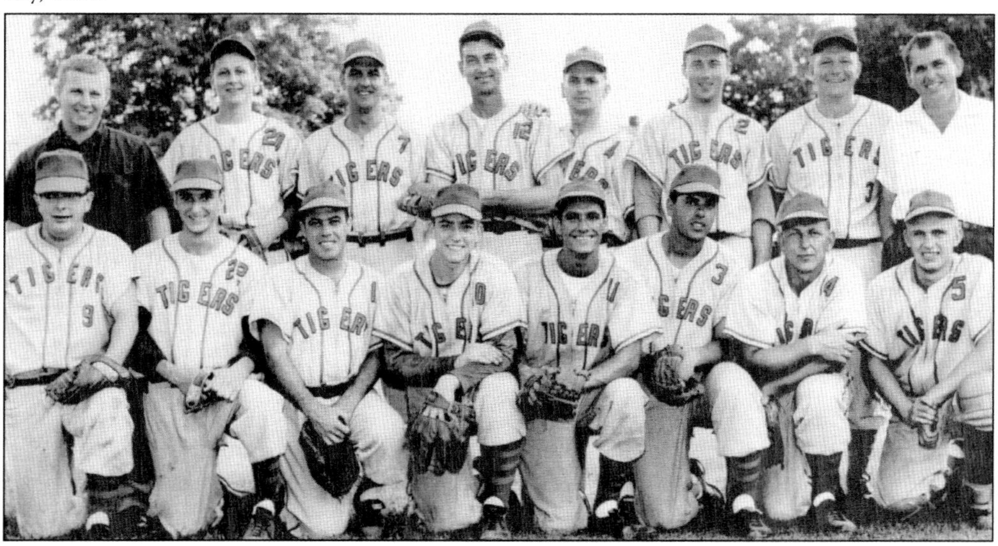

Nearly a decade later, in 1959, legendary manager Max Lesniak (second row, right) and Dan Dulchinos (first row, third from left) remained. By then, the young men playing for the Tigers were talented college athletes. Today, in its 75th anniversary year, the Chicopee Falls Club sponsors 42 teams for girls and boys in the six to 16 age group—15 in baseball, 10 in soccer, and 17 in basketball.

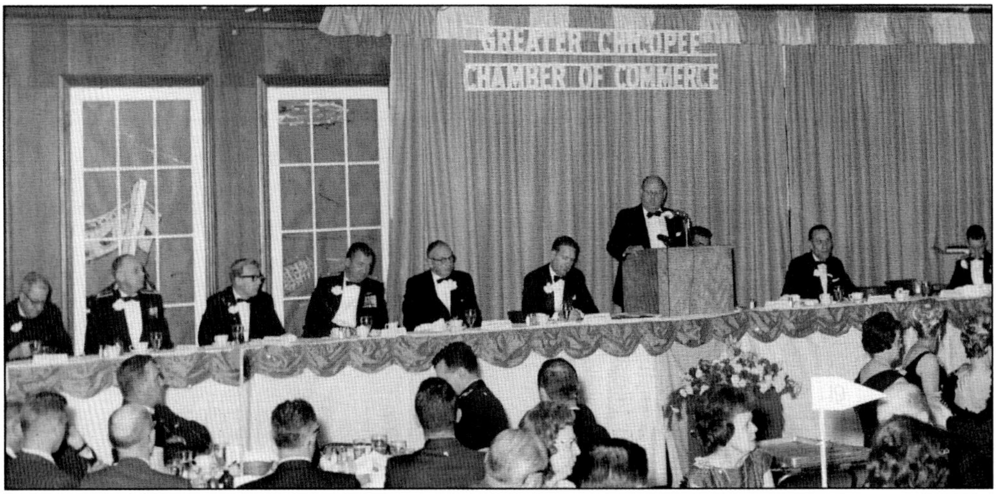

Former Chicopee fire chief Ernest A. Laflamme was the leading Franco-American candidate. In a stunning upset, career politician "Big Ed" Lysek topped the ticket with 4,858 votes to Laflamme's 4,275 votes, with Mayor Grocki a distant third with 3,255 votes. Lysek's promise to reduce the property tax by $10 helped defeat Laflamme in the city's closest election in history. Lysek is at the podium speaking to the chamber of commerce.

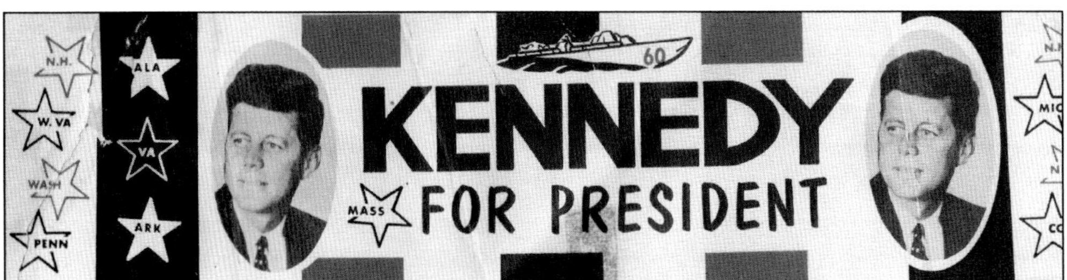

A year later, John Fitzgerald Kennedy, the junior senator from Massachusetts, defeated Vice Pres. Richard Nixon by fewer than 120,000 popular votes. During the presidential election campaign, Kennedy charged that under the Republicans, the United States had lost ground to Russia in the Cold War. Kennedy's reference to the "Missile Gap" became an important issue in the election of 1960.

Three

THE 1962 MISSILE CRISIS
1961–1965

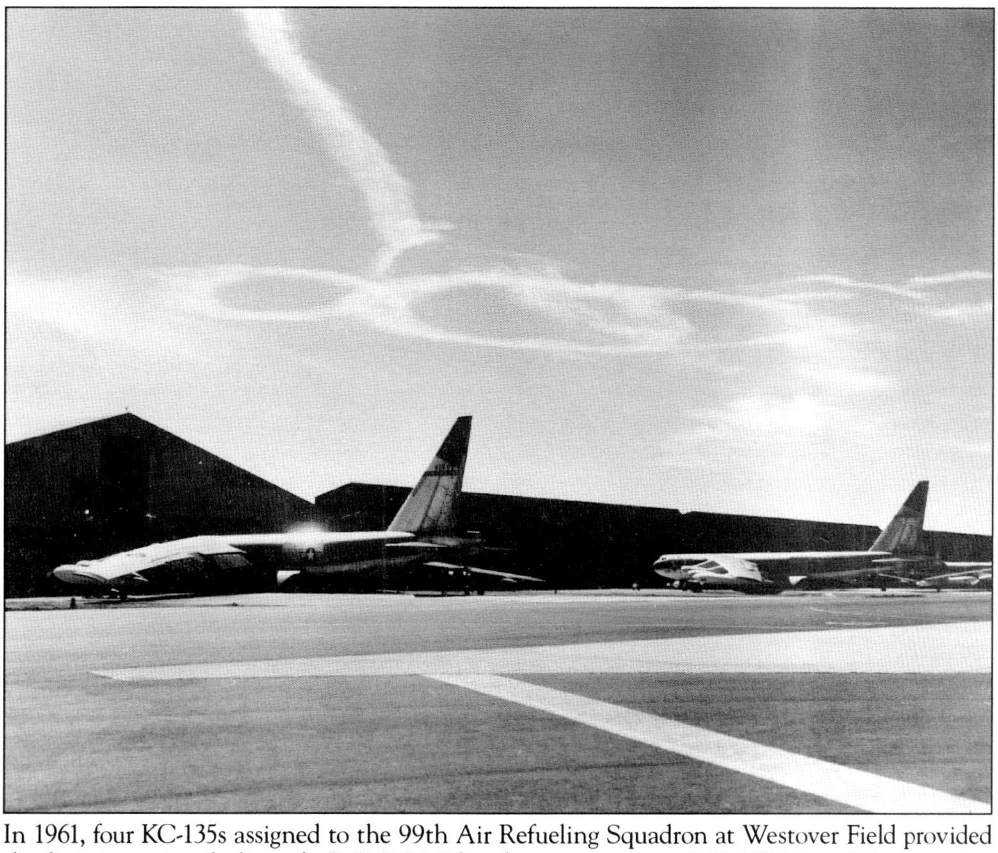

In 1961, four KC-135s assigned to the 99th Air Refueling Squadron at Westover Field provided the first air-to-air refueling of a B-52G SAC bomber carrying two GAM-77 Hound Dog missiles. The plane carried the missiles to the coastal waters of Cape Canaveral Florida for a successful launching and free flight down the Atlantic Missile Range.

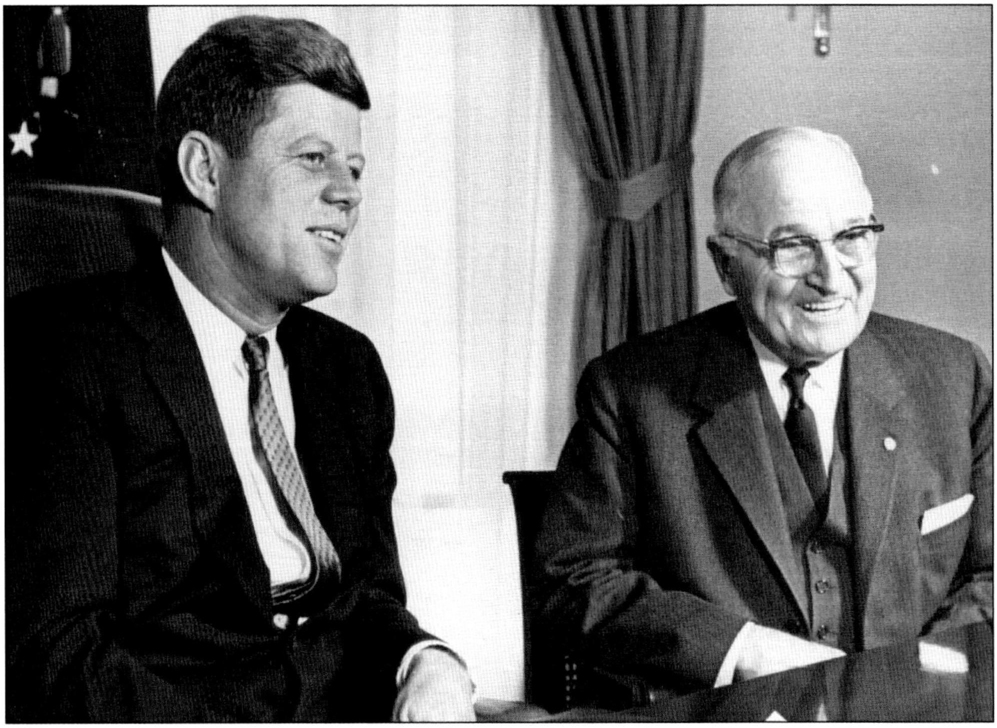

Pres. John Kennedy (photographed in the Oval Office with former president Harry S. Truman) promised to lead Americans to a "new frontier." The new president believed that under the Republicans, the nation had lost ground to the Russia in the Cold War. In Vienna, Austria, Kennedy met Russian Premier Nikita Khrushchev. Hardliners in the Soviet leadership will badly miscalculate the resolve of the young American leader.

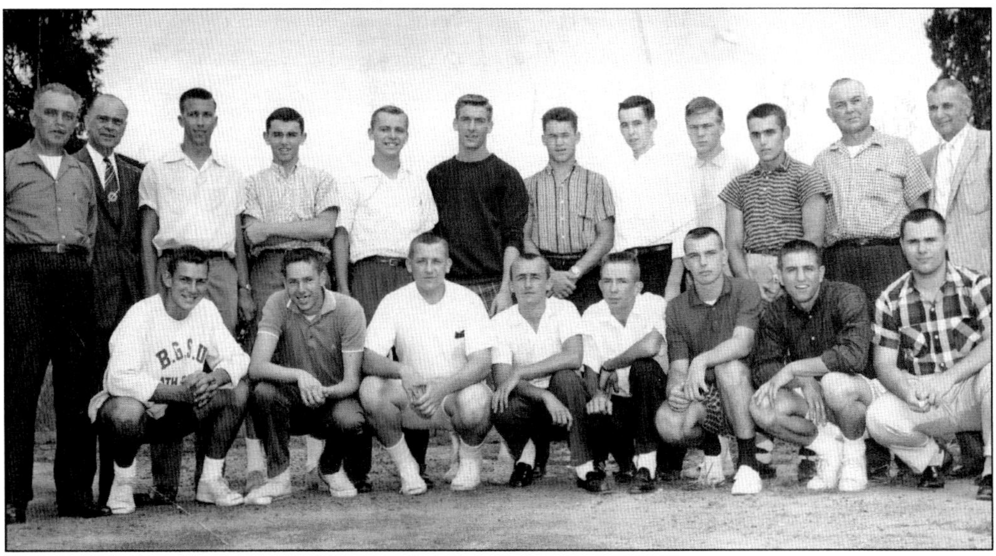

The 1961 Chicopee High School baseball team won the first of three consecutive state championships. Pictured here, the Chicopee Post 452 Massachusetts Legion baseball championship team takes time out before traveling to Keene, New Hampshire, to represent the state in the New England Championships, a first for Chicopee's "Boys of Summer."

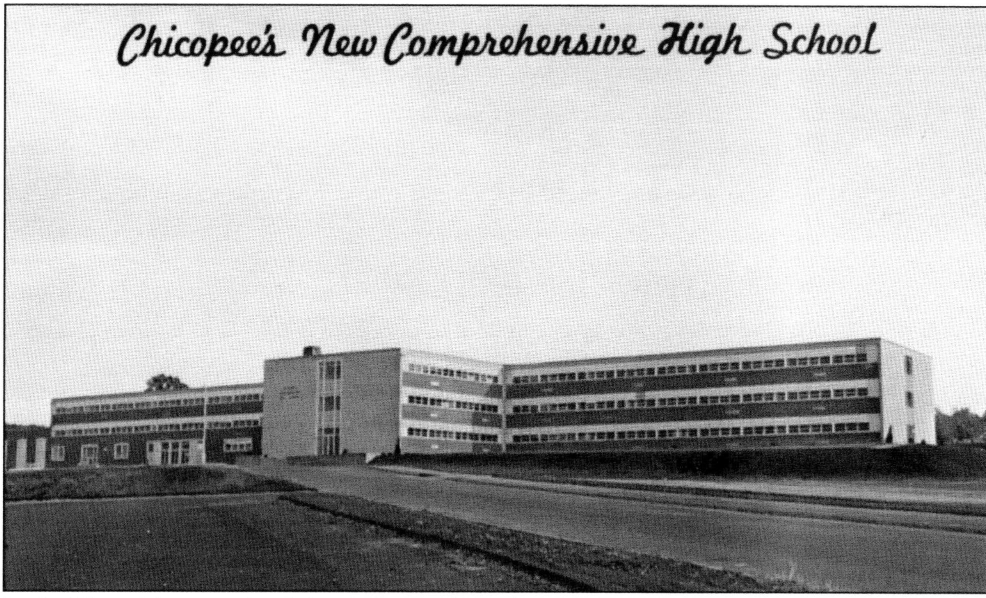

In the United States, schools located on military bases were operated by the local school system. Federally impacted areas' funds paid teachers and fully funded base construction. The Strategic Air Command wanted its teenaged Air Force dependents to become a part of the local community. When the new Chicopee Comprehensive High School opened in 1962, there were more than 400 youngsters enrolled who were military dependents.

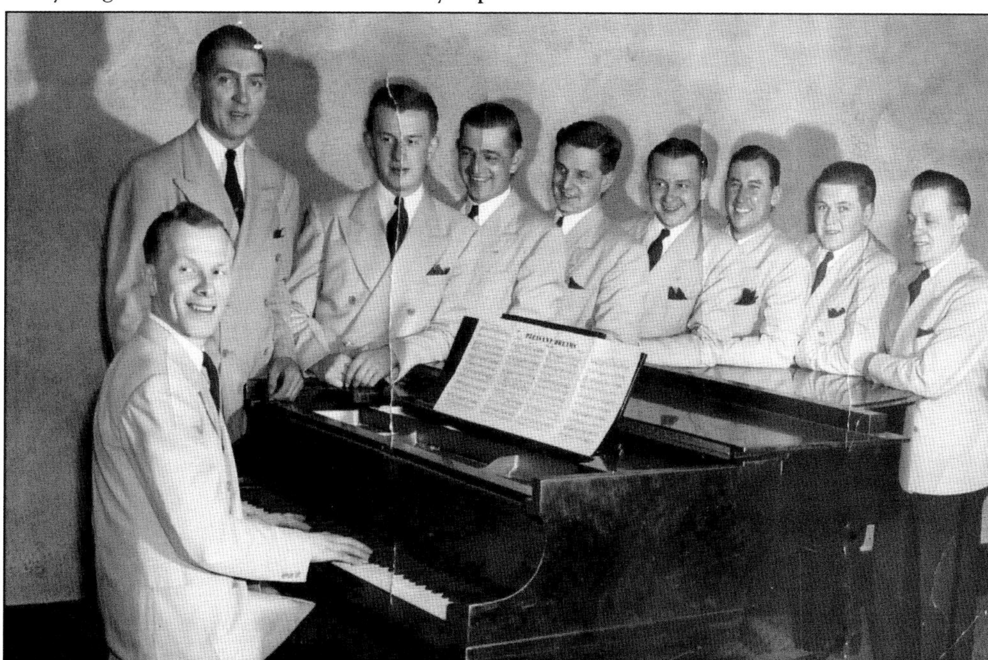

Stanley Ziemba, the member of a prominent Polish American family, was named to head the new high school. Pictured here at the piano, the first-generation American was an accomplished musician. The institution in the Aldenville section of the city was New England's first truly comprehensive high school.

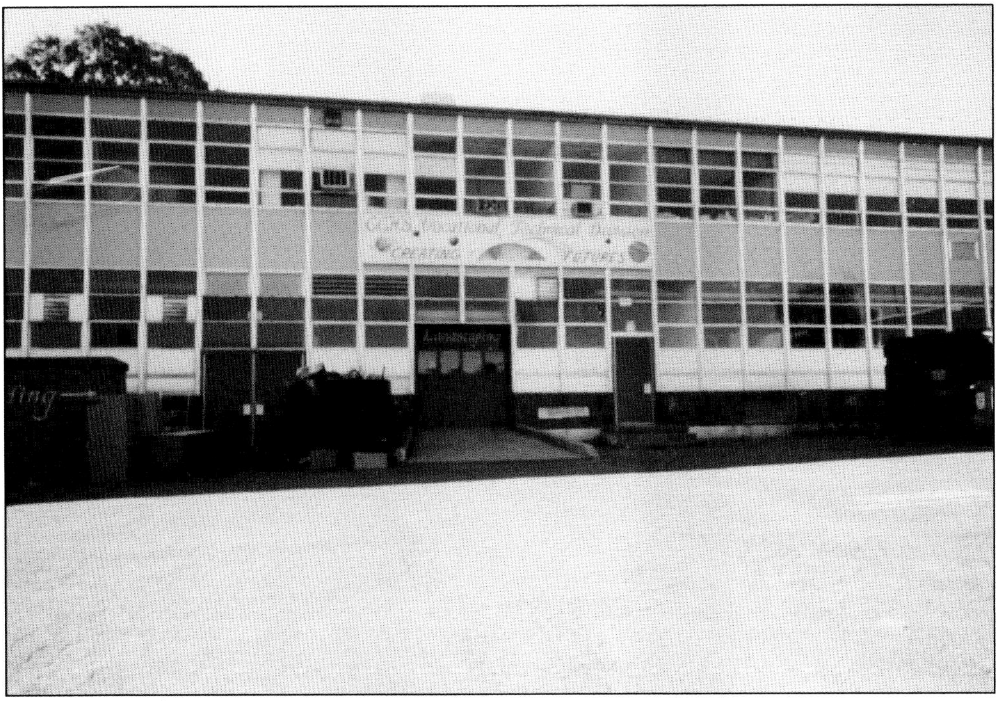

The new school was a comprehensive high school. Dr. James B. Conant, the president of Harvard University, wrote a national best seller supporting the integration of academic and vocational technical education under one school roof. Chicopee was one of the nation's first communities to adapt the concept.

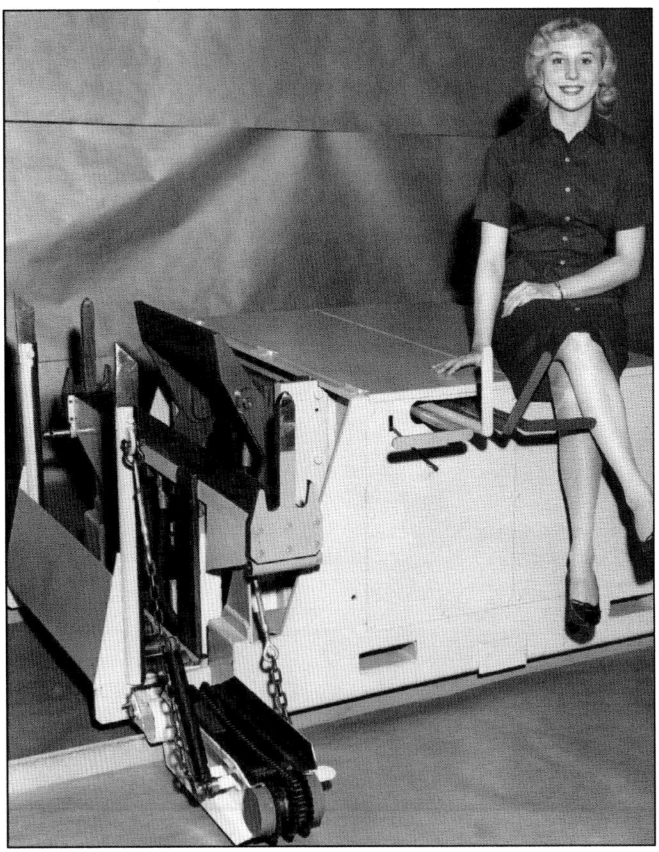

Barbara Stec, the office manager at Chicopee's McKinstry Metal Works, poses atop a newly designed extruder machine. The local company designed the prototype and manufactured the machines for the plastic division of the Monsanto Chemical Company in Springfield, Massachusetts. The industrially prominent Roy family operated the McKinstry Works in the Willimansett section of the city.

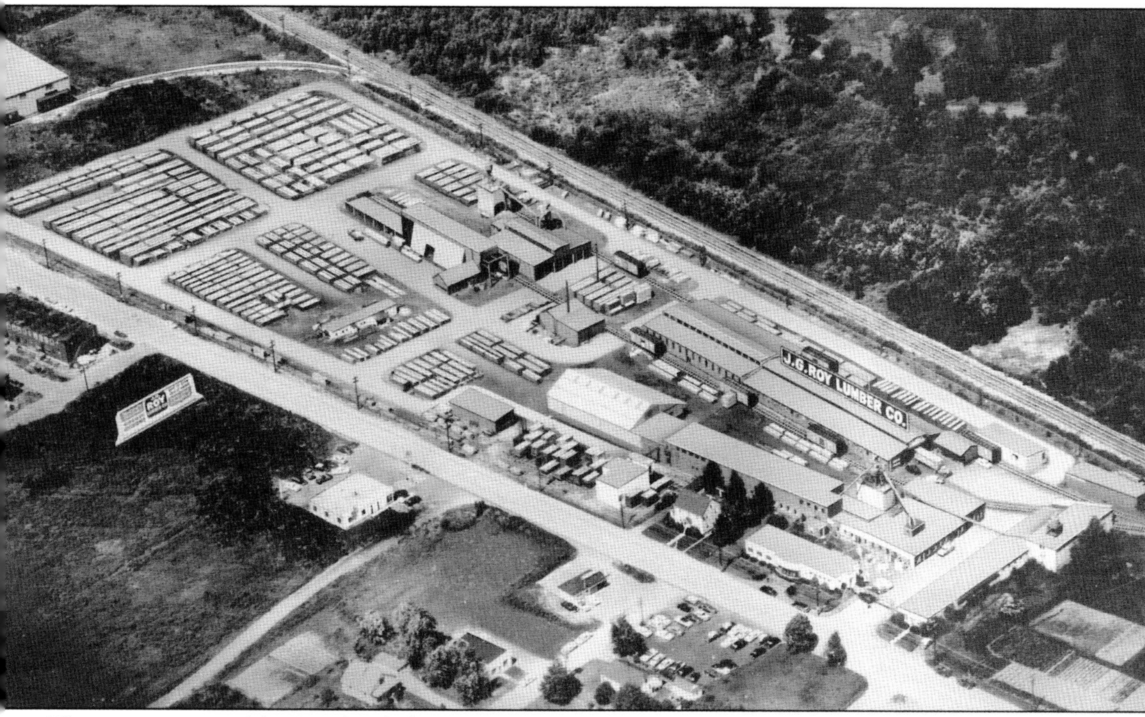

The success story of the Roy family began in the construction business. In the 1940s, the company was one of the major contractors involved in the development of the Northeast Army Air Corps facility in Chicopee. The company built housing and barracks for the Army Corps of Engineers and was a major supplier of building materials for the base. In 1942, the company was called upon for an emergency $25,000 construction job on the base. Roy Construction built a German prisoner of war facility at Westover Field. In the 1960s, a considerable portion of Meadow Street was consumed by J.G. Roy Lumber Yard. The facility was a wholesale and retail operation with manufacturing capabilities and its own rail spur. The company helped meet the demand created by the record levels of new home construction in Chicopee and the suburbs.

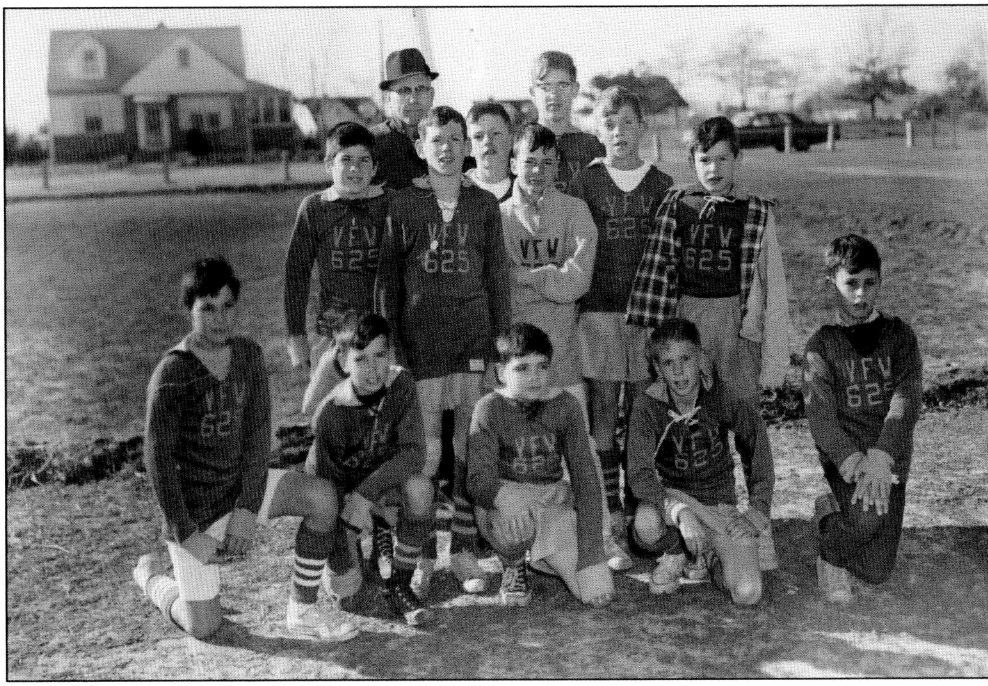

The Chicopee Soccer Association was established about the same time Chicopee High School began playing the sport on the varsity level. By the 1960s, youth soccer had arrived. Pictured here, a bevy of future high school stars were members of VFW Post 625's undefeated 11–13 champions.

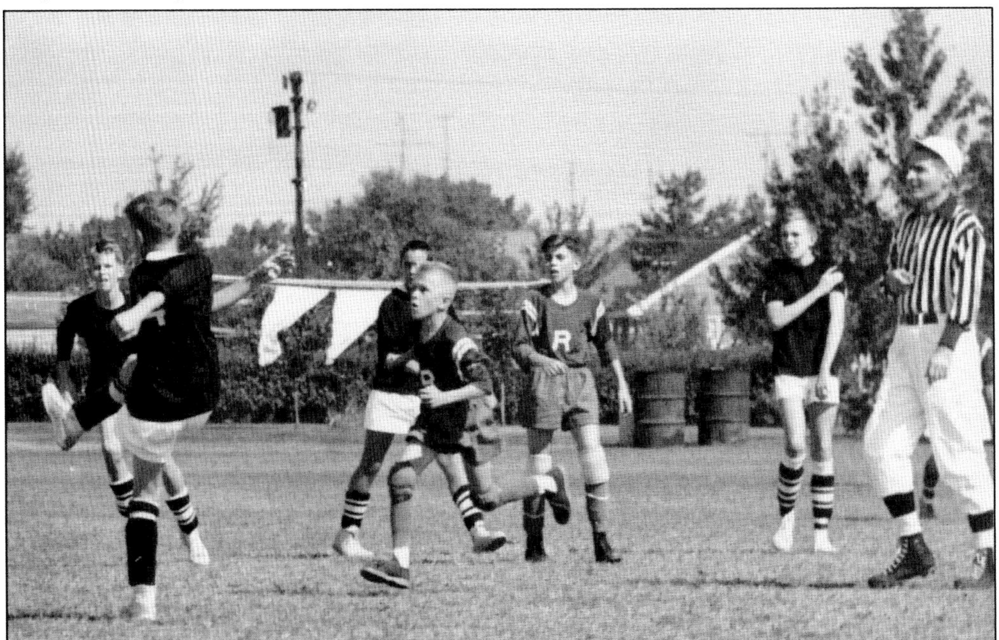

Brooks Field in Chicopee Falls was the city's first park exclusively devoted to the new sport of soccer. In Chicopee, the introduction of youth soccer was the result of the single-minded efforts of Alfred Allen. He taught school in East Longmeadow, was a member of the Chicopee School Committee, and lived near Brooks Field. Pictured here, Allen officiates a boys' game.

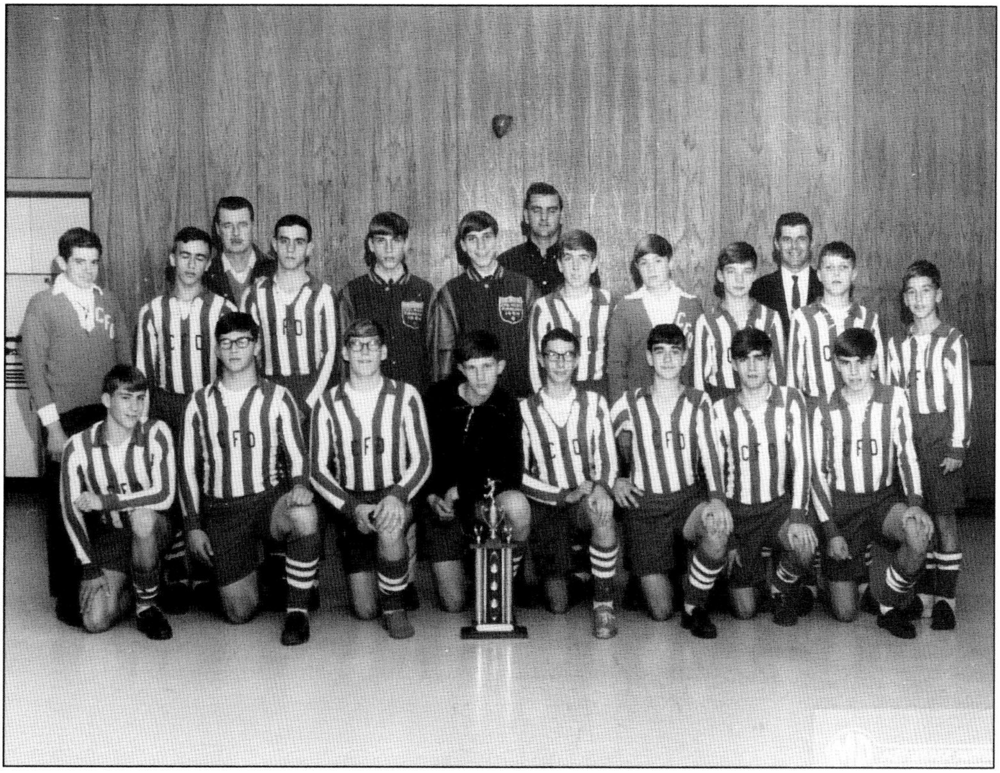

In 1960, Chicopee joined West Springfield and Ludlow to play in the National Midget Soccer Tournament against teams from New York and Pennsylvania. The Chicopee Fire Department squad pictured here won the National Junior Tournament. The coaches in the third row are, from left to right, Harvey Rock, Robert McIntyre Jr., and Donald Howe.

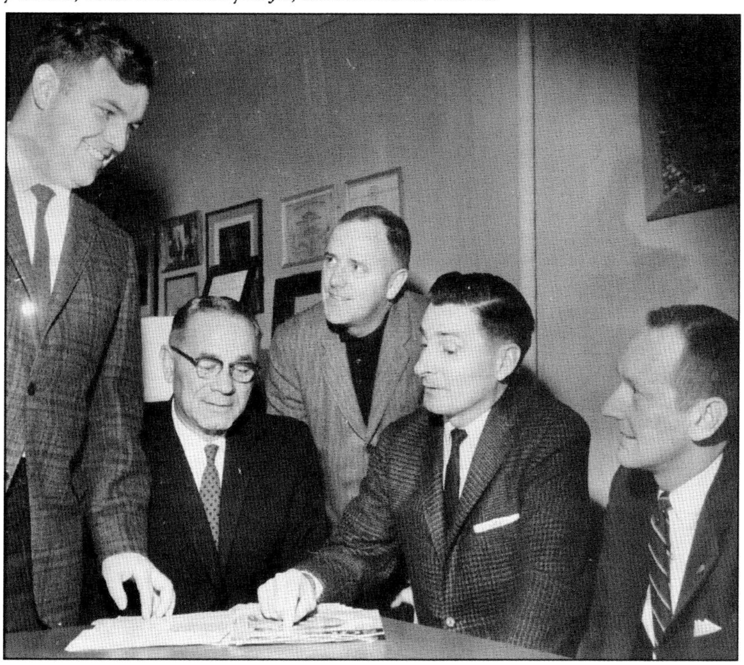

The Chicopee Soccer Association needed a reliable fundraising instrument to underwrite its ambitious program. The International Soccer Association agreed to furnish two foreign teams for a game in Chicopee. In this photograph, committee members are making plans for the big match between Ireland and Czechoslovakia.

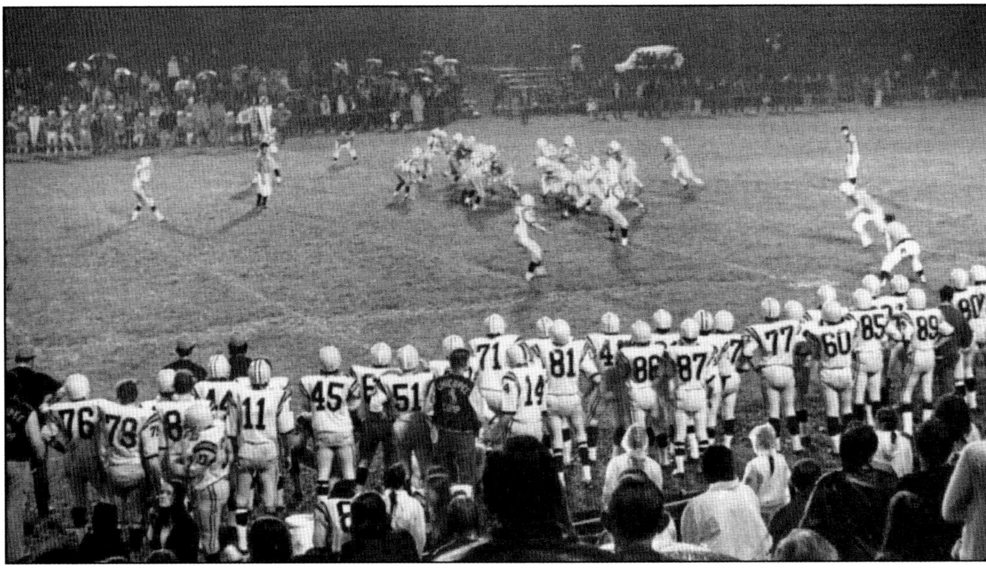

Chicopee mayor Edward Lysek spearheaded a plan to install lights at the city's premiere sports venue, Szot Park. In this picture, the Chicopee Comp Colts football team plays a Friday night game. Under the lights on July 23, 1961, came 8,000 fans from as far away as upstate New York to see a team from Communist Czechoslovakia play the Shamrock Rovers of Dublin, Ireland.

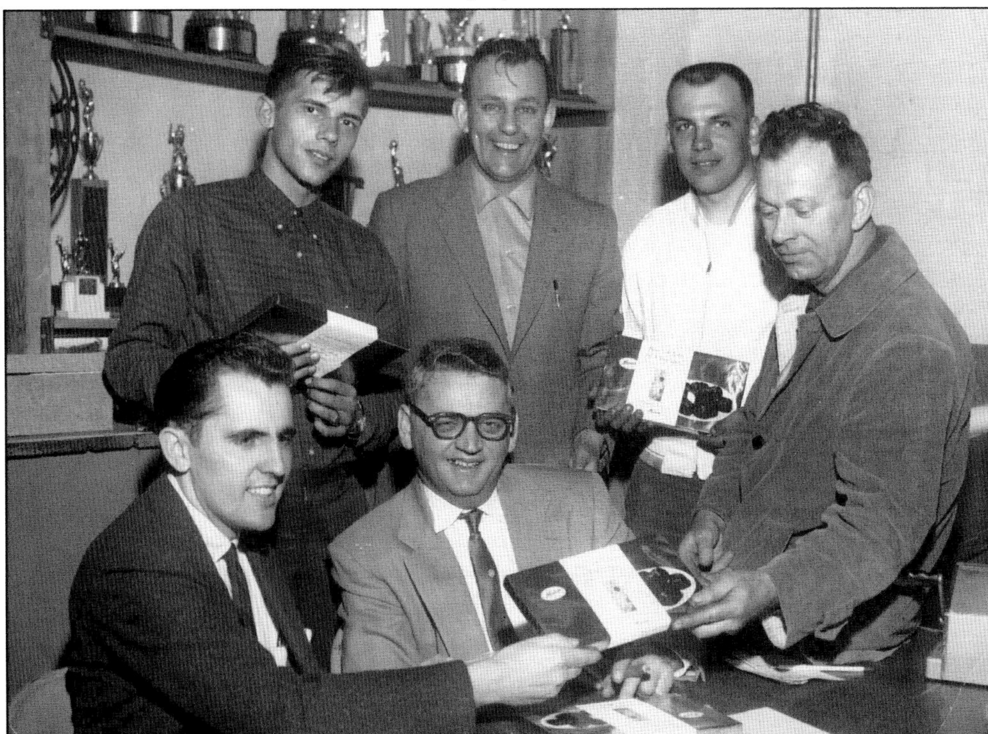

Members of the Chicopee Boys Club Executive Board join Alfred Dzialo (second row, second from left) in promoting the club's 10th anniversary candy sale. The club was organized in 1952. The city provided the fledging unit with a clubhouse at the old Grape Street firehouse.

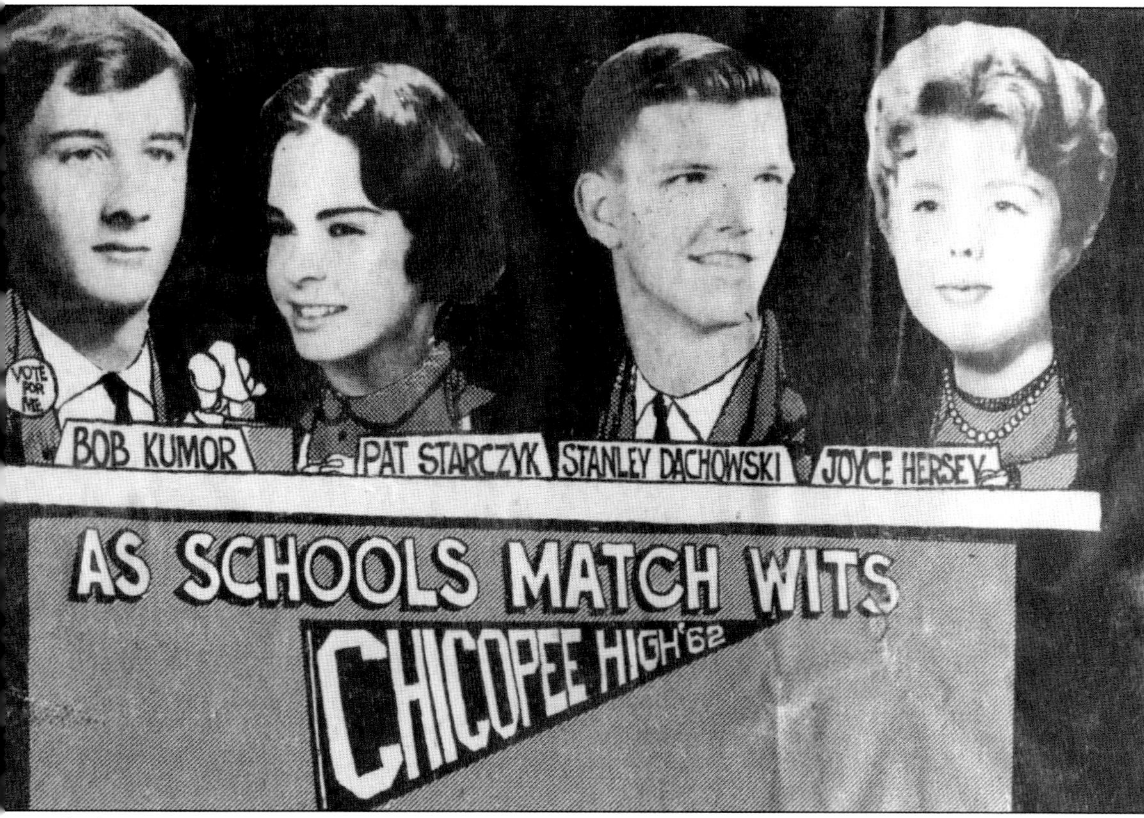

The longest-running program on Pioneer Valley television is the high school quiz competition called *As Schools Match Wits*. In 1962, the young team from Chicopee High School swept the initial year's competition. In the historic opening match, Chicopee faced Ludlow High School, a powerhouse in quest of a fifth-straight victory. That night, Patricia Starzyk and Joyce Hersey answered key questions late in the match to lead a spirited comeback. In those days, one team was equipped with buzzers, the other with bells, and the team that buzzed or rang first got a shot at the question. For the next eight weeks, the star of the team would be a fuzzy-cheeked 11th grader named Bob Kumor. While Kumor is remembered as the team's go-to guy, Hersey, Stefanik, and Stanley Dachowski provided a balance that monopolized winning and forced Channel 22 to retire the undefeated Pacers and change the show's format. The team's stunning victory buoyed community pride giving the young scholars admiration usually reserved for athletic standouts.

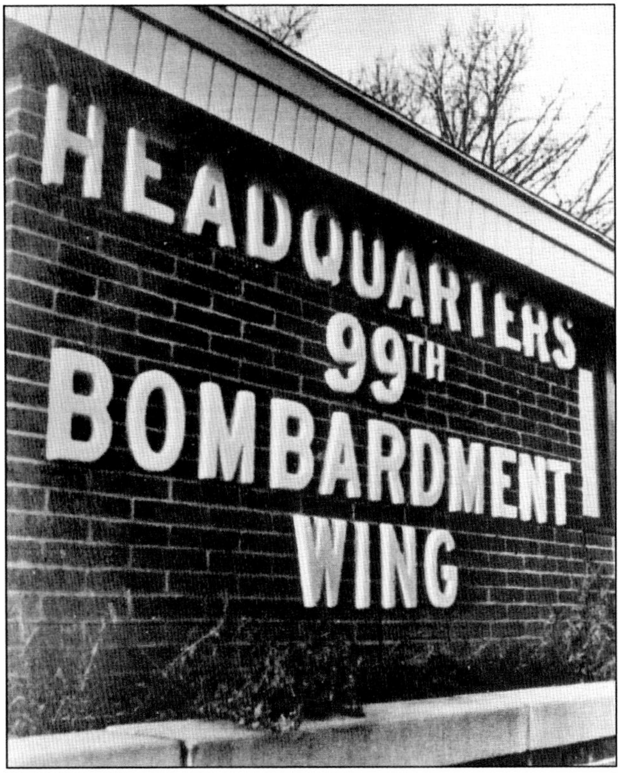

Newsweek magazine reported that a young Massachusetts senator urging, "Lets get this country moving again," marched jauntily into the White House, only to lose the summit facedown with Khruschev in Vienna. The meeting resulted in a Soviet decision to place missiles on the island of Cuba. For six days in October, the 99th Bombardment Wing was on a nuclear war alert on the Tobacco Plains of Chicopee, Massachusetts.

The main gate was closed; armed soldiers patrolled the perimeter as the largest US Air Force facility on the East Coast was in the center of the Cold War's most dangerous crisis. The crewmembers of the 99th Bombardment crews were always on 24-hour alert, ready to launch their aircraft.

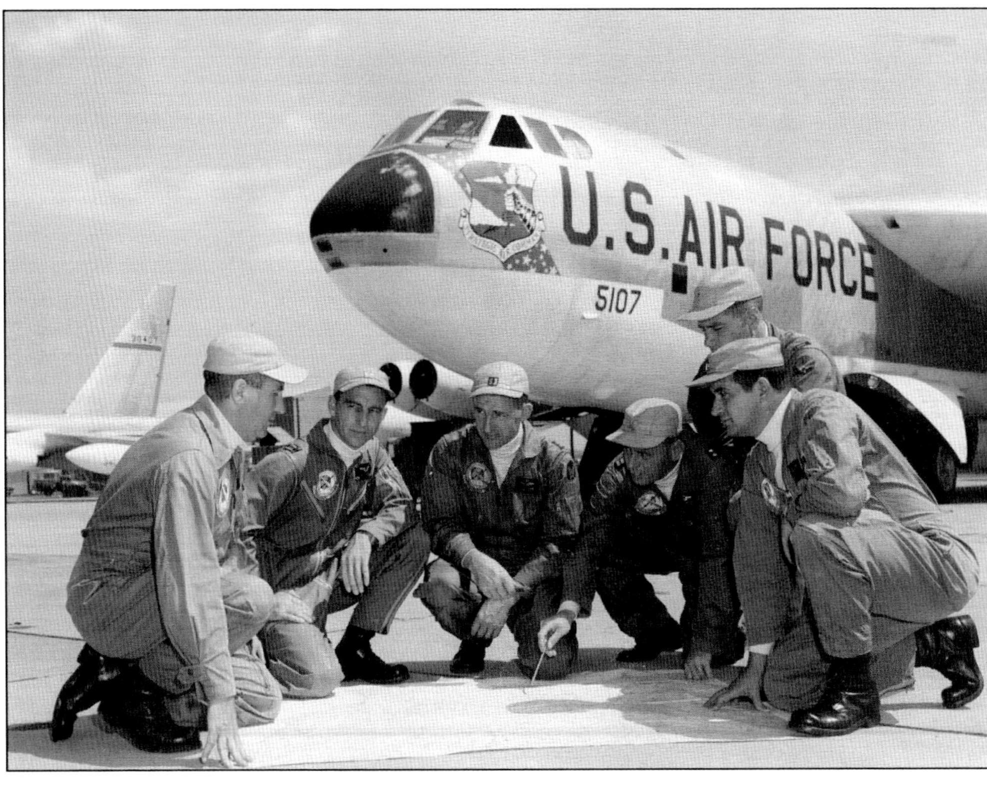

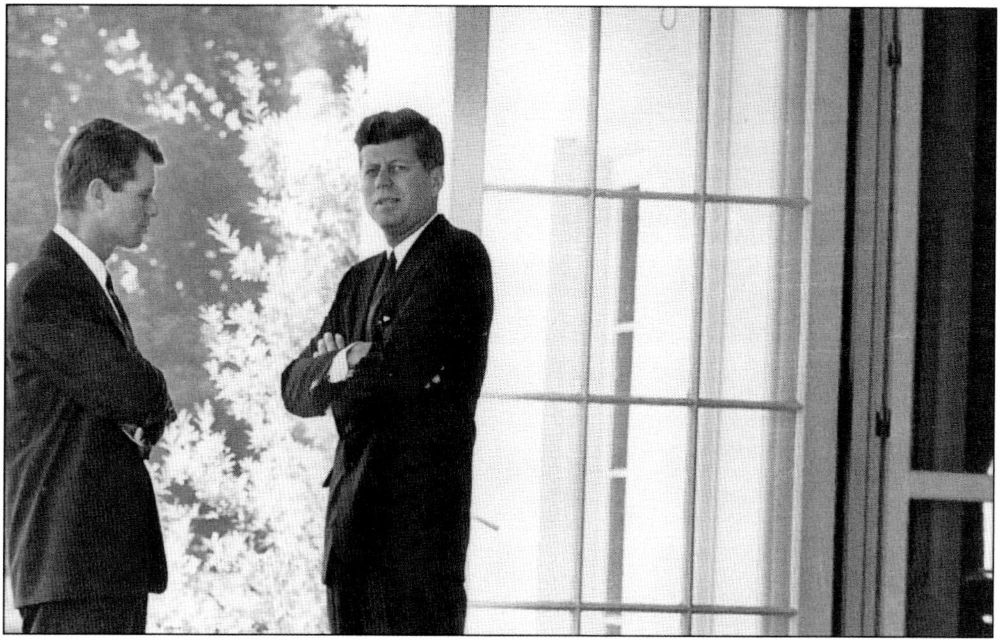

Attorney general Robert Kennedy confers with his brother as nuclear war seemed only hours away. The US Navy was ordered to turn back all ships delivering Russian missiles to Cuba. *Newsweek* magazine observed: "Then Khrushchev blinked, and shipped the missiles back to Russia. For Jack Kennedy and his Camelot-on-the-Potomac, it was a shining moment of triumph."

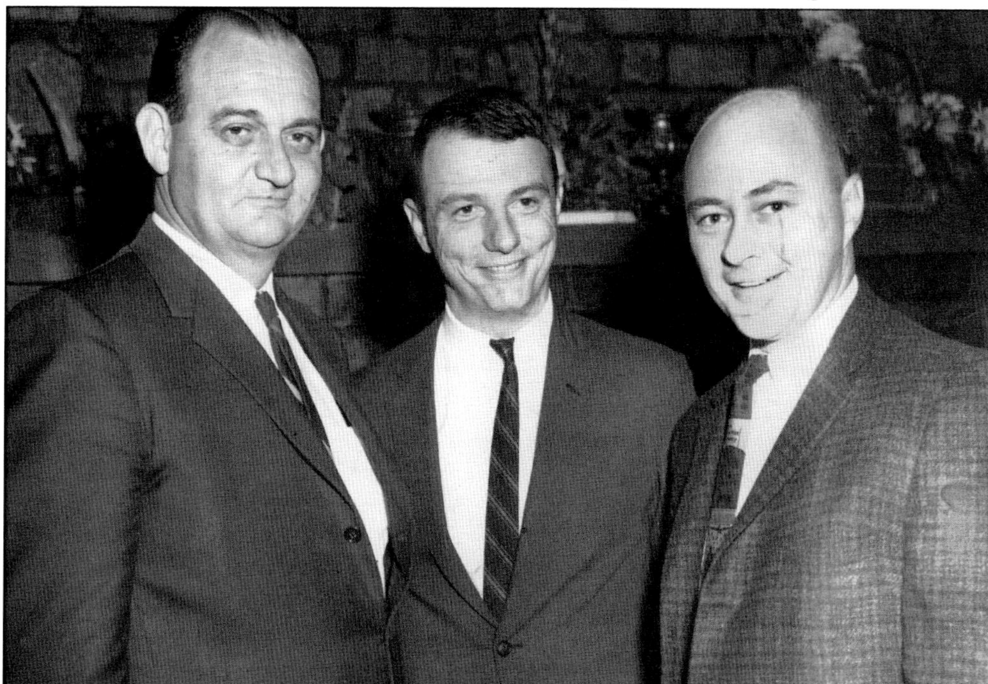

At the monthly meeting of the Chicopee Bar Association are, from left to right, Wilfred P. Conlin, Robert A. Gelinas, and Robert L. Nowak. Attorney Conlin, a highly respected member of the local bar, mentored several young local attorneys in his Grove Street law office.

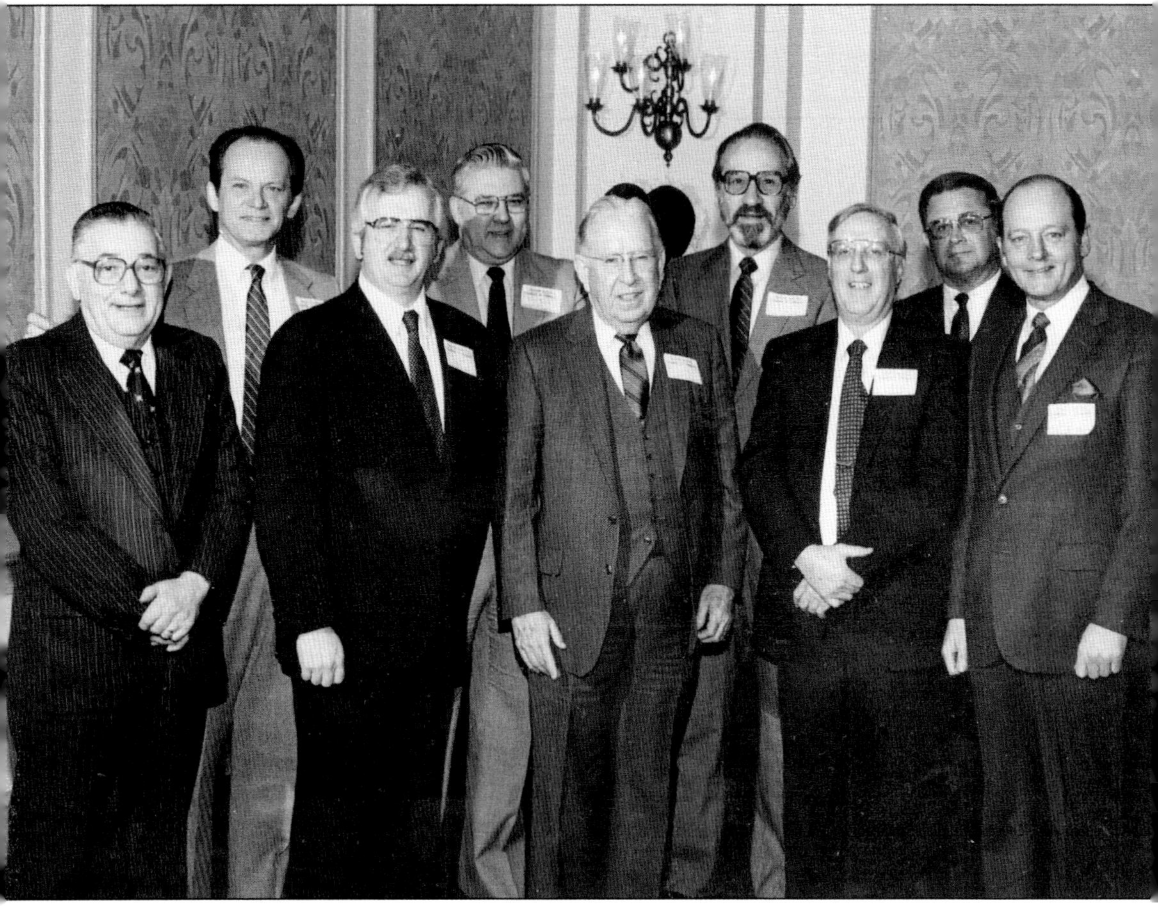

In 1957, the state completed the Massachusetts Turnpike. In Chicopee, exits 5 and 6 were the sites of major development projects. At the junction of the turnpike at exit 6, a new world-class hotel was constructed by the Schine Hotel Corporation. The very impressive facility featured a circular building in the center of the complex, the Phineus Fogg Ballroom, decorated with memorabilia from the Academy Award–winning film *Around the World in 80 Days*. In October 1962, the room was host to Charter Night, a spiffy black-tie affair that celebrated the establishment of the Chicopee Chamber of Commerce. In this historic photograph taken 20 years later, nine past presidents pose. From left to right are (first row) Paul Psilos, Roy Scott, Thomas Murphy, Irving Rosazza, and Edward Bys; (second row) Ned Wright, Walter Mrozinski, Francis Balicki, and Joseph Topor.

Edward Fitzgerald and Ted Jamrog are all smiles as they meet the new Miss Chicopee. The newly formed chamber of commerce added a junior chamber of commerce unit to promote the new image of the fastest-growing city in Massachusetts. Dorothy Kwiecien proved to be an outstanding representative of her hometown.

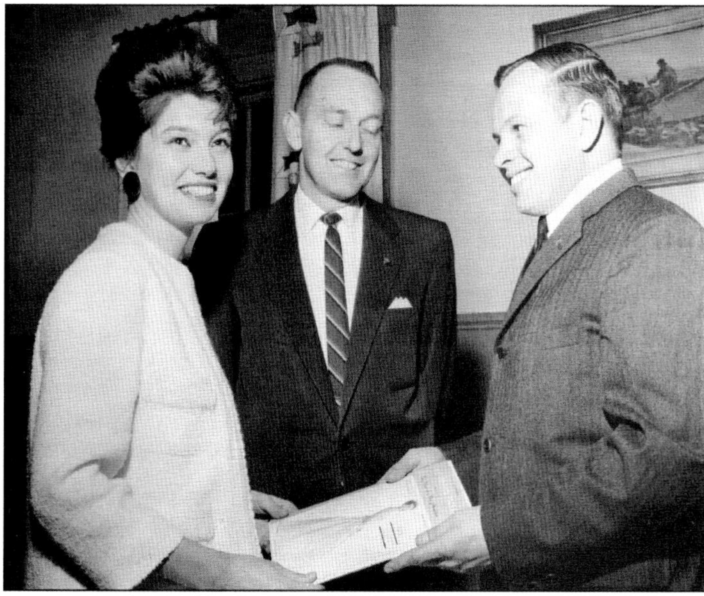

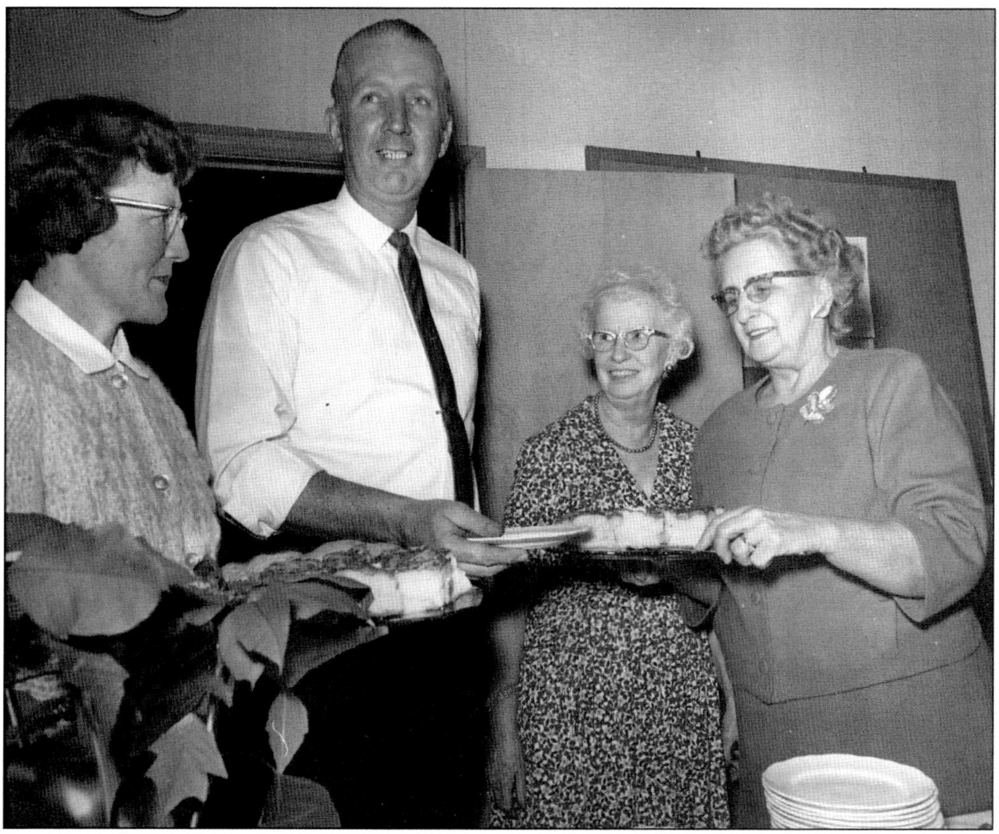

In 1891, Rev. Newton Black personally supervised the building of the Grace Episcopal Church on Springfield Street. Here, Chicopee School historian Dick Haslam joins members of the executive committee of the Grace Episcopal Church in Chicopee. From left to right are Mrs. William Rosendale, Mrs. Ellen Rice, and Mrs. Paul Richards.

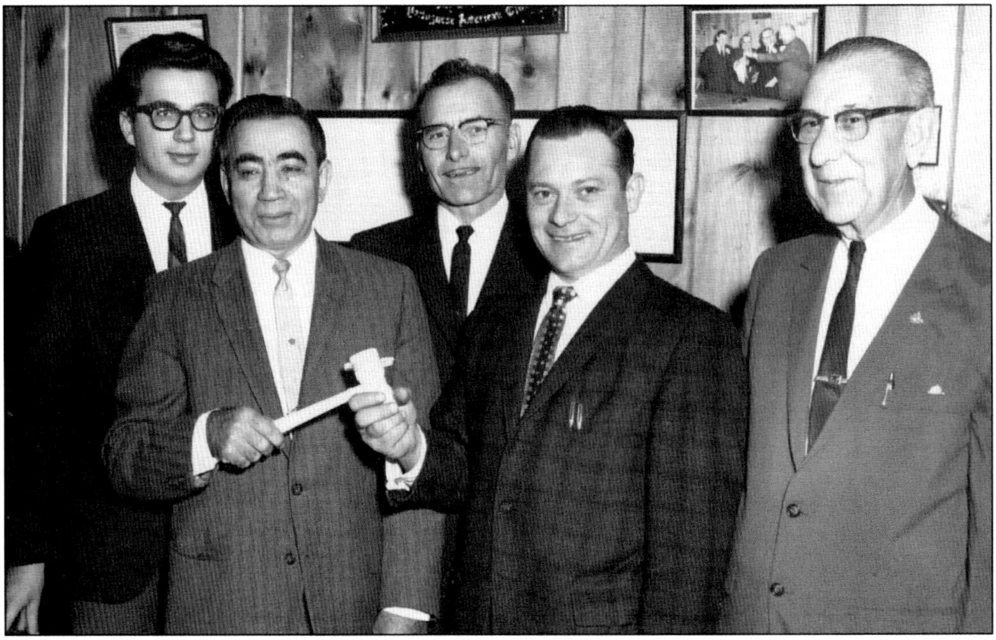

In the 1850s, Portuguese immigrants began settling in Massachusetts coastal towns and working in whaling and fishing communities. In 1890, a second wave of immigrants settled in towns along the Connecticut River. Pictured here at induction ceremonies, Anzio Antonia holds the gavel. In the 1960s, the club built a modern banquet facility on Exchange Street in Chicopee Center.

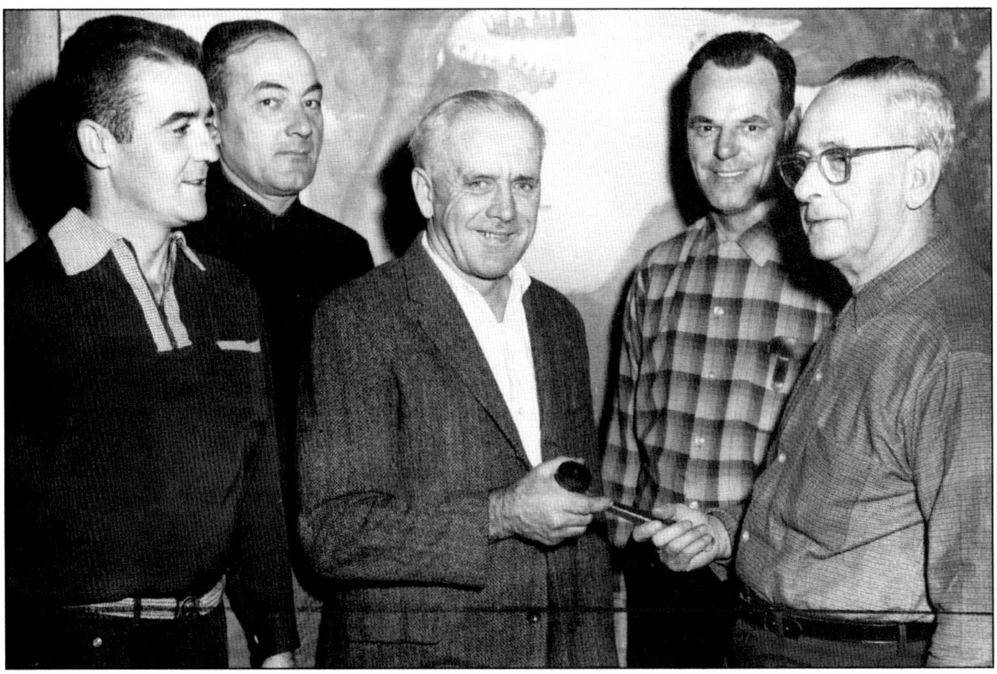

Chicopee roofing contractor Frederick Lonczak (center) accepts the gavel. Lonczak was the long-serving president of the Chicopee Sportsman Club. Following World War II, the club purchased a large parcel of land in Granby, Massachusetts. The club has served the needs of Chicopee sportsmen for more than six decades.

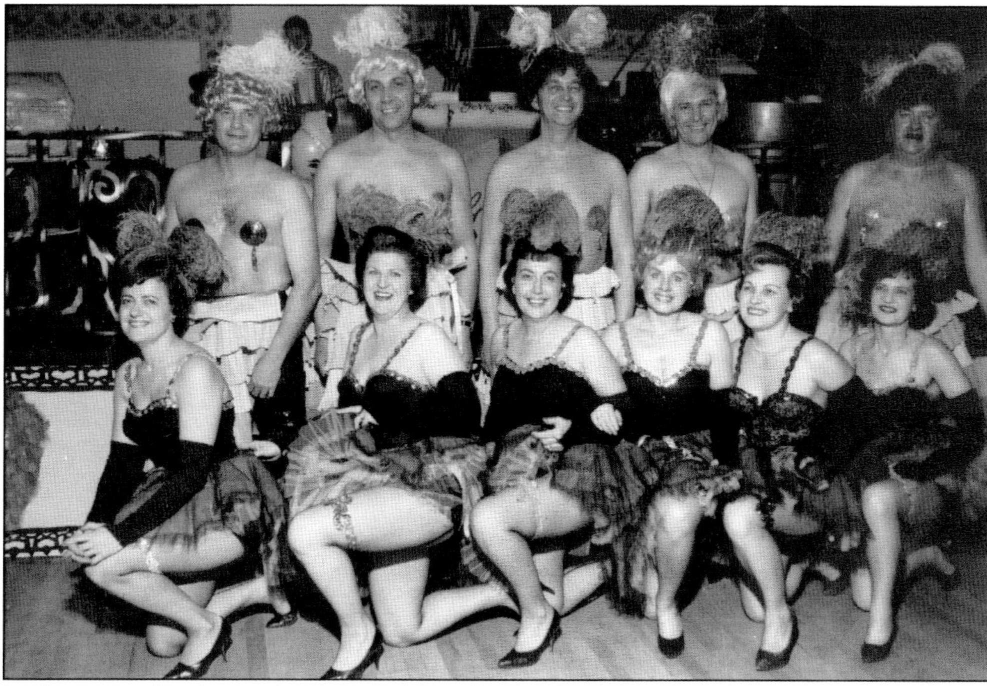

In the 1960s, the place to be on Saturday night was the Elks Lodge on Granby Road. The city's "movers and shakers" took time off to let their hair down and have a good time. They call themselves the "Saturday Nighters."

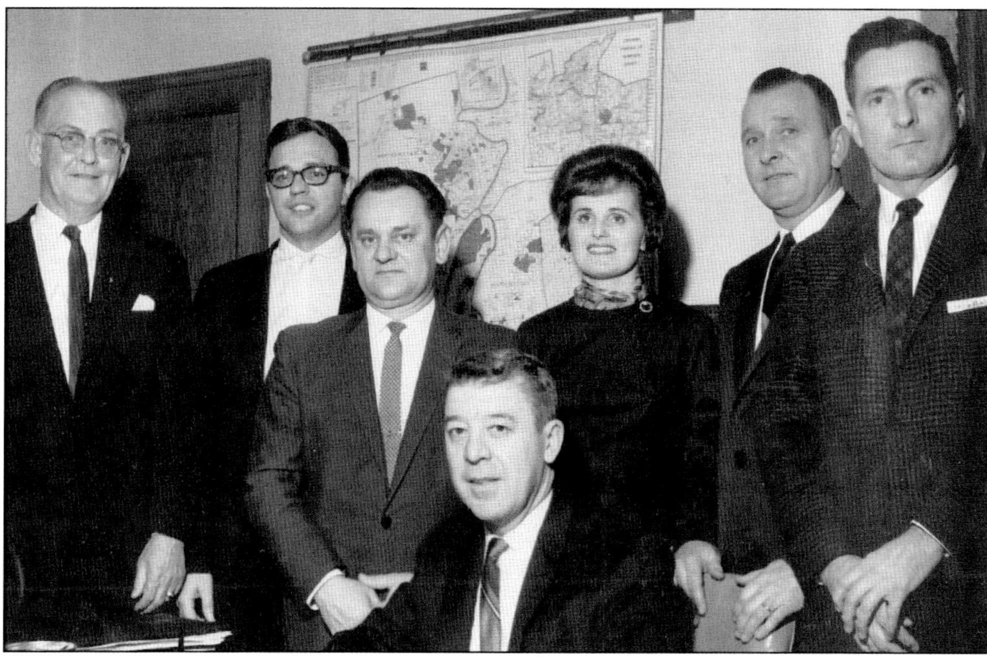

Supt. John Fitzpatrick is pictured here with members of the school committee. From left to right are Fitzpatrick, Dr. Roger Parenteau, Stanley Pierog, Roger Turgeon (seated), Josephine Kord, Theodore Les, and Alfred Allen. During Fitzpatrick's tenure, the city completed 11 school construction projects.

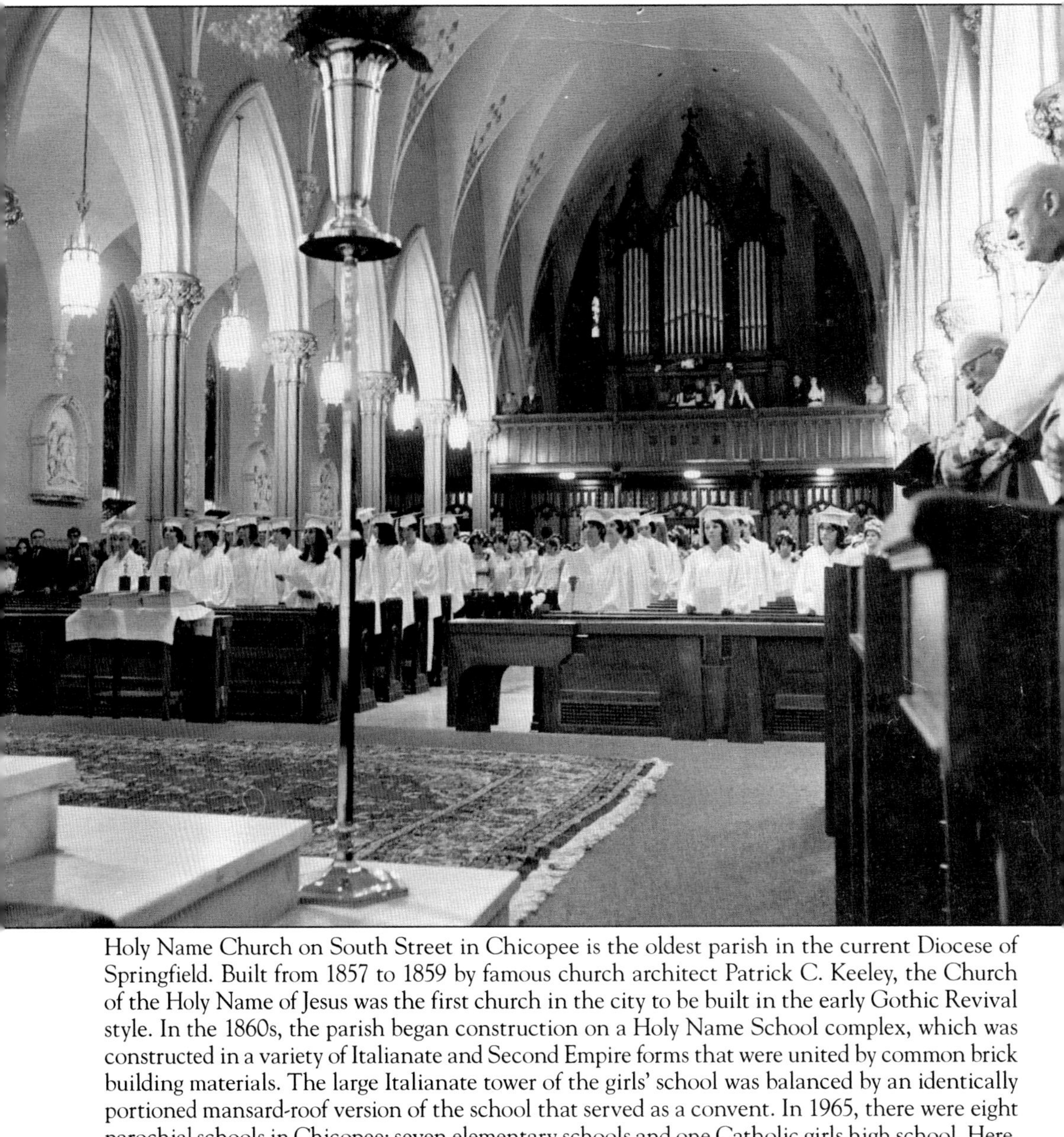

Holy Name Church on South Street in Chicopee is the oldest parish in the current Diocese of Springfield. Built from 1857 to 1859 by famous church architect Patrick C. Keeley, the Church of the Holy Name of Jesus was the first church in the city to be built in the early Gothic Revival style. In the 1860s, the parish began construction on a Holy Name School complex, which was constructed in a variety of Italianate and Second Empire forms that were united by common brick building materials. The large Italianate tower of the girls' school was balanced by an identically portioned mansard-roof version of the school that served as a convent. In 1965, there were eight parochial schools in Chicopee: seven elementary schools and one Catholic girls high school. Here, graduates of the Holy Name High School receive their diplomas in the historic church.

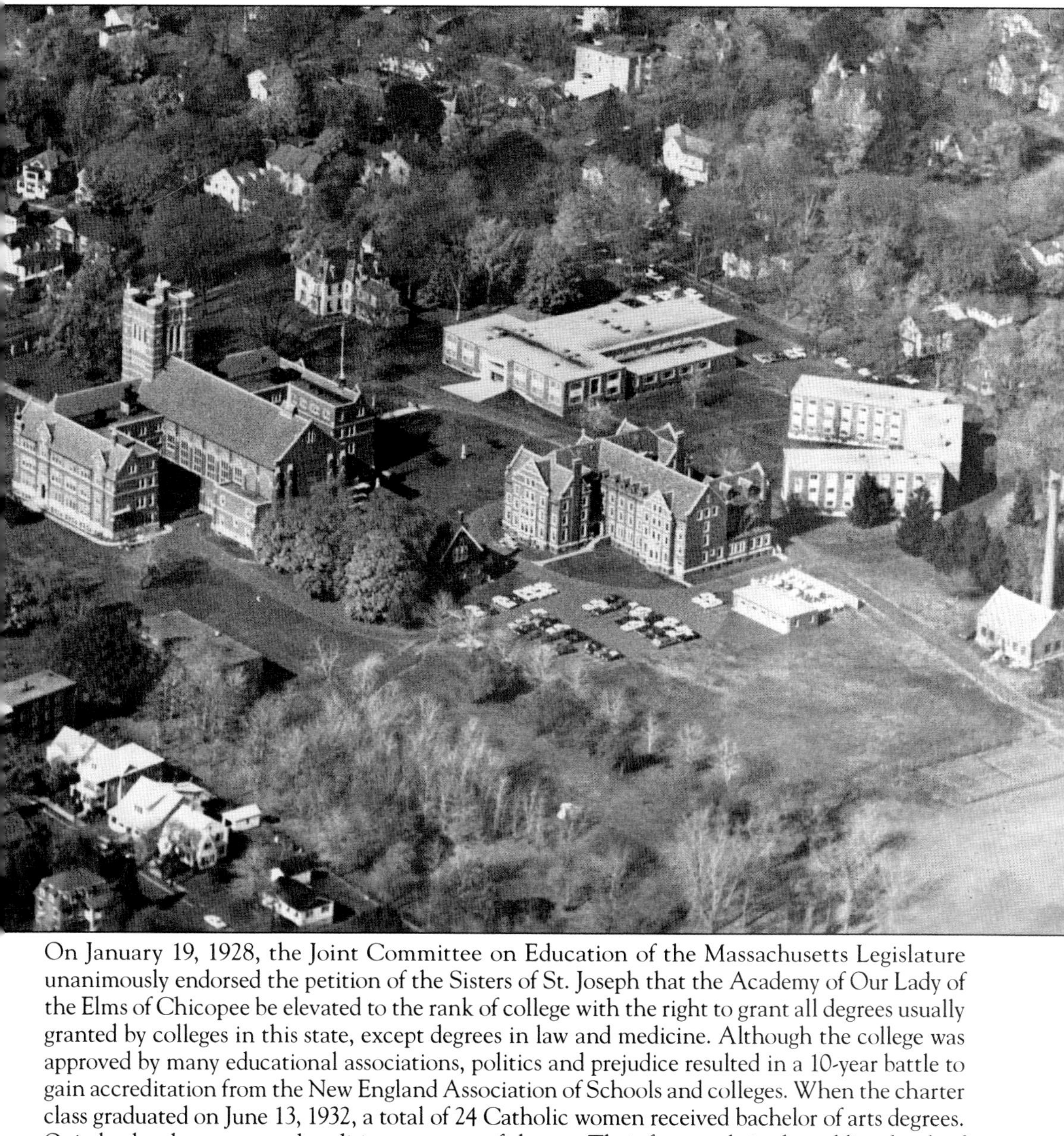

On January 19, 1928, the Joint Committee on Education of the Massachusetts Legislature unanimously endorsed the petition of the Sisters of St. Joseph that the Academy of Our Lady of the Elms of Chicopee be elevated to the rank of college with the right to grant all degrees usually granted by colleges in this state, except degrees in law and medicine. Although the college was approved by many educational associations, politics and prejudice resulted in a 10-year battle to gain accreditation from the New England Association of Schools and colleges. When the charter class graduated on June 13, 1932, a total of 24 Catholic women received bachelor of arts degrees. Quietly, they began a proud tradition as agents of change. Their future role in the public schools of Massachusetts cannot be understated. In the 1960s, under the leadership of Rev. Thomas Devine, the College of Our Lady of the Elms launched an unprecedented expansion program. For the first time, the college was able to access federal funding for the construction of new dormitories and an impressive new student center, shown center right.

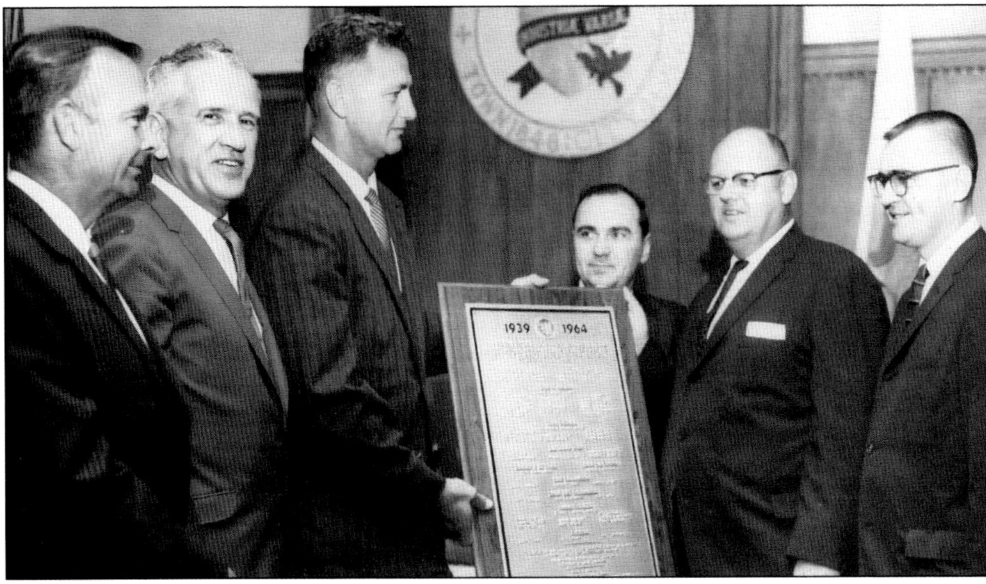

Chicopee Mayor Edward Lysek is pictured (second from right) with Westover's 25th Anniversary Committee. In 1965, the "Big Ed" Lysek era was coming to an end, and the outgoing mayor was wrong a good deal of the time, but from his "bully pulpit" in Market Square, he was difficult to challenge. And perhaps to no one's surprise, he had carried out or had in the works everything he said he was going to do.

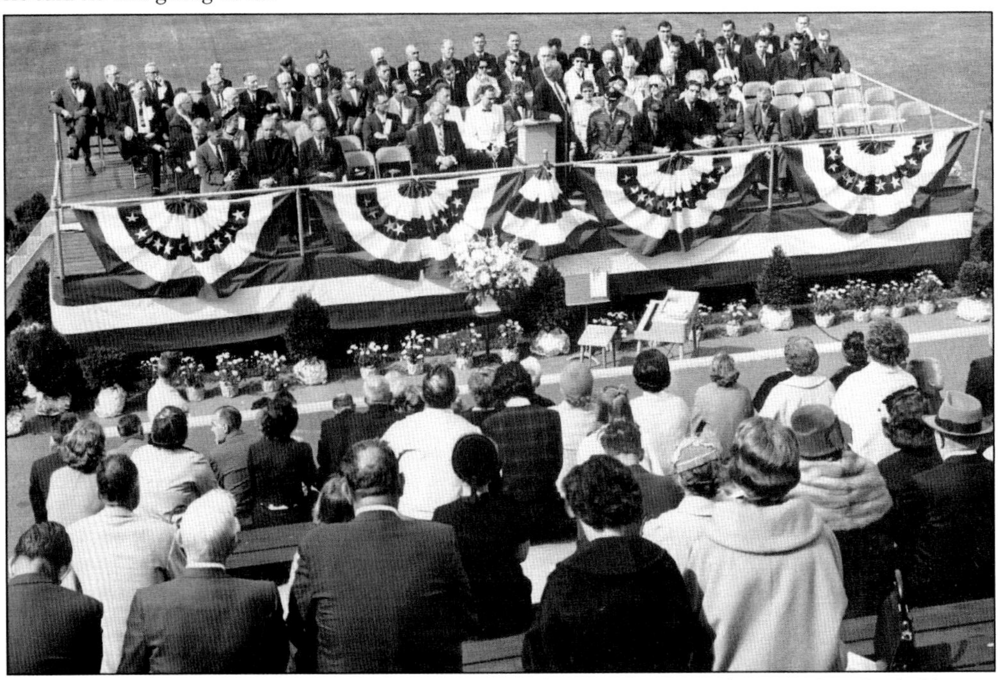

On September 13, 1964, city, state, and national leaders were in attendance at Szot Park. Former Chicopee mayor Anthony J. Stonina, standing at the rostrum, is shown addressing the hundreds at the afternoon ceremonies commemorating the silver anniversary of Westover Air Force Base. Mayor Stonina received an Air Force Scroll of Appreciation, the Air Force's highest award bestowed on a civilian.

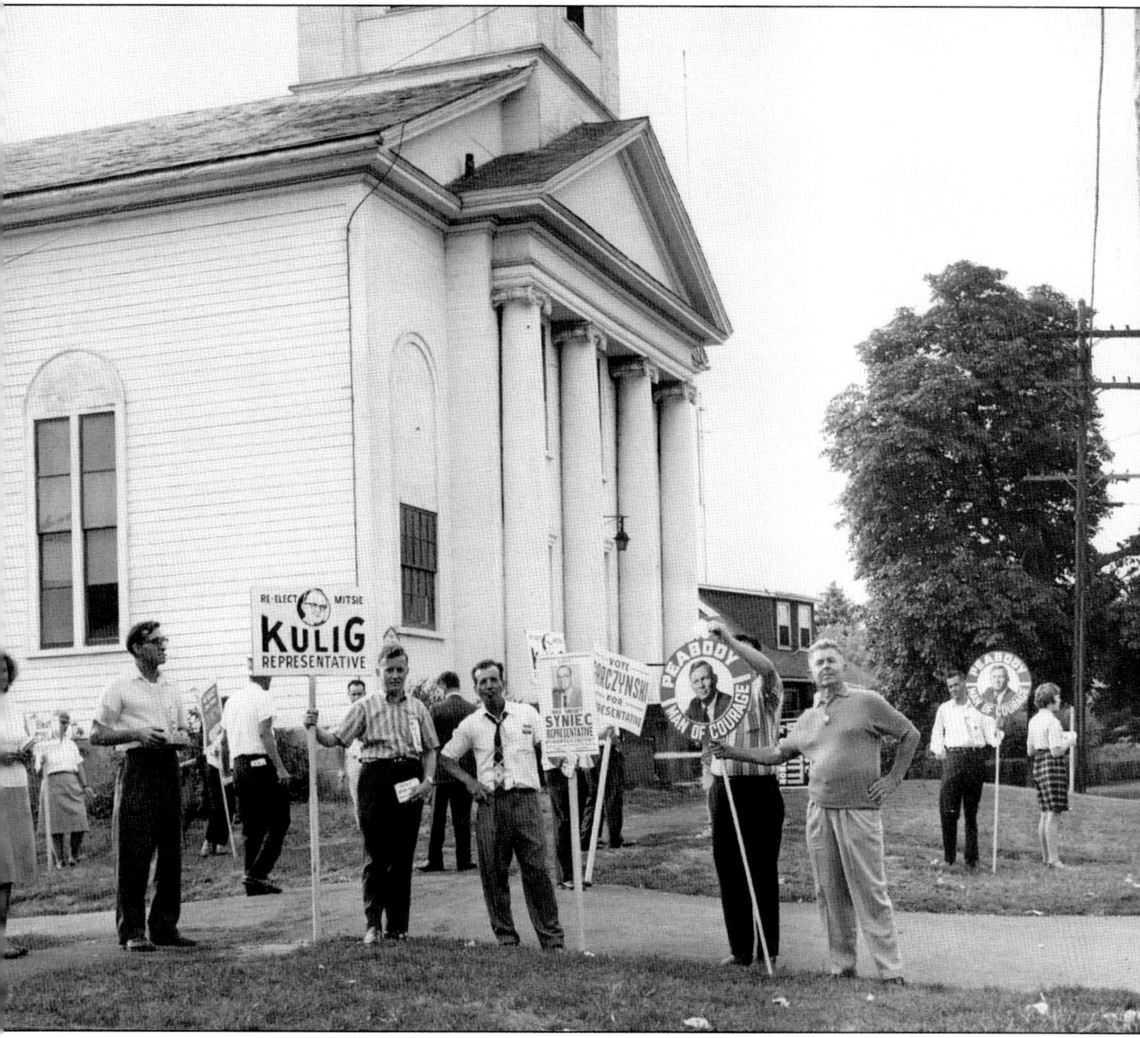

Chicopee's historic First Congregational Church on Chicopee Street served for decades as a Ward 3 polling place. This classic picture captures the spirit of Chicopee's fierce electoral landscape in the 1960s. It was an era when Chicopee's voter turnouts in statewide elections frequently topped 80 percent participation by the community's registered voters. Even with an overwhelming number of registered Democrats, the citizenry frequently supported liberal Republican candidates for governor. For decades, Western Massachusetts voters have viewed the motives of the political class in Boston with a considerable margin of disrespect. Consequently, statewide candidates never took the local electorate for granted in the 1960s. During the election season, serious statewide candidates sought the support of local activists. In the fiercely combative statewide elections of the 1960s, local activists surround the historic basement voting station, voicing support for their favorite candidates.

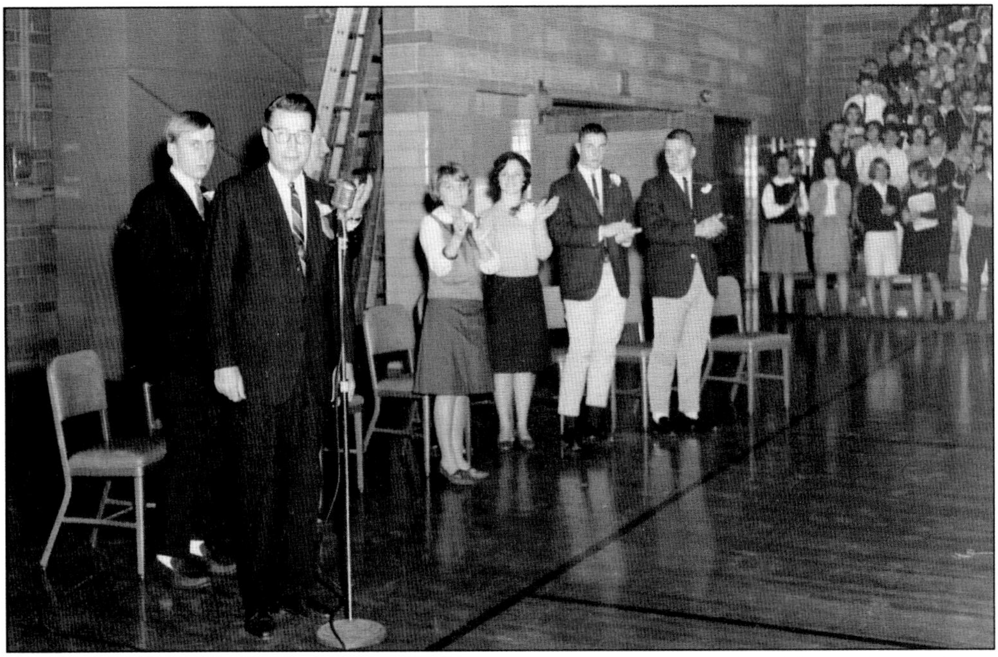

On Veterans Day 1964, the brand new Chicopee Comprehensive High School football team played its first game against crosstown rival Chicopee High School. Prior to the contest, both schools hosted an exchange rally. Here, Chicopee High School principal Henry B. Fay welcomes the Chicopee Comprehensive delegation to the exchange rally in the Chicopee High School gym.

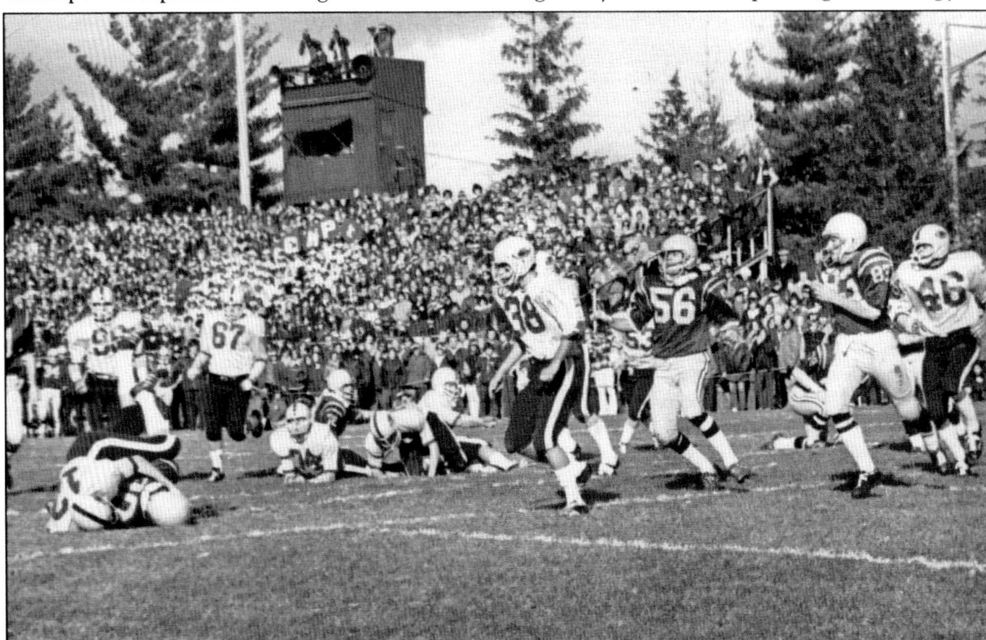

The Colts emerged victorious by a score of 13-6. Following the game, Mayor Edward Lysek unwrapped a 19th-century Ames saber as the huge crowd watched. The glorious relic of Chicopee's rich industrial past instantly became the community's symbol of gridiron supremacy as the mayor presented the saber to the winning team.

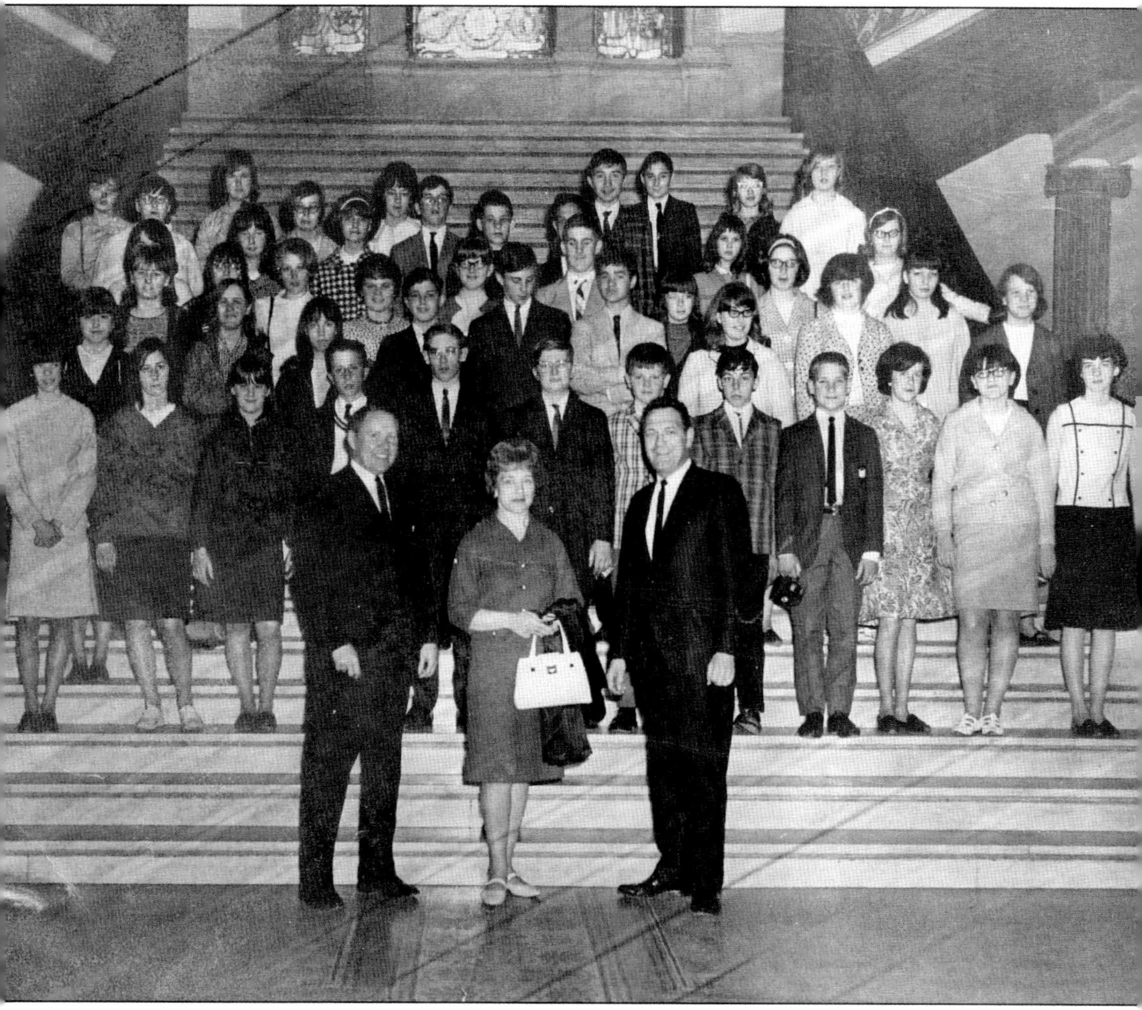

On January 5, 1891, Chicopee industrialist George S. Taylor became the first mayor of the new city of Chicopee. In 1910, a new school was built on Belcher Street in Chicopee Falls. The school committee named the building in Taylor's honor. Taylor remains the only chief executive so recognized. Members of the George S. Taylor School's student council visit the Massachusetts State House. In the first row are, from left to right, Principal Joseph Kosiorek, Emily Ziemba, Parent Teacher Association executive board member, and Massachusetts Rep. Stephen Chmura. The students were well aware that their venerable old school was slated for demolition in 1970. The decision to remove the school was based on the obvious age of the structure and its location in the center of the urban renewal area. Unfortunately, the argument that the building was unsound proved untrue. Large crowds watched for several days as a wrecking contractor spent nearly a week trying to knock down the building.

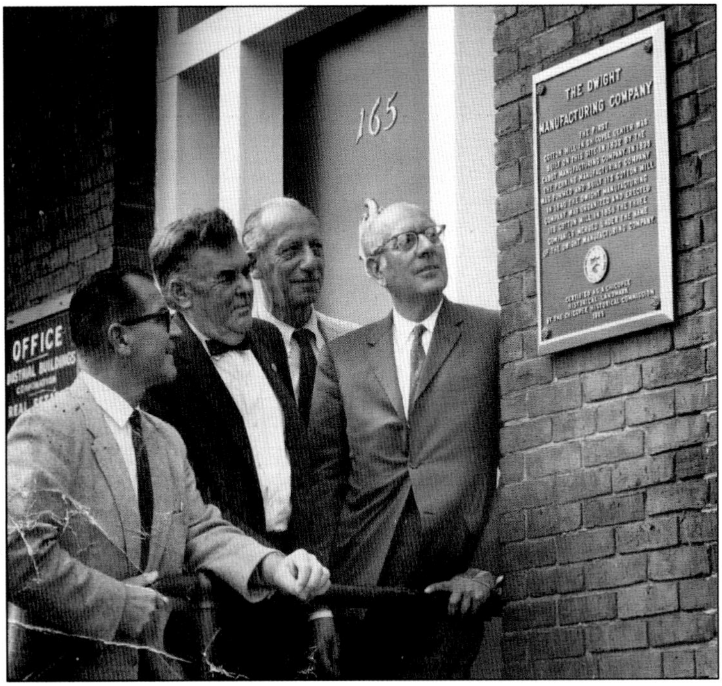

In 1965, the newly formed Chicopee Historical Commission initiated a program of placing historic plaques on some of the community's historic treasures. Here, commission chairman Thaddeus M. Szetela (far right) and historian Winthrop McKinstry (second from right) join Industrial Building Company executives Archie Burak (second from right) and Jullian Sagalyn (first from right) in observing the Dwight Manufacturing Company Plaque.

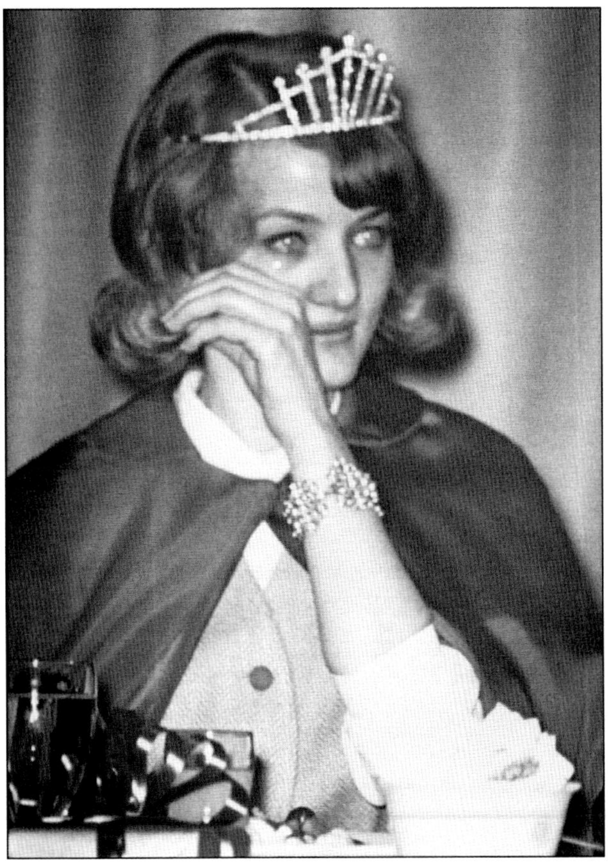

Judith O'Connor, the 1965 Chicopee Coleen, wipes away a tear. A graduate of Chicopee Comprehensive High School, O'Connor led the Chicopee delegation for the St. Patrick's Day Parade in Holyoke, Massachusetts. Since 1954, the city's business community has enthusiastically supported the event.

Four

Urban Renewal 1966–1970

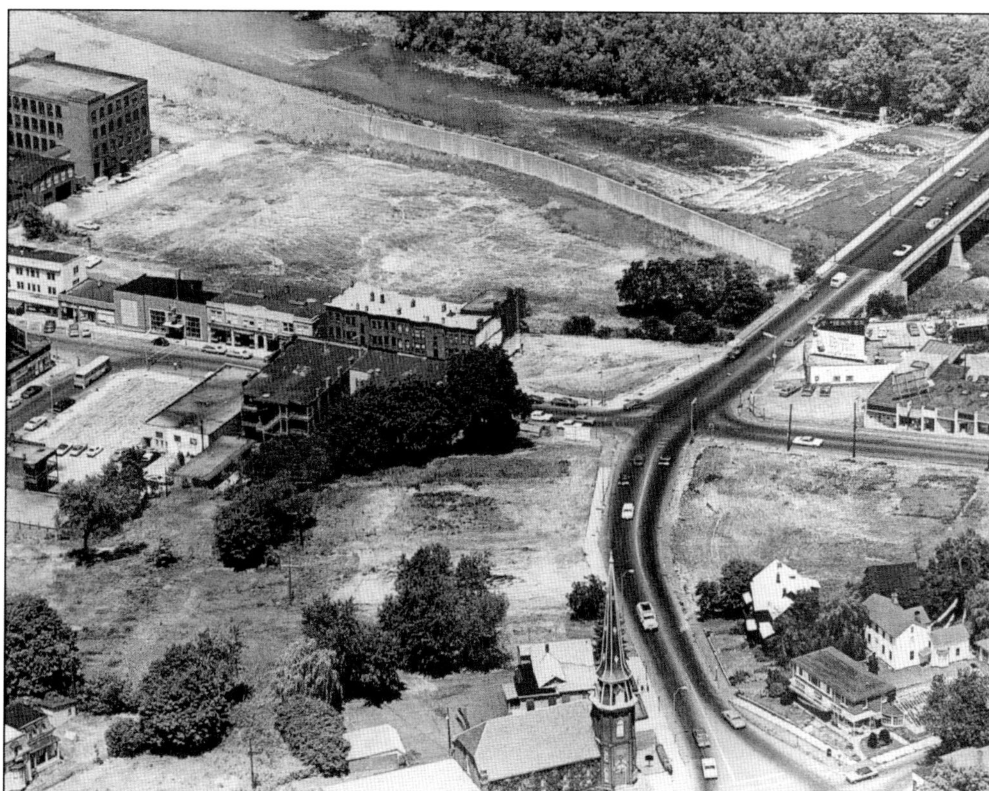

The Chicopee Redevelopment Authority was acting as the liaison among business, industrial, and residential interests in Chicopee Falls. At the heart of the revitalization effort were the Uniroyal Company's plans to construct a new $12-million automated tire warehouse in the "China Town" section of the falls.

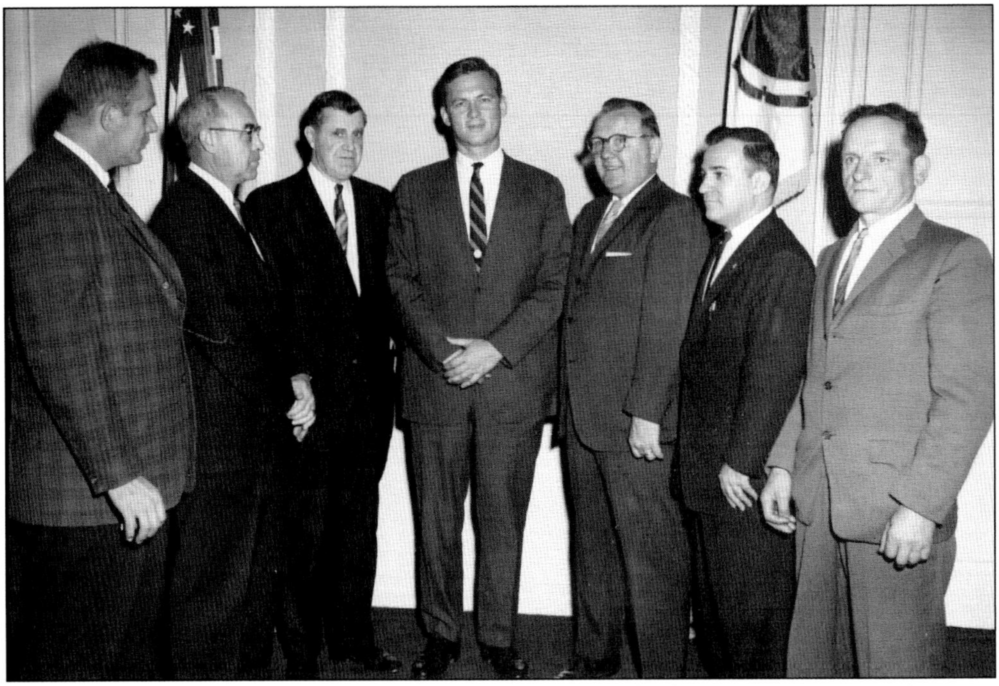

Massachusetts governor Endicott "Chub" Peabody was running for the US Senate in 1966. Governor Peabody is in the center, and at his immediate right is Rep. Mitzi Kulig. The Democratic governor would be soundly defeated by Republican Edward Brooke, the Massachusetts attorney general.

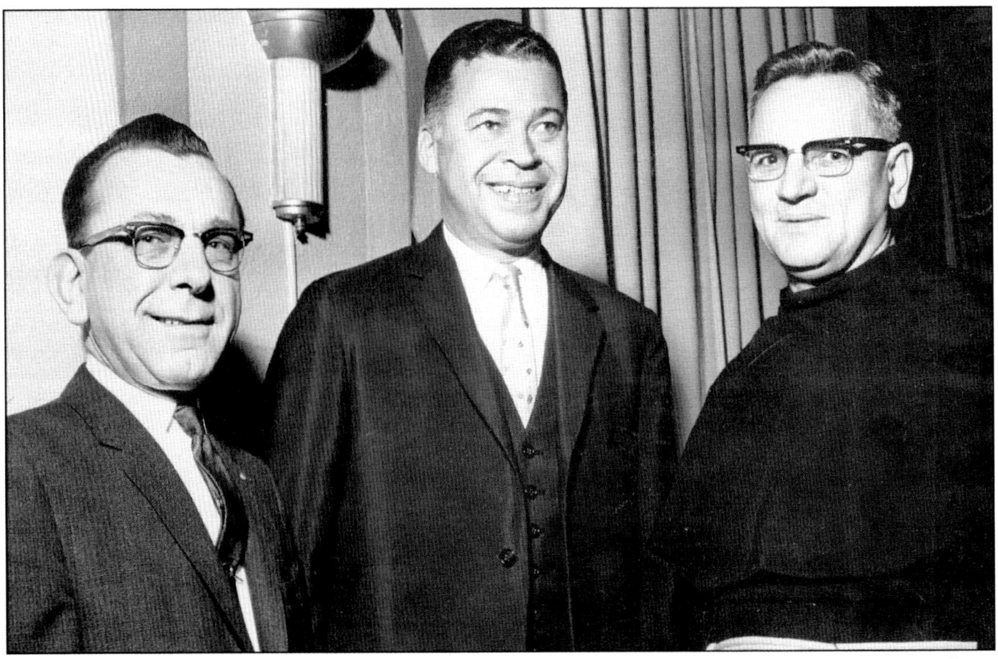

Pictured at the St. Stanislaus Holy Name Society Father's Day Communion Breakfast are, from left to right, chairman Stanley Bragiel, Sen. Edward Brooke, and the society's moderator, Rev. Francis Kasprzak. Breakfast speaker Senator Brooke was the first African American elected to the US Senate by a popular vote.

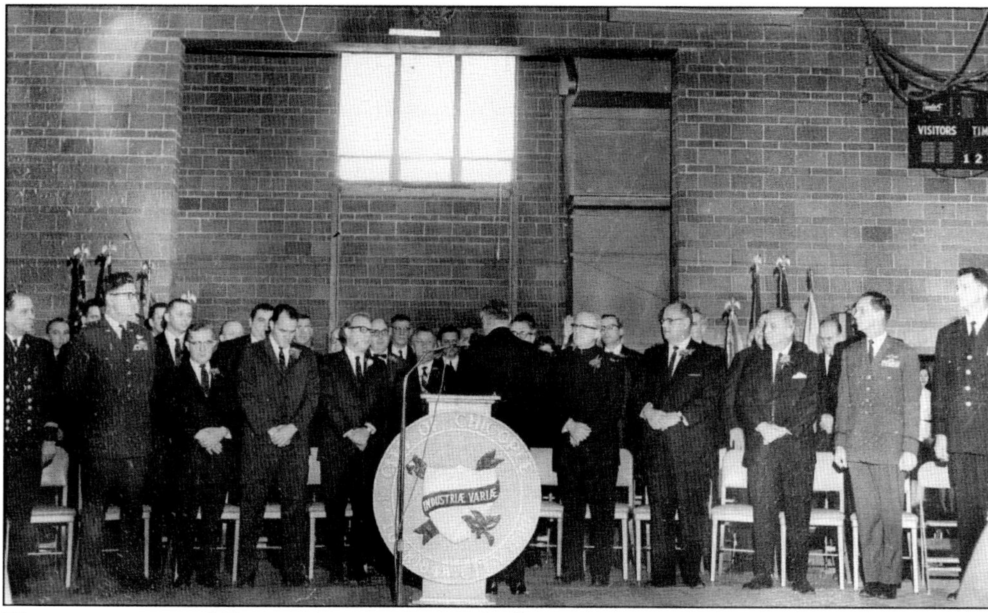

The inauguration of Chicopee's new mayor took place in the Chicopee High School gymnasium. The city's youthful Mayor Richard "Whitey" Demers enthusiastically laid out his plans for the city. Highlighting the expansion efforts at the Fisk Tire Company, Piels Brewery, American Bosch, and the Bay State Refining Company, he was optimistic about the community's economy.

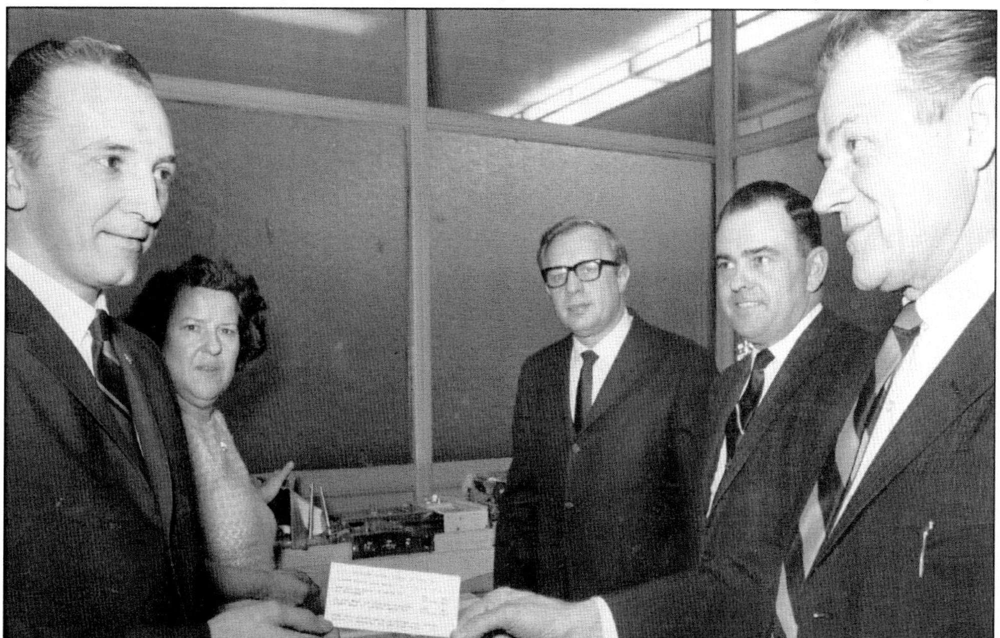

The city of Chicopee joined the national discussion regarding the advent of "paid" television. The mayor appointed Donald Heroux to lead the local Cable Television Committee. Pictured from left to right are Donald Heroux, committee secretary Dorothy Metzger, Mayor Richard Demers, assistant manager Herve Plasse, and manager of the Chicopee Electric Light Department John Korkosz.

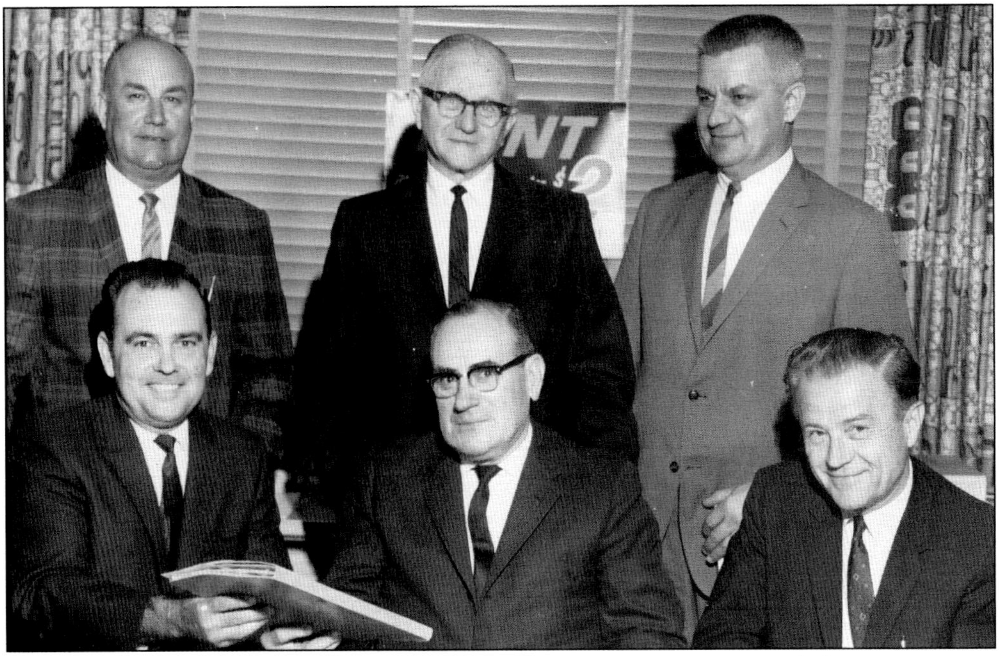

In 1895, Chicopee became the first city in Massachusetts to own a municipal electric company. The company was an immediate success, maintaining low rates and providing outstanding service. The electric light commission (pictured here) faced a complex decision regarding the establishment of a municipally owned local cable television system 70 years later. The issue was finally settled by the Federal Communications Commission (FCC) in Washington, DC.

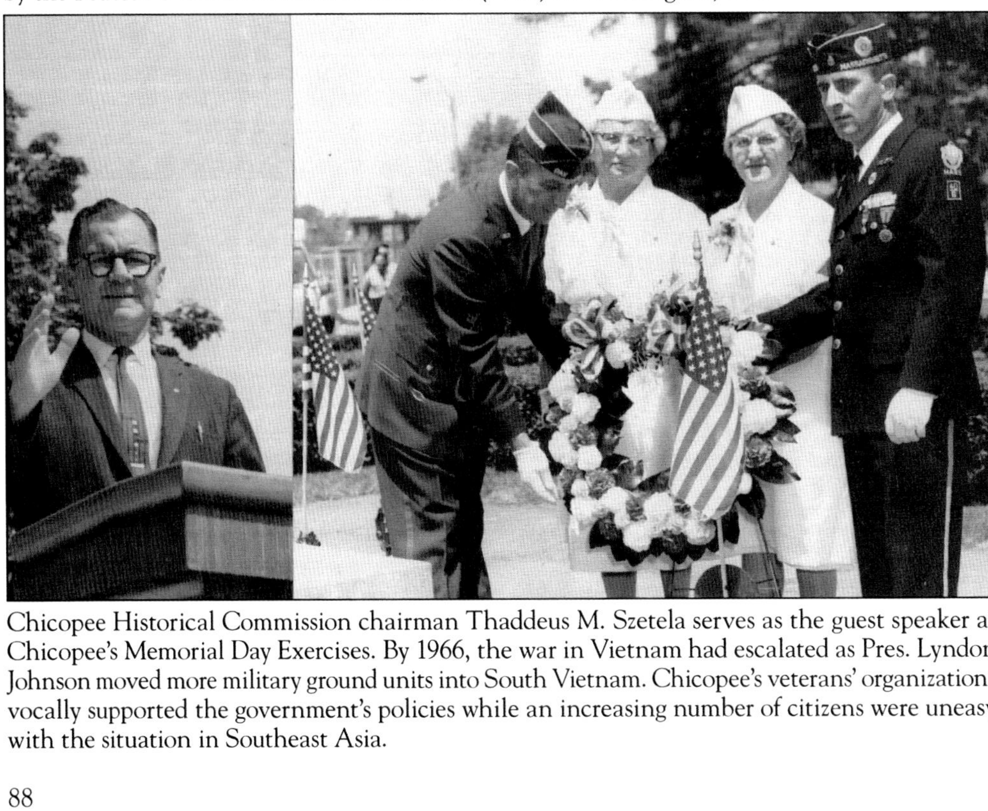

Chicopee Historical Commission chairman Thaddeus M. Szetela serves as the guest speaker at Chicopee's Memorial Day Exercises. By 1966, the war in Vietnam had escalated as Pres. Lyndon Johnson moved more military ground units into South Vietnam. Chicopee's veterans' organizations vocally supported the government's policies while an increasing number of citizens were uneasy with the situation in Southeast Asia.

Sgt. Robert R. Litwin, of 905 Montgomery Street, was killed in a savage battle in Dak To, Vietnam, on June 22, 1967. He was a member of the CO.A 503rd Infantry, 173rd Airborne Brigade. The Distinguished Service Cross was awarded posthumously to Sergeant Litwin's widow, the former Theresa Robak. The new elementary school constructed in Ward 6 was named in his honor.

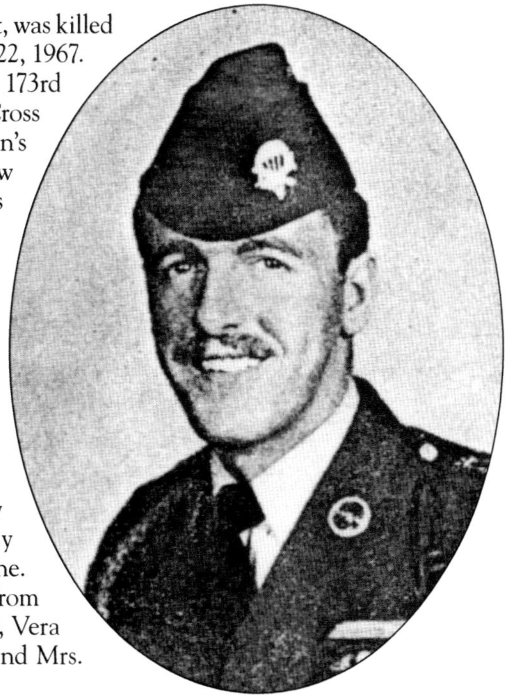

The Friends of the Retarded group was officially chartered in 1967. The organization established Sunshine Village, a community-based facility to provide a sheltered workshop and activity development center on 10 acres at 75 Litwin Lane. Kerry-Ann Casey (far right) is pictured with, from left to right, committee members Joseph Casey, Vera Lafleur, Mrs. Max Pietras, Mrs. Albert Fish, and Mrs. Burton Hurst.

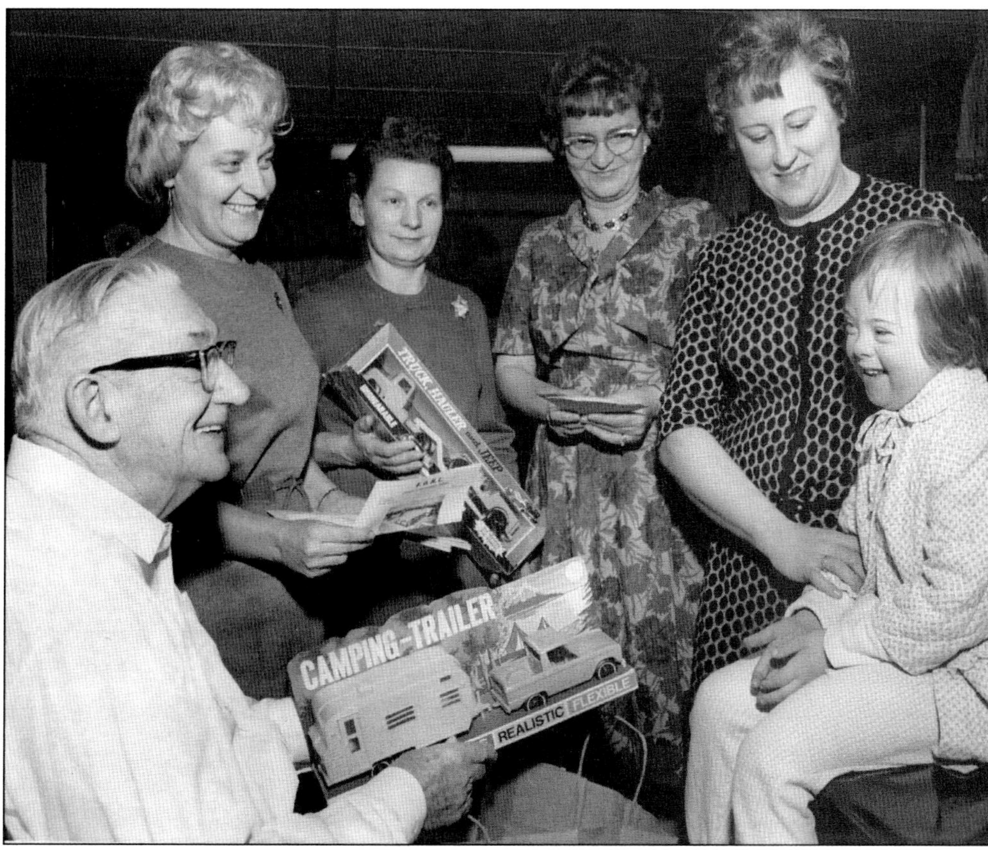

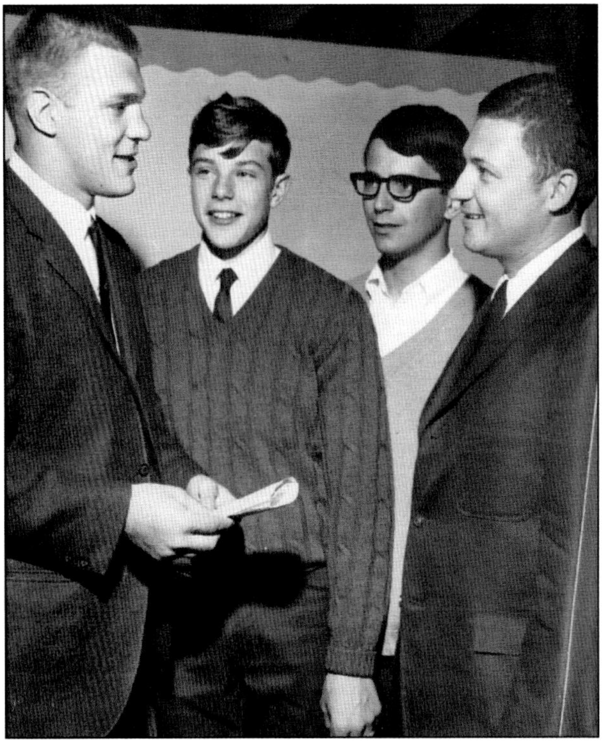

Bill Budness (left) was the guest speaker at a Chicopee High School Sports Night. Budness, a 1960 graduate of the high school, went on to captain the Boston University football team. In 1967, he was performing at the next level as a member of the Oakland Raiders of the American Football League. In 1968, he played in the second Super Bowl game against the Green Bay Packers.

Anthony "Tony" Kumiega (center) is the guest speaker at the Belcher School PTA. A three-sport standout at Chicopee High School, Kumiega was recipient of the Bronislaw J. Stepczyk Scholar Athlete Award in 1958. He played college football at Michigan State University. Here, his audience is enthralled with his stories of "Big 10" football.

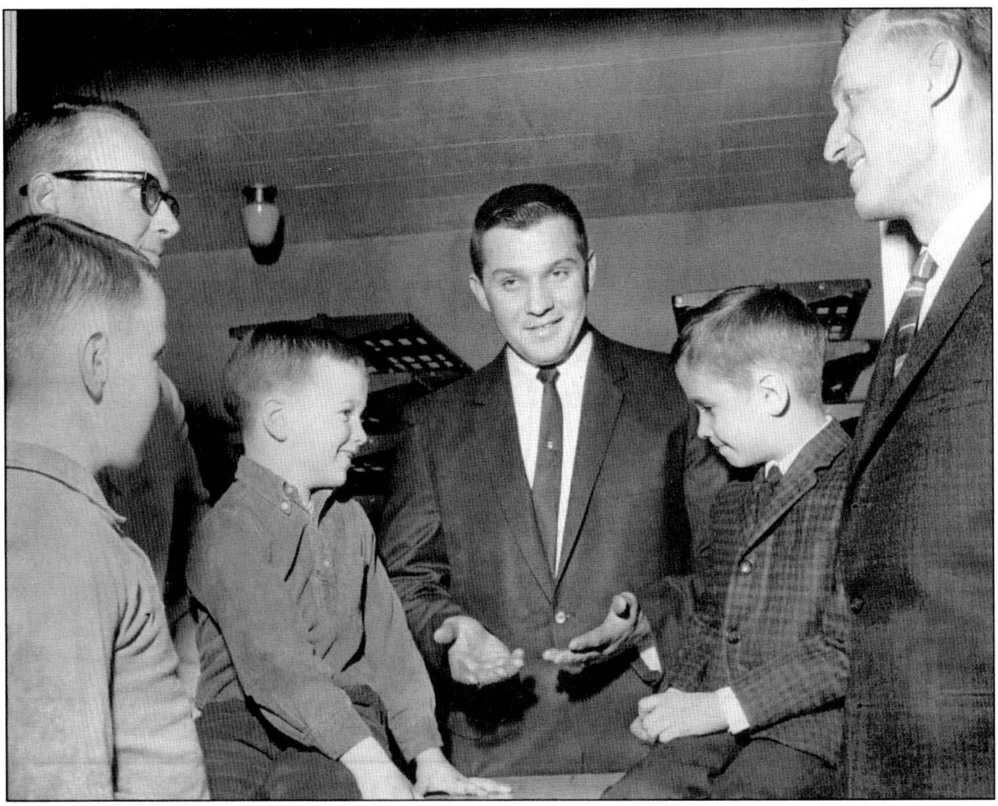

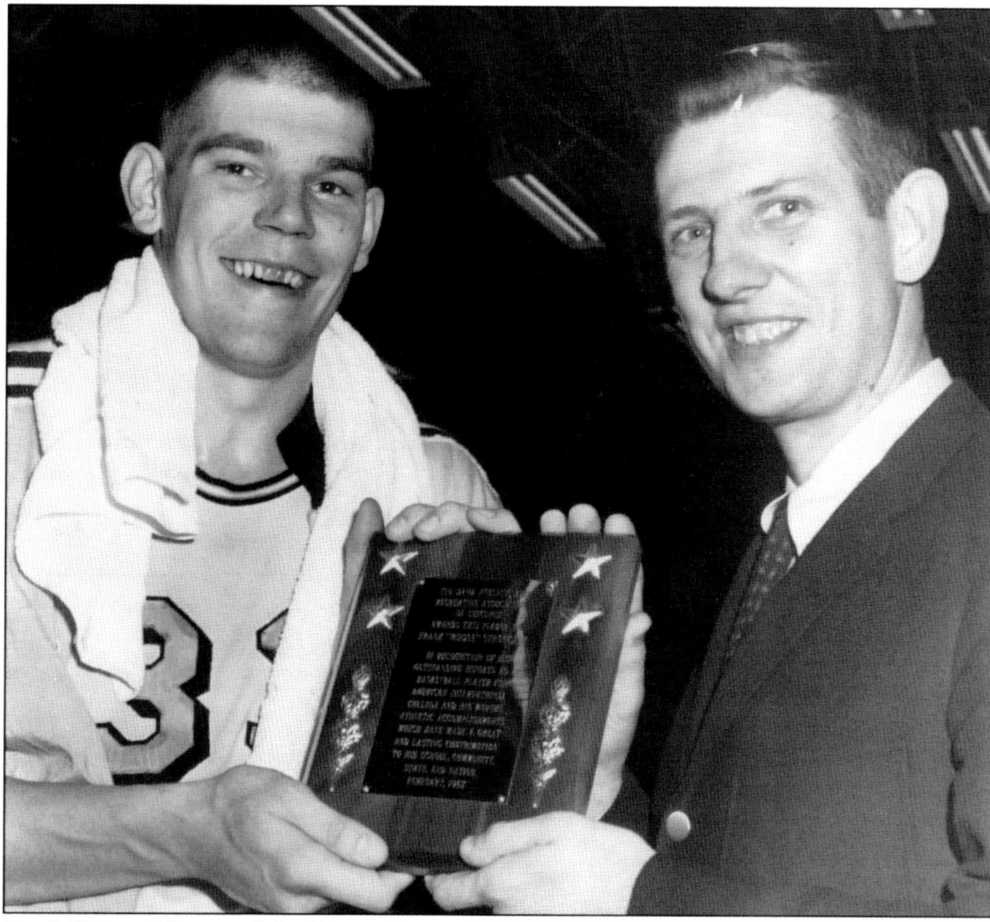

Frank "Moose" Stronczak had been a bigger-than-life figure during his basketball career at Chicopee High School. Pictured here, Stronczak (left) is recognized for his outstanding contributions to the basketball program at American International College in Springfield, Massachusetts. Making the presentation is Stanley Lusnia, the president of the Dana Athletic and Recreation Association (DARA) of Chicopee.

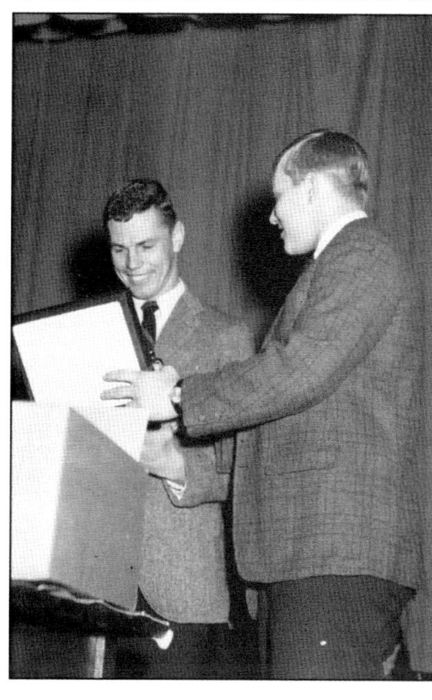

Ron Nizankiewicz (left) accepts an award from the 1967 Chicopee High School football team. Making the presentation is Kenneth Cyboron, the team's cocaptain. Nizankiewicz won the Stepczk Award as the community top high school athlete 10 years earlier for his play on the football field. Following a successful career at Springfield College, he returned to the high school as a teacher and coach.

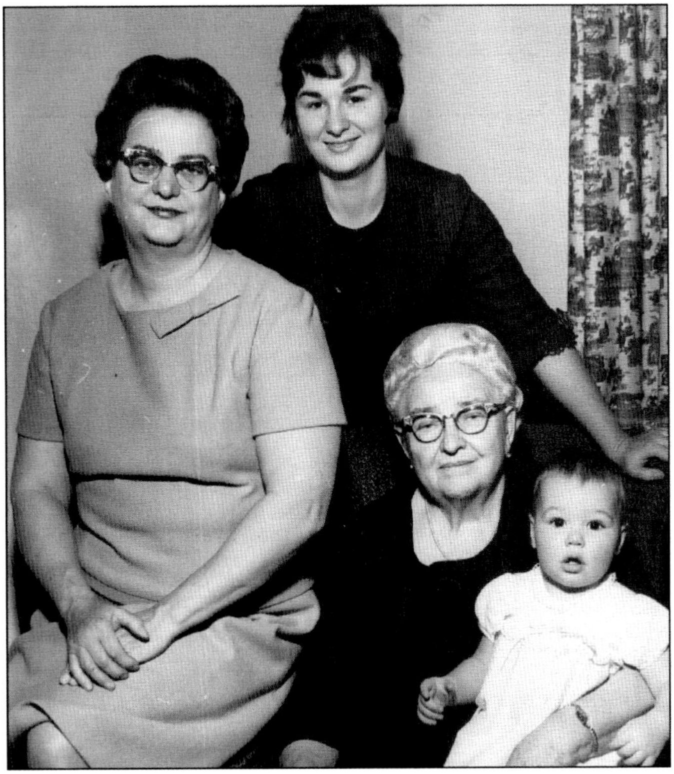

Shown from left to right are four generations of a Chicopee family, including grandmother Francis Galica, granddaughter Nancy Underwood, great-grandmother Rose Stylar, and baby Lynn Underwood. Stylar's great-granddaughter graduated from the Rhode Island School of Design in Providence, Rhode Island.

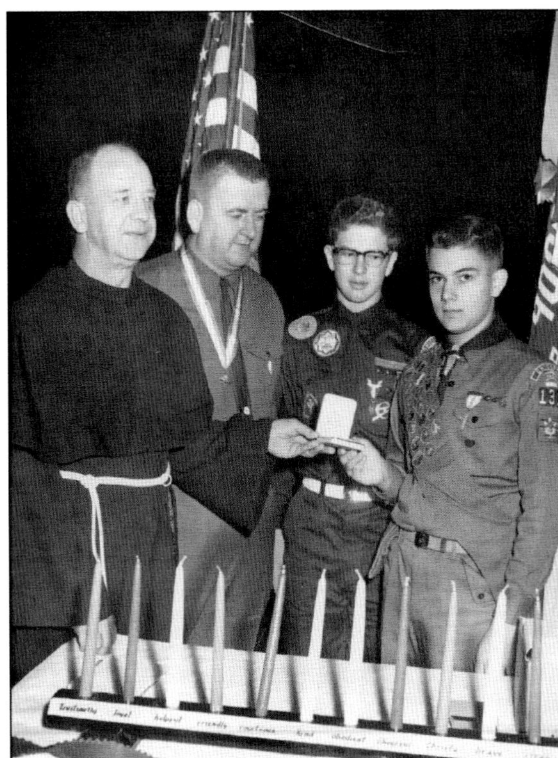

Shown from left to right, pastor of St. Stanislaus church Rev. Emil Majchrzak joins Scoutmaster Chester Sroka, honoring Thomas Paci, and Joseph Wasowicz for successfully attaining the rank of Eagle Scout. In the 1960s, all of Chicopee's Catholic parishes sponsored Scout troops.

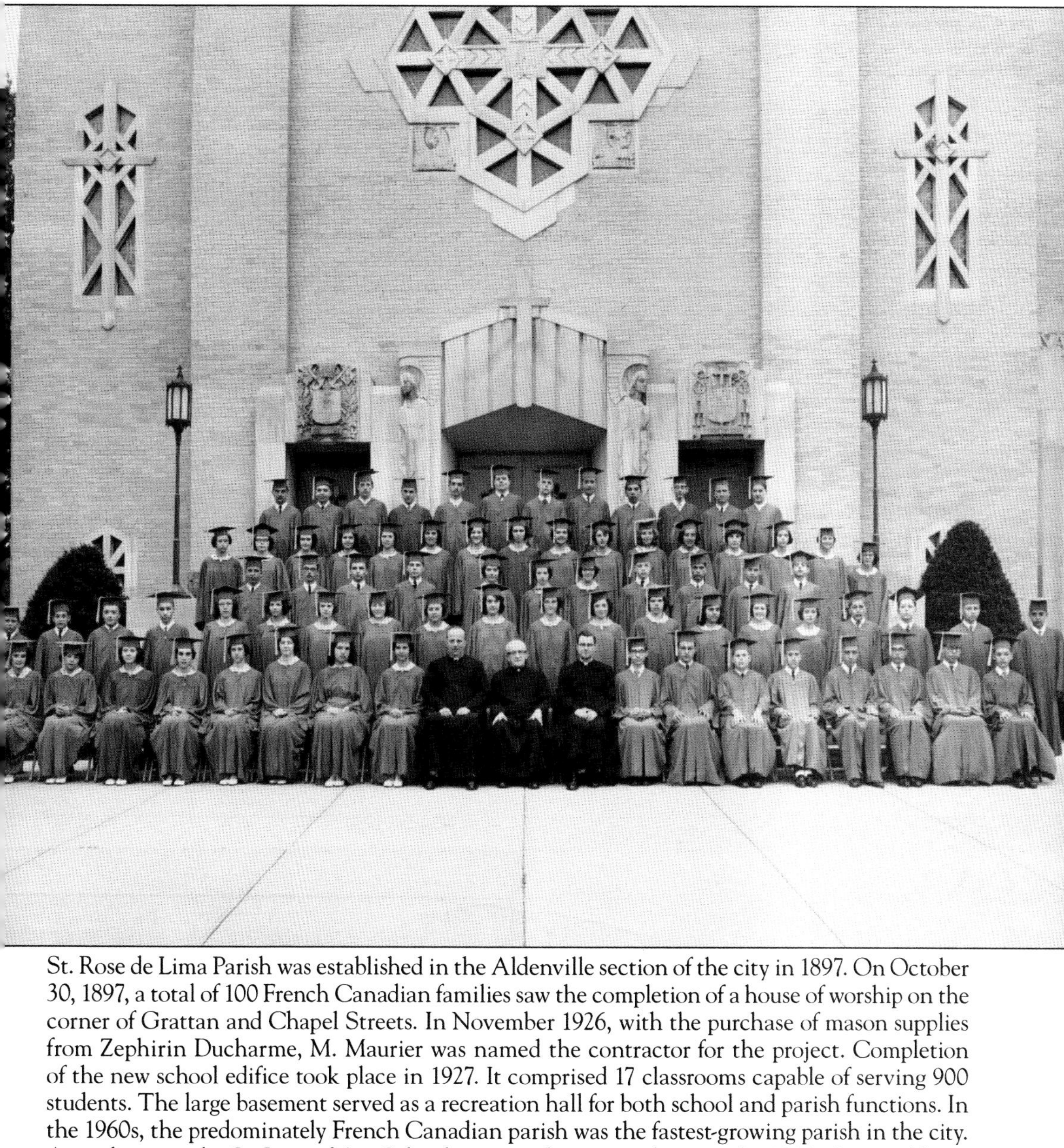

St. Rose de Lima Parish was established in the Aldenville section of the city in 1897. On October 30, 1897, a total of 100 French Canadian families saw the completion of a house of worship on the corner of Grattan and Chapel Streets. In November 1926, with the purchase of mason supplies from Zephirin Ducharme, M. Maurier was named the contractor for the project. Completion of the new school edifice took place in 1927. It comprised 17 classrooms capable of serving 900 students. The large basement served as a recreation hall for both school and parish functions. In the 1960s, the predominately French Canadian parish was the fastest-growing parish in the city. Attendance at the St. Joan of Arc School was matching records set in the 1930s. Pictured here, an eighth-grade graduating class poses for the traditional picture in front of the church.

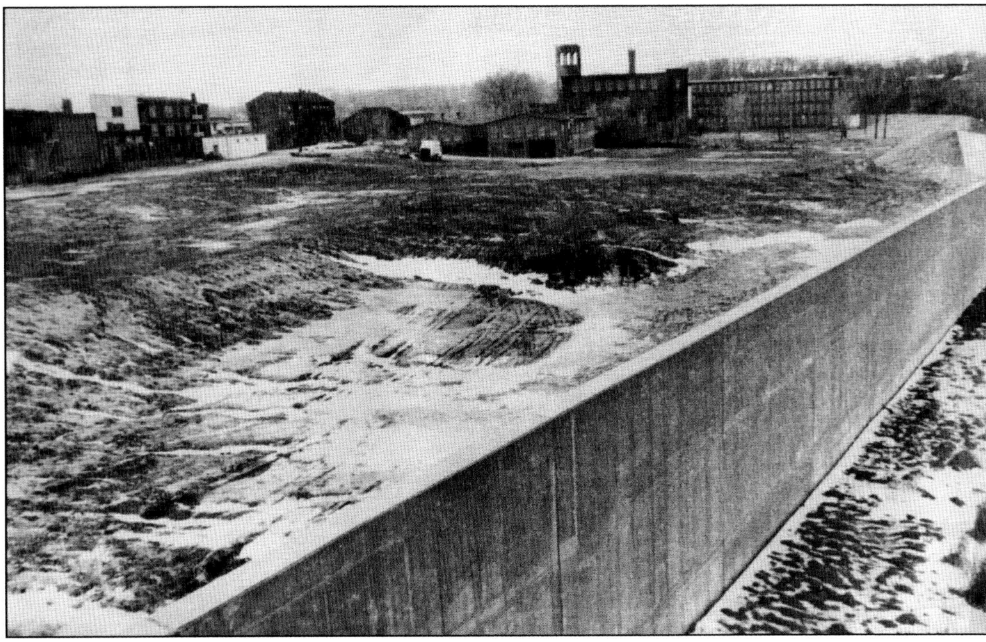

On June 19, 1968, a general-alarm fire destroyed the abandoned Savage Arms River Plant in Chicopee Falls. The fire consumed the entire four and a half acres adjacent to the newly constructed concrete dike on the Chicopee River. The building itself was part of the city's urban renewal project and had been slated for demolition. Local pundits referred to the vacant lot as "instant urban renewal."

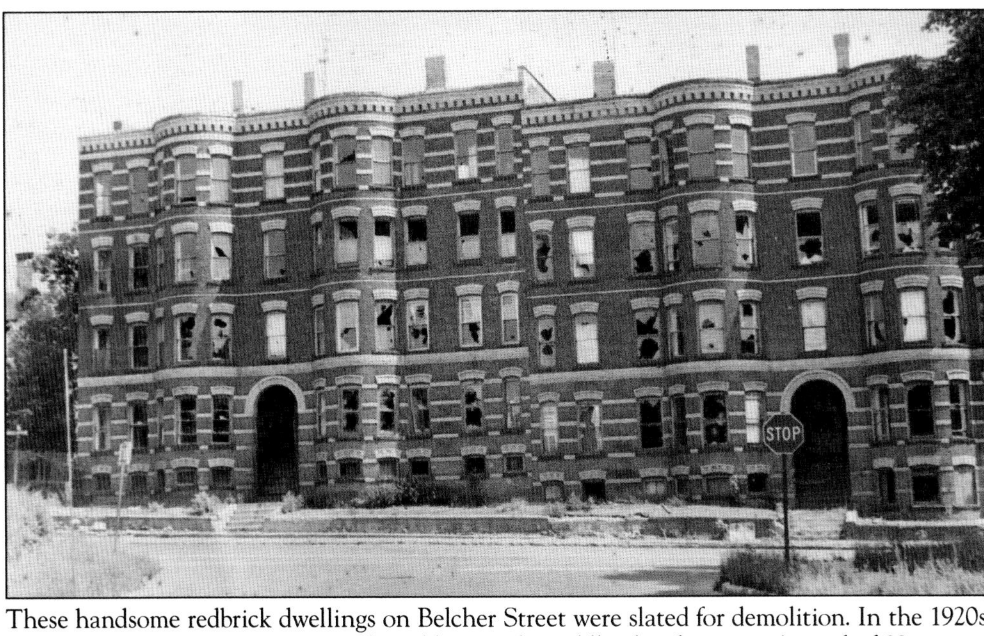

These handsome redbrick dwellings on Belcher Street were slated for demolition. In the 1920s, the Beauchamp Apartments were desirable upscale middle-class housing. A total of 82 acres of the oldest section of Chicopee Falls was slated for rebuilding, including a widening of Broadway Street from 46 feet to 100 feet under a federal road-building program.

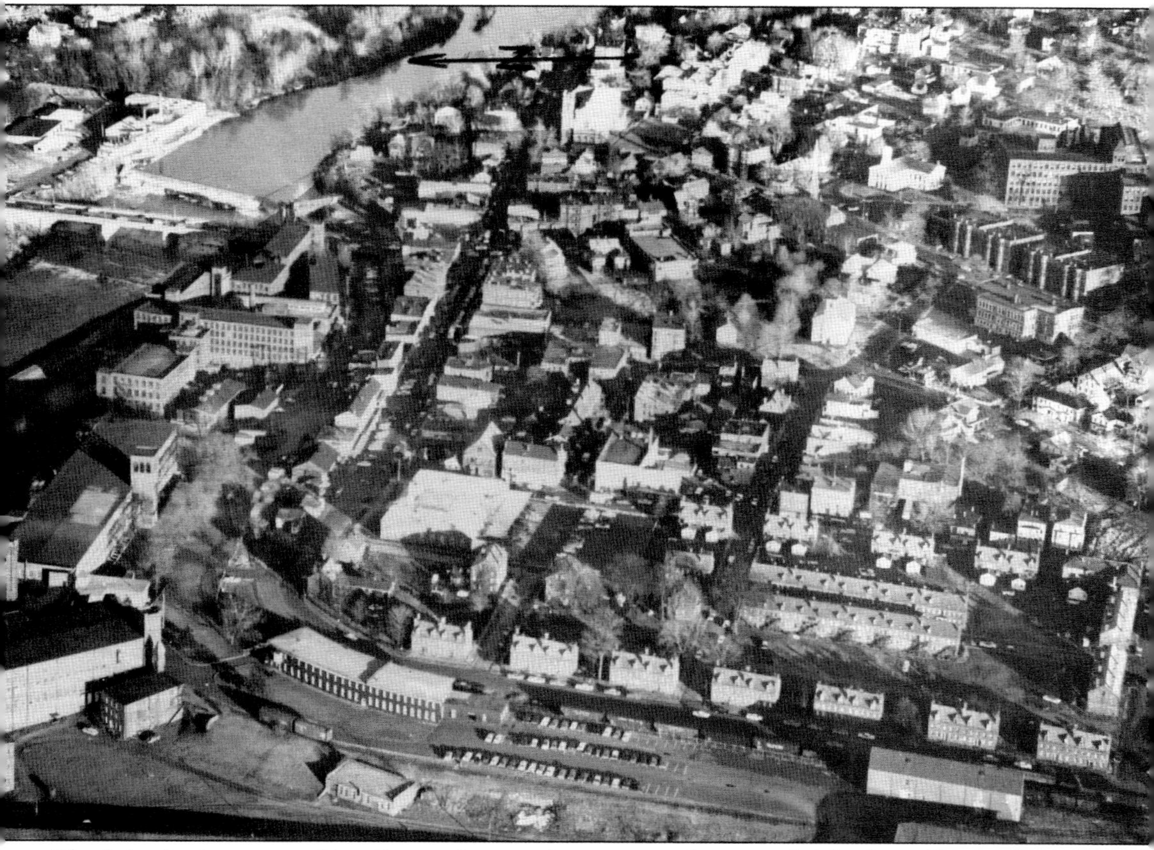

The federal urban renewal law financed a complex program that provided funding allowing the city to buy and destroy dilapidated buildings while constructing needed parks, playgrounds, schools, and public safety complexes and assisting in the establishment of new commercial, industrial, and retail facilities. Unfortunately in Chicopee Falls, the municipal government was poorly equipped to meet the challenges of the new program's extensive oversight provisions. Urban renewal arrived with several strings attached. The federal government had waded into the murky world of local politics. The majority of the residential and business structures in the shaded area of the picture were slated for eventual demolition. The Savage Arms Hill Plant slated for demolition will be replaced by garden-type apartments for those displaced by urban renewal. In addition to the construction of a new Uniroyal Tire Warehouse, plans included a new $1-million central post office and a new shopping center.

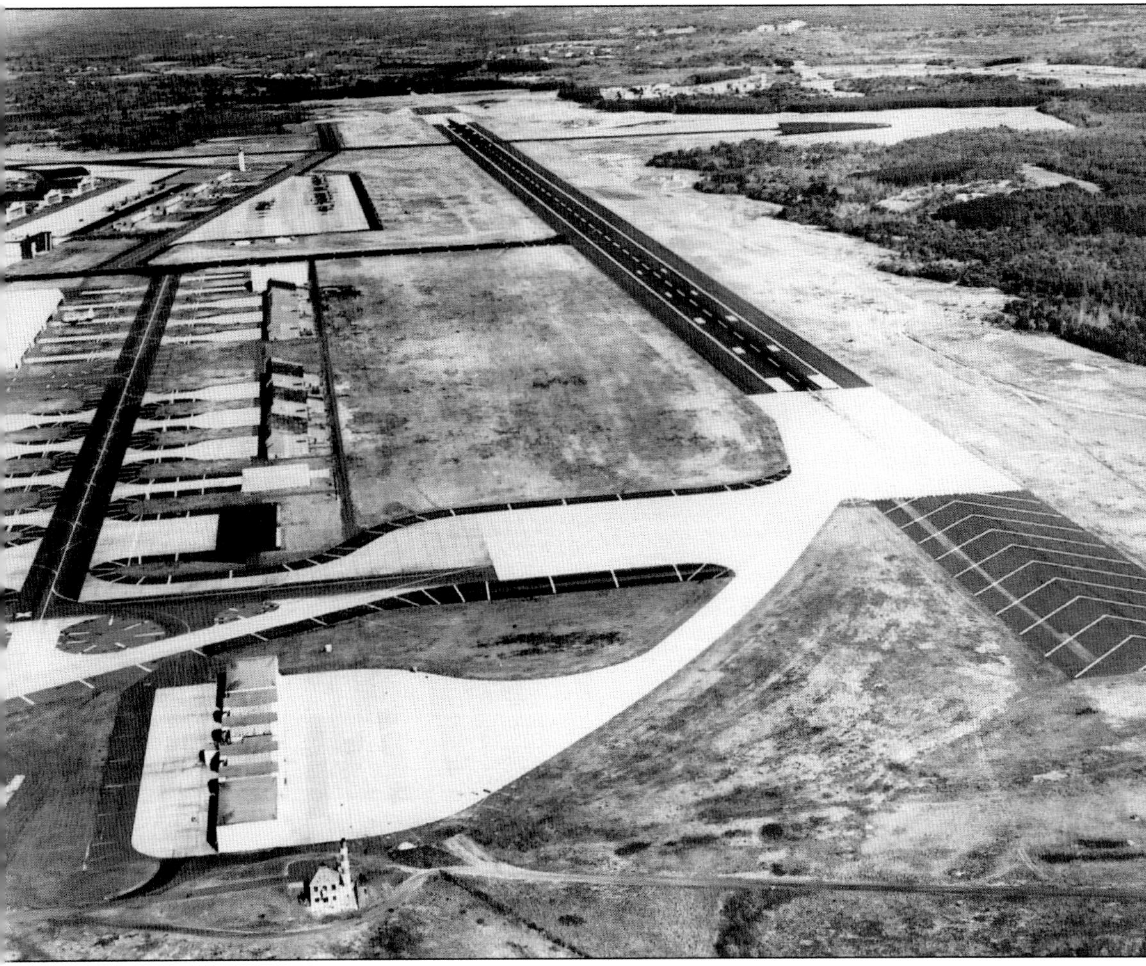

During most of Lyndon Johnson's presidency, Westover remained a training-and-preparedness facility. When it was announced that planes from Westover were going to Southeast Asia, protestors began to appear outside the main gate on James Street. As the war was quickly becoming the most unpopular war in American history, the Chicopee base was targeted by an increasing number of well-organized activists. In 1967, the 35 B-52s of the 99th Bombardment Wing were assigned to Anderson Air Force Base in Guam. Flying from the island of Guam and from Thailand, the planes made more than 3,600 bombing runs over North Vietnam during their six-month tour of duty. During those days, the skies over Chicopee were quiet for the first time in 25 years.

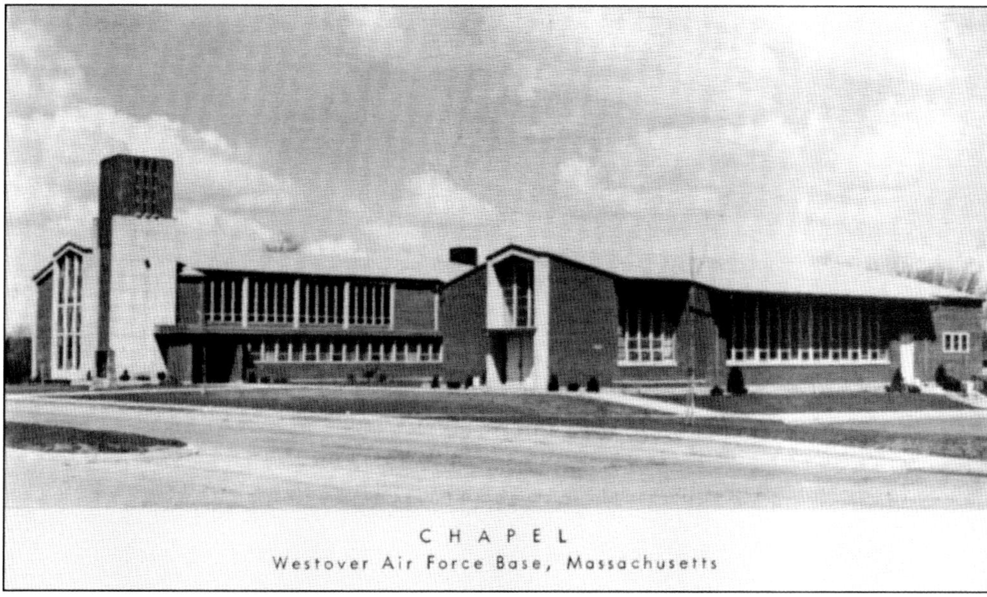

While the 99th Bombardment Wing was overseas, the families of the aircrews remained at the base. The base chapel played a very important role in the lives of military families. In March 1970, the 99th was again deployed to bases in the Western Pacific in support of Operation Arc Light.

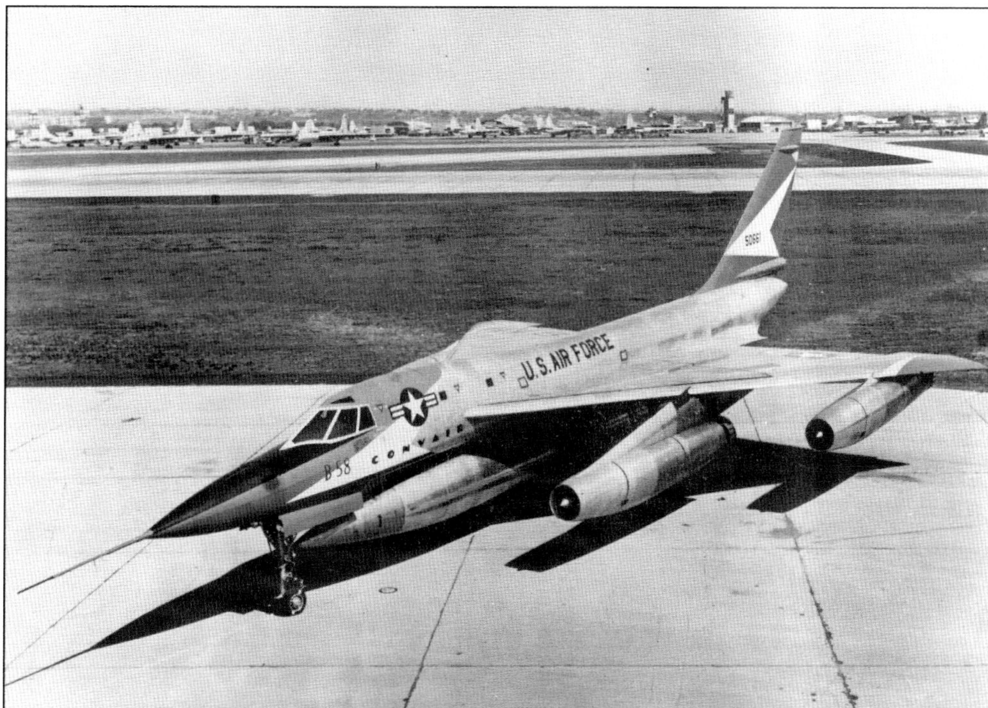

Poised on the tarmac at Westover Air Force Base is an extraordinary supersonic B-58 bomber, the fastest warplane in the nation's arsenal. The aircraft shared top billing with actor Henry Fonda in the thrilling Cold War film *Fail-Safe*, which tells the story of a squadron of Air Force bombers who were accidentally sent to bomb the Soviet Union.

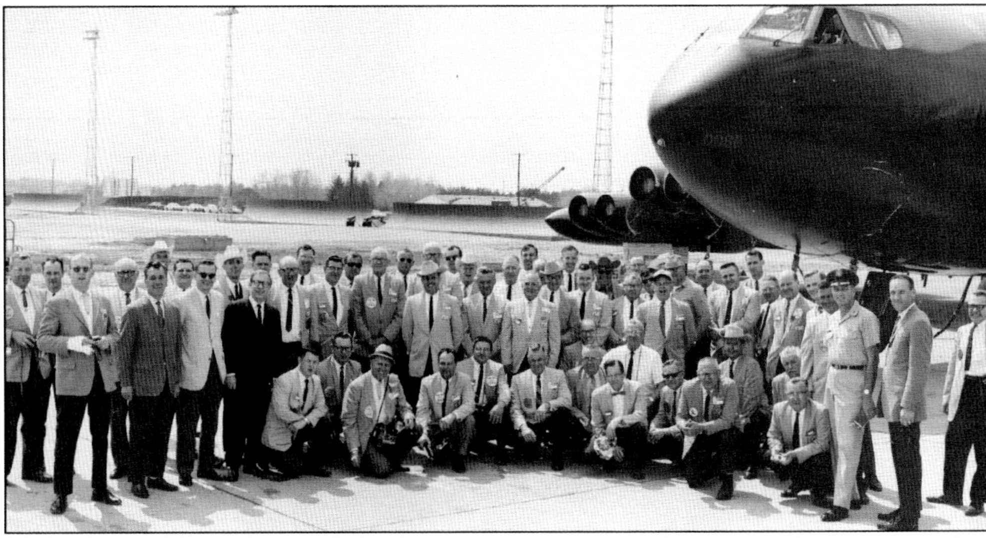

On May 18, 1967, the Iowa Caravan, a delegation of Midwest Chamber of Commerce members arrived at Westover Air Force Base. The visit was part of a public relations program sponsored by the US Air Force. Mayor Richard Demers (left in dark suit) was on hand with Chicopee Chamber of Commerce members to welcome the visitors.

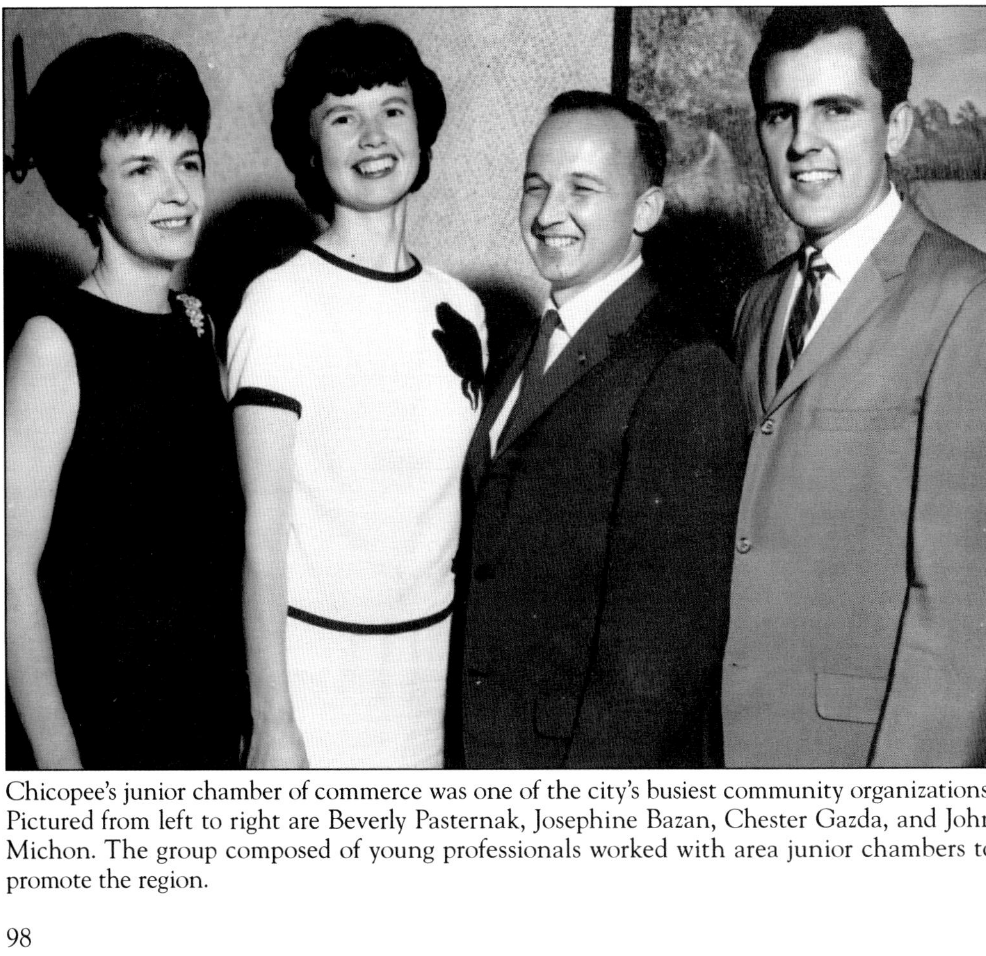

Chicopee's junior chamber of commerce was one of the city's busiest community organizations. Pictured from left to right are Beverly Pasternak, Josephine Bazan, Chester Gazda, and John Michon. The group composed of young professionals worked with area junior chambers to promote the region.

Jennie Chieka greets arrivals at the Chicopee Lodge of Elks Hawaiian Night. The lodge on Granby Road was famous for its Saturday night parties. In the 1960s, the Elks Lodge was a place where community leaders networked, socialized, and gave back to friends and neighbors.

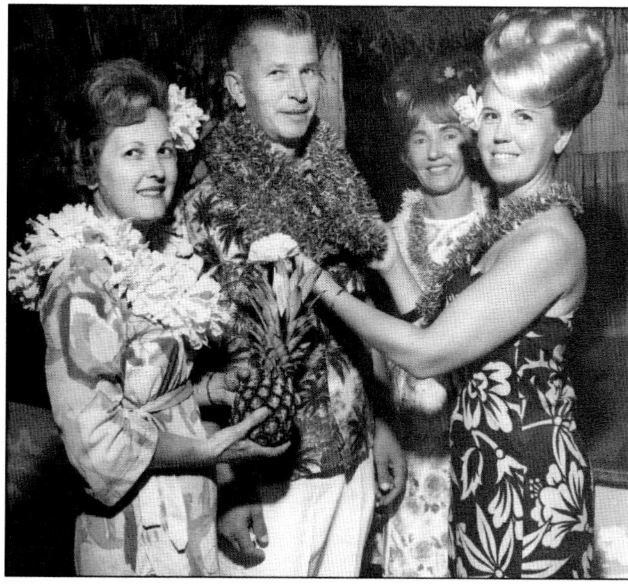

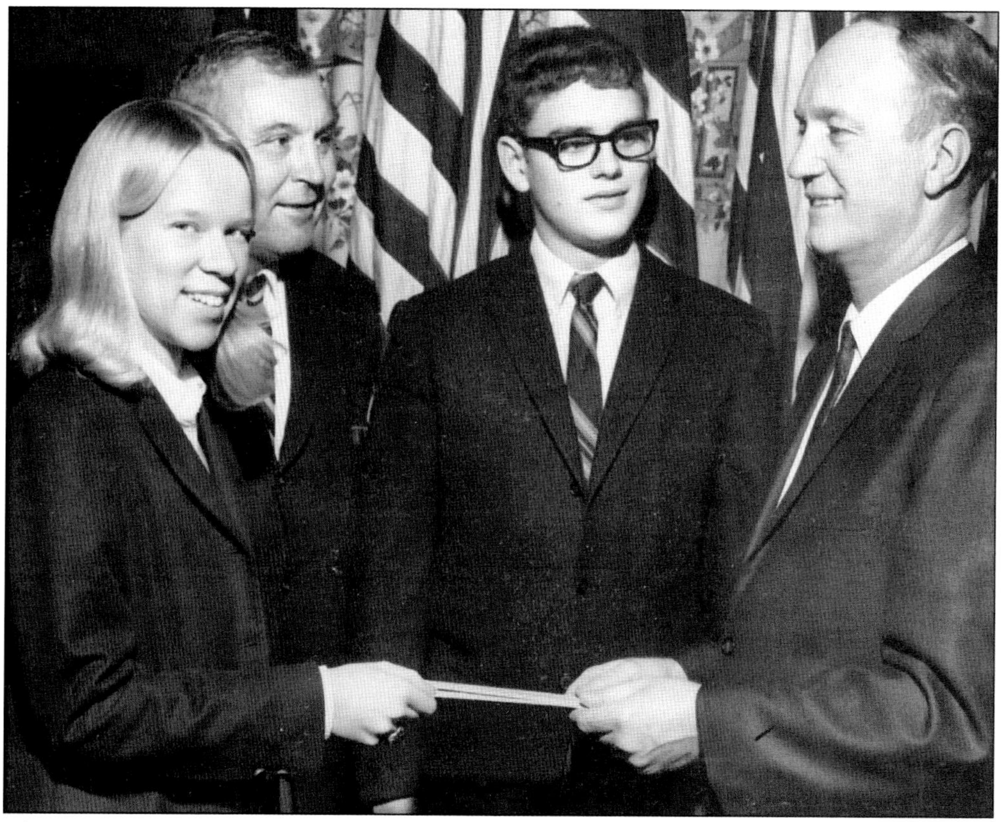

The Benevolent and Protective Order of Elks was a nationwide patriotic organization dedicated to supporting the nation's next generation. On a monthly basis, the Chicopee Lodge recognized the student of the month at the city's two high schools. From left to right are Wanda Ziemba (Chicopee High School), youth chairman Ted Budynkiewicz, Mike Jones (Chicopee Comprehensive High School), and treasurer John Stachowicz.

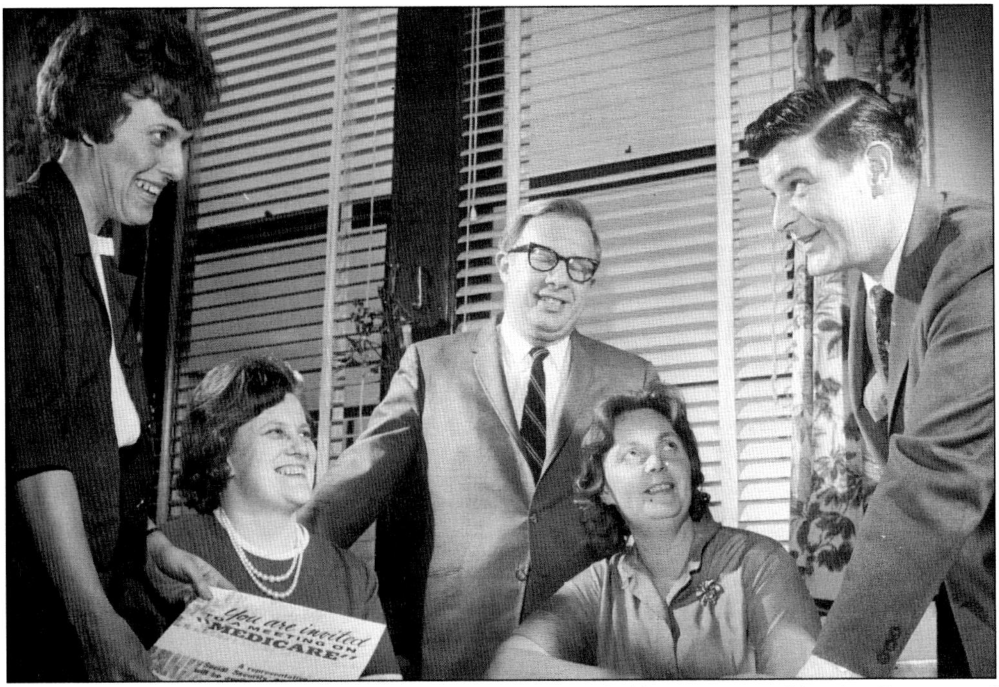

Medicare, a program of health benefits for persons 65 and older, was passed by the Congress of the United States in 1965 and went into operation on July 1, 1966. By the end of the year, more than two million Americas had received hospital services. Pictured here, Mayor Richard Demers (center) announces a series of local meetings to introduce the new program.

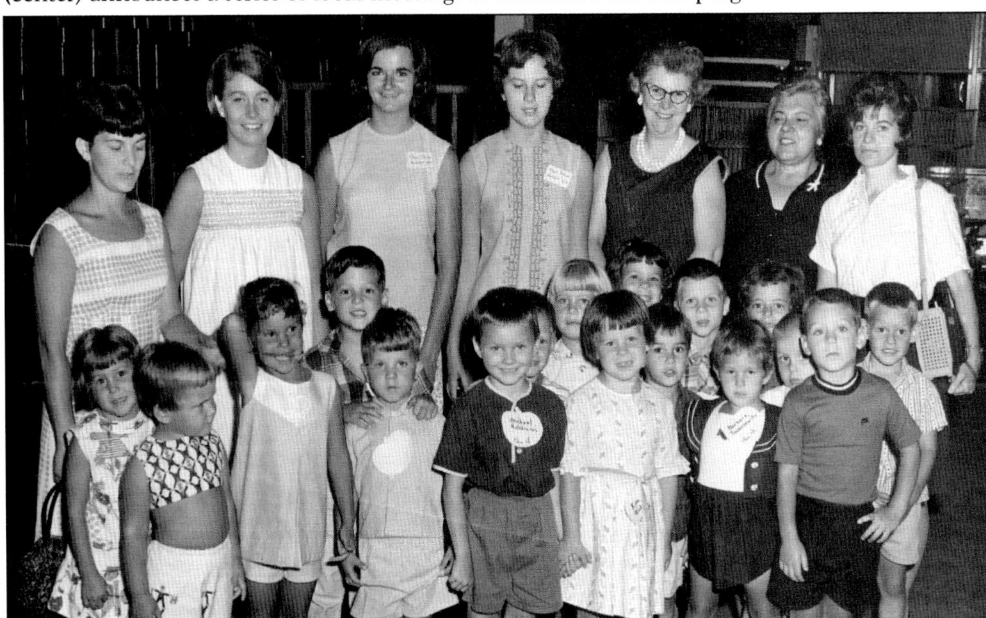

A new federally financed preschool effort called Project Head Start enrolled more than 500,000 youngsters in an eight-week summer program. Here, a group of children from the Chicopee Street, Kirby, and Chapin Schools tour the Friendly Ice Cream Plant in Wilbraham, Massachusetts with their teachers.

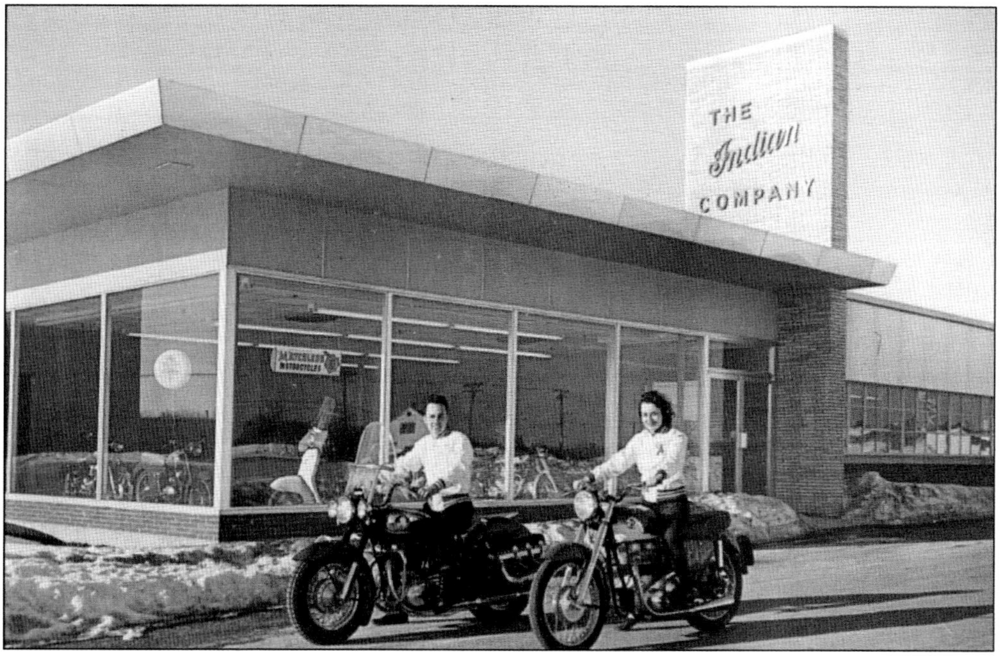

The Hendee Manufacturing Company in 1923 was renamed the Indian Motorcycle Company. The Springfield, Massachusetts, company closed in 1953, after supplying motorcycles for the police departments of 38 states and 2,000 towns across the country. In the 1960s, the company reopened in Chicopee Falls, Massachusetts.

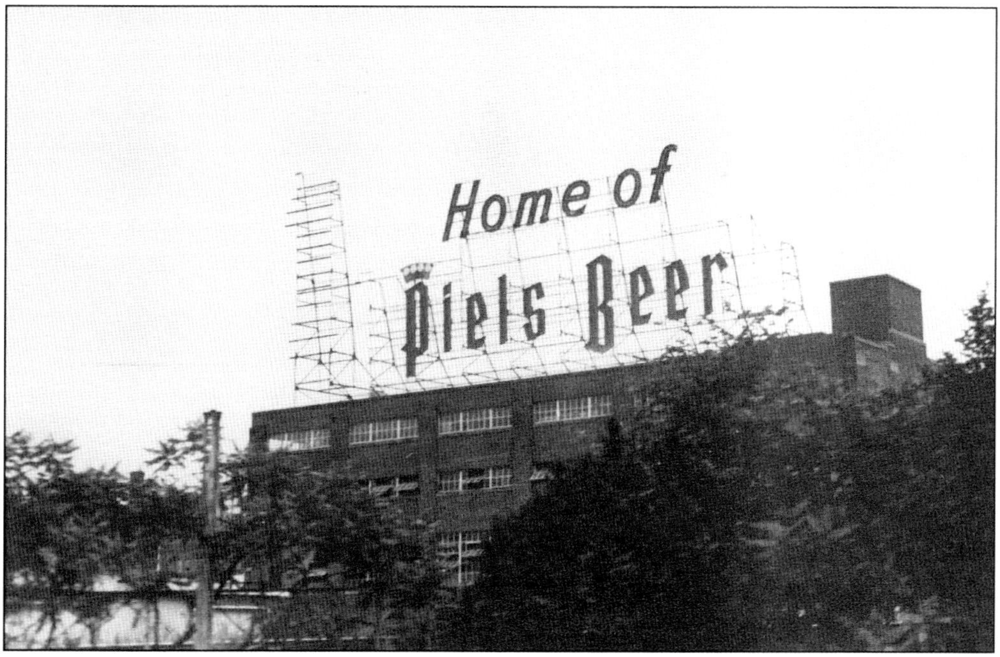

In the 1960s, the Piels Brewery had a successful television and radio campaign featuring two animated characters called Bert and Harry Piel. At that time, the company acquired the Hampden Brewing Company in Willimansett, Massachusetts. In 1973, the brand was sold to the F.M. Shaffer Brewing Company, and the local plant was closed.

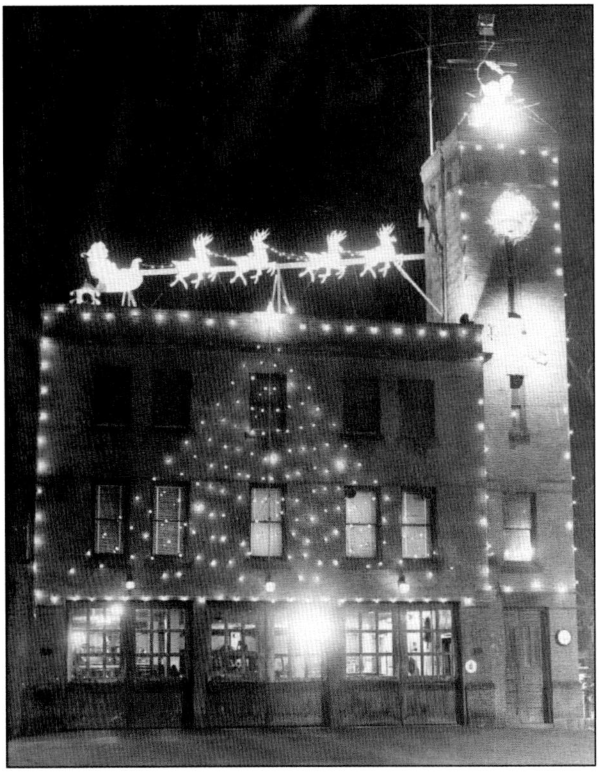

The Cabot Street Fire Station was built in 1892 on the site of the old Unitarian Church. In the 1960s, the city's fire stations engaged in a friendly competition. Each fire company, with an eye to originality, decorated their stations during the Christmas season.

As early as 1848, the Central Fire District was established by the mill owners in Chicopee Falls. Here, fire chief Edward Borowiec (seated) introduces the city's new firefighters to Mayor Richard Demers. Standing from left to right are Jean Lefebvre, Donald Roy, Richard Roy, Ronald Gioscia, Richard Tenczar, and Earl Racine.

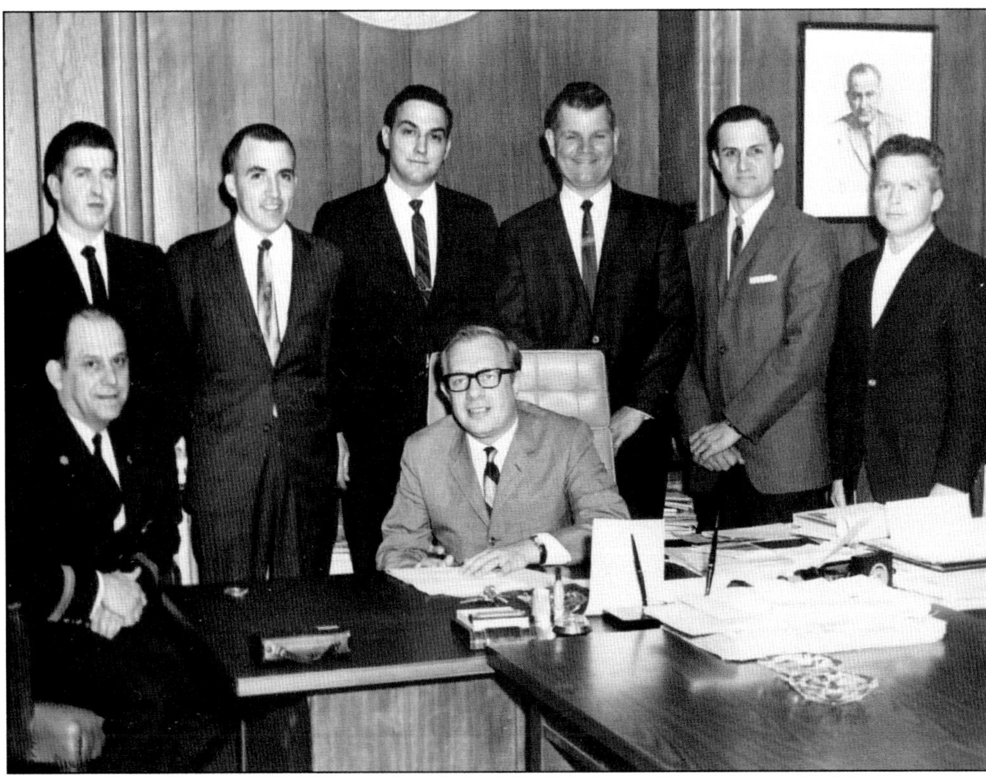

Bishop Christopher J. Weldon takes time out from his busy schedule to present diplomas at the College of Our Lady of the Elms in Chicopee. On March 24, 1950, Monsignor Weldon was consecrated a bishop in St. Patrick's Cathedral in New York. He was installed as the fourth Bishop of Springfield four days later. In 1967, the Springfield clergyman was dealing with significant racial problems.

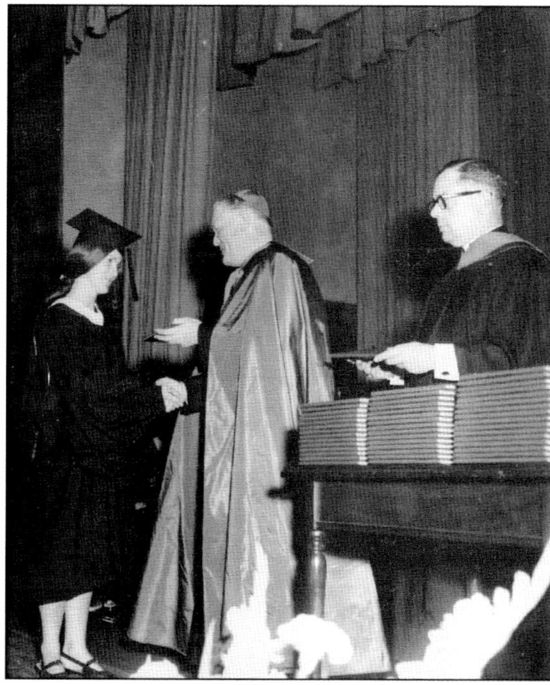

Chicopee's Girl Scouts were city officials for the day. Shown from left to right, Maureen McDowell replaces Judge James Landers, Capt. Edward Rojowski at the traffic bureau is replaced by Joyce Hebert, city prosecutor Alphonse Turcotte is assisted by Denise Dion, and Susan Mantler replaces John Moylan as city solicitor.

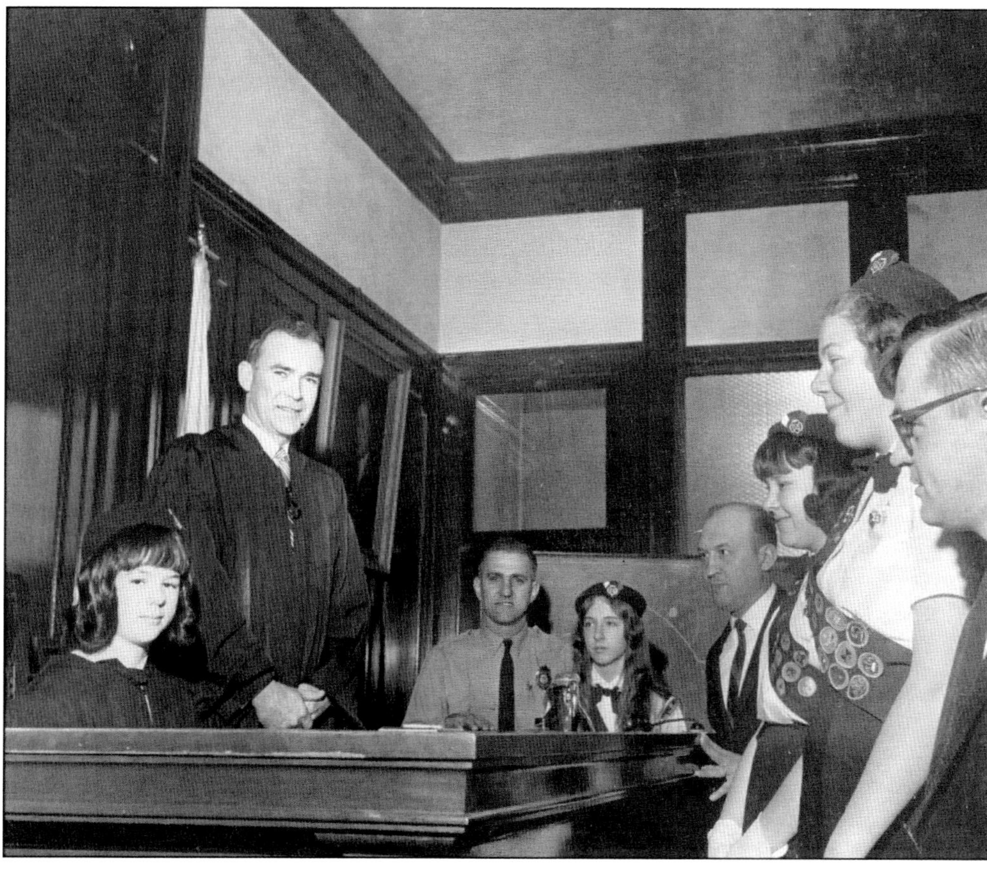

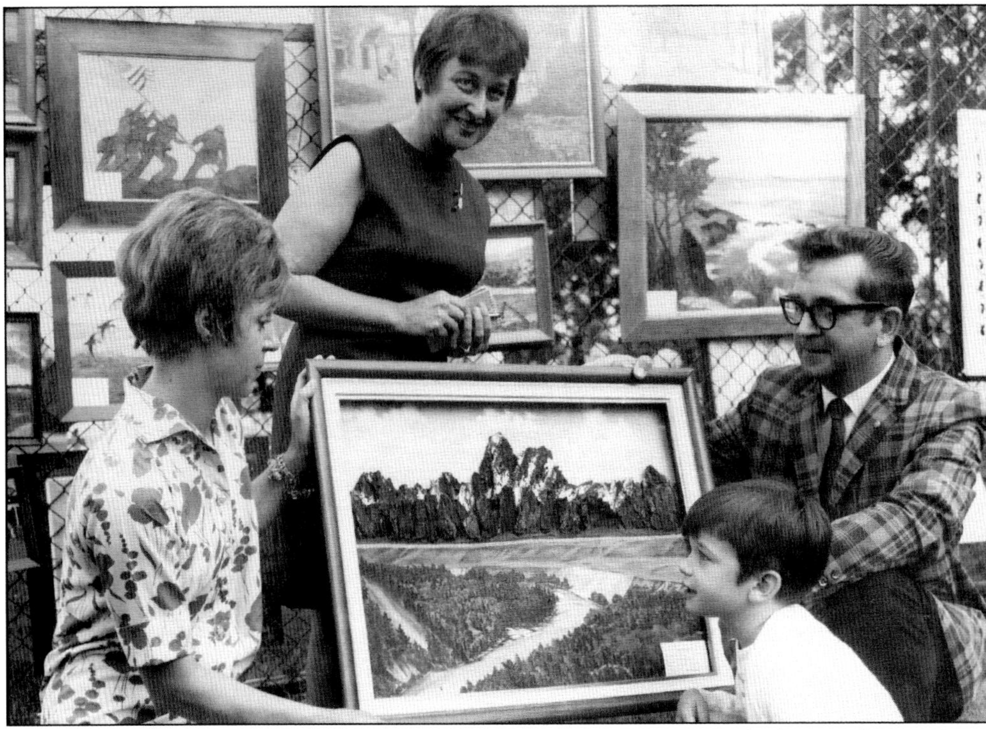

On an afternoon in late June 1894, by invitation, 12 women met at the home of Mrs. Henry Tabor on Cochran Street. On August 1, 1894, the ladies signed the charter of the Chicopee Falls Women's Club, the oldest continuous women's organization in the city. In 1967, the club sponsored its first annual Art Festival at Szot Park in Chicopee.

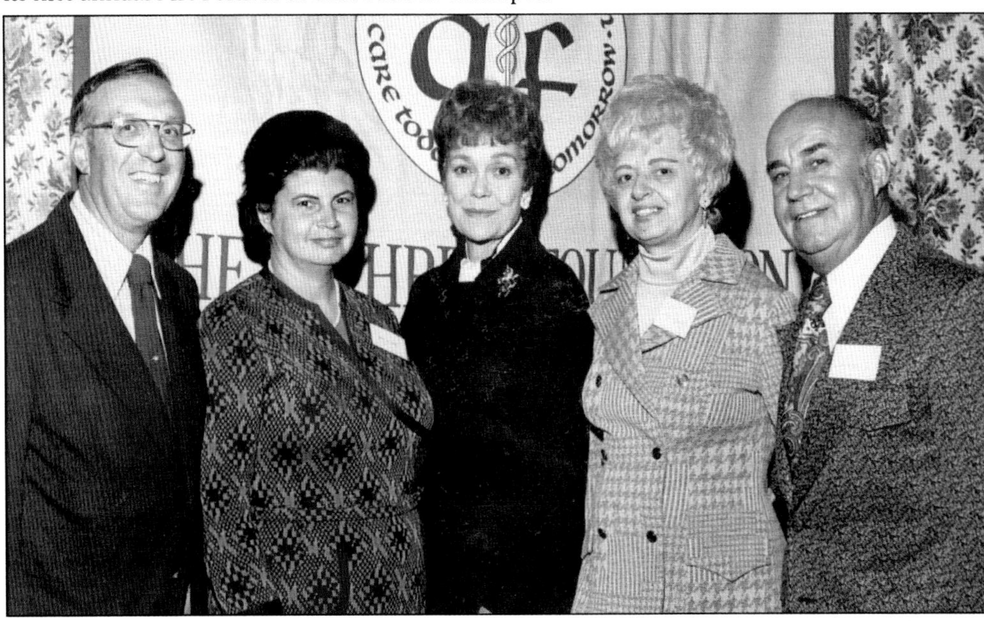

Actress Jane Wyman, the national spokesperson for the Arthritis Foundation, visited Chicopee. Here, she joins members of the organization's local unit. From left to right are Irving Rosazza, Lauria Demers, Wyman, and Mr. and Mrs. Rene Harnisch.

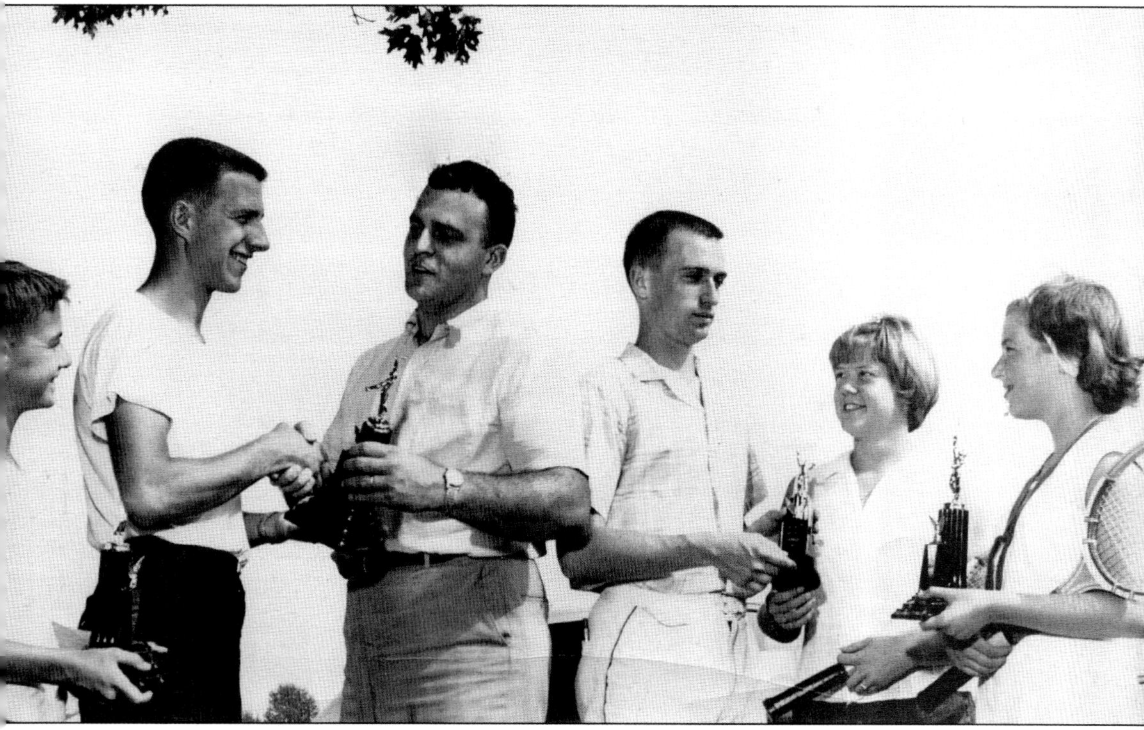

Richard Chapdelaine (center left) and Paul Lebeau (center right) recognize the winners in the Annual Tennis Tournament at Ray Ashe Park in Aldenville. Lebeau, a Chicopee educator, would coach the Chicopee Comprehensive High School girls' softball team for two decades. In the 1960s, Mayor Edward Lysek and his successor, Richard Demers, offered unstinting support for the expansion of the city's recreational facilities. The decade saw the construction of adult swimming pools in every section of the city. Both administrations upgraded the city's outstanding public parks, making them the envy of the entire region. The city lent its full support for the new sport of soccer, establishing fields in every section. Szot Park, the premiere baseball facility in western Massachusetts was equipped with lights for night games. On Burnett Road, the long-awaited Chicopee State Park opened in the Cooley Brook section of Johnny Cake Hollow. In the far end of the hollow, the Chicopee Country Club welcomed local golfers. In the 1970s, the city's two high schools established girls' varsity teams in field hockey, basketball, soccer, tennis, and softball.

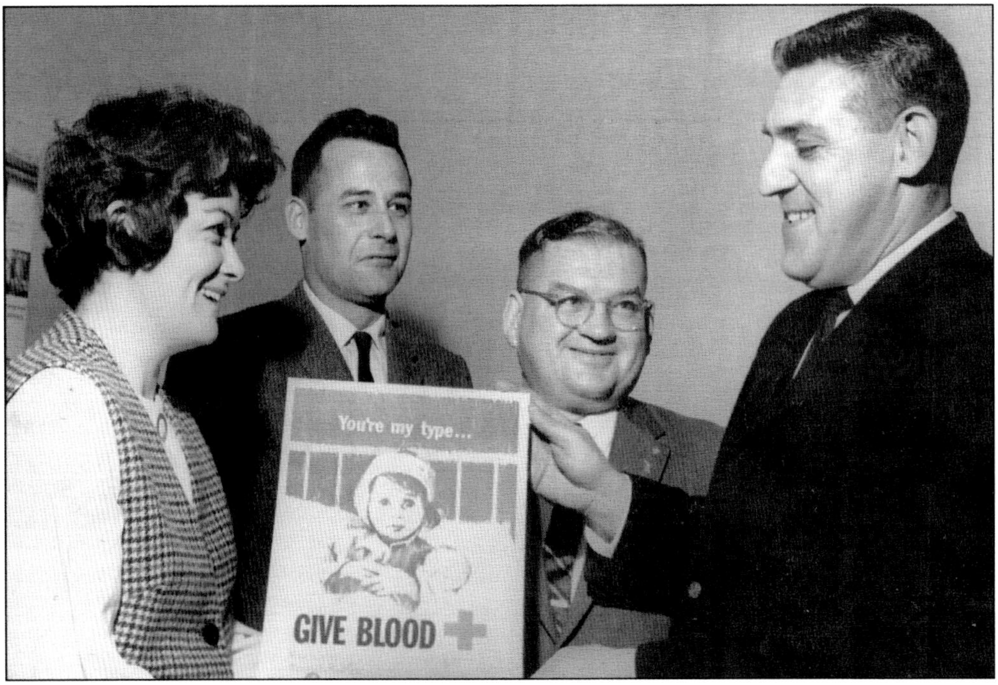

In this publicity photograph, Chicopee Teacher's Association president Edwin Orlowski (right) is urging community support for the association's annual blood drive. At the time, the association was engaged in first-time contract negotiations with the Chicopee School Committee.

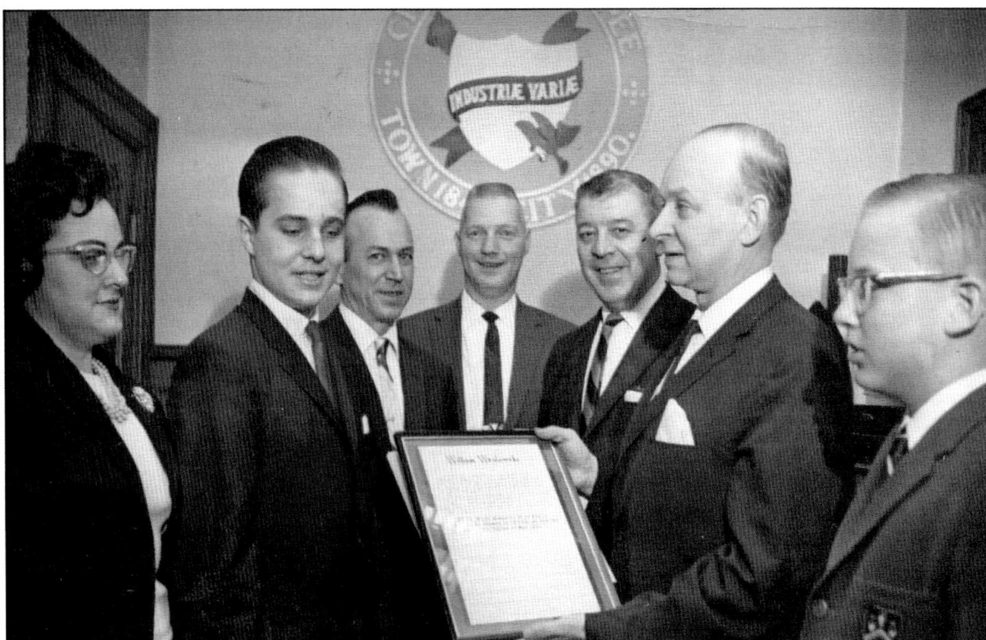

Chicopee Comprehensive High School Student William Weslowski is honored by the Chicopee School Committee as his parents and younger brother look on. The young man, blind since birth, is recognized for his outstanding academic achievements and his selection to the high school all-state band.

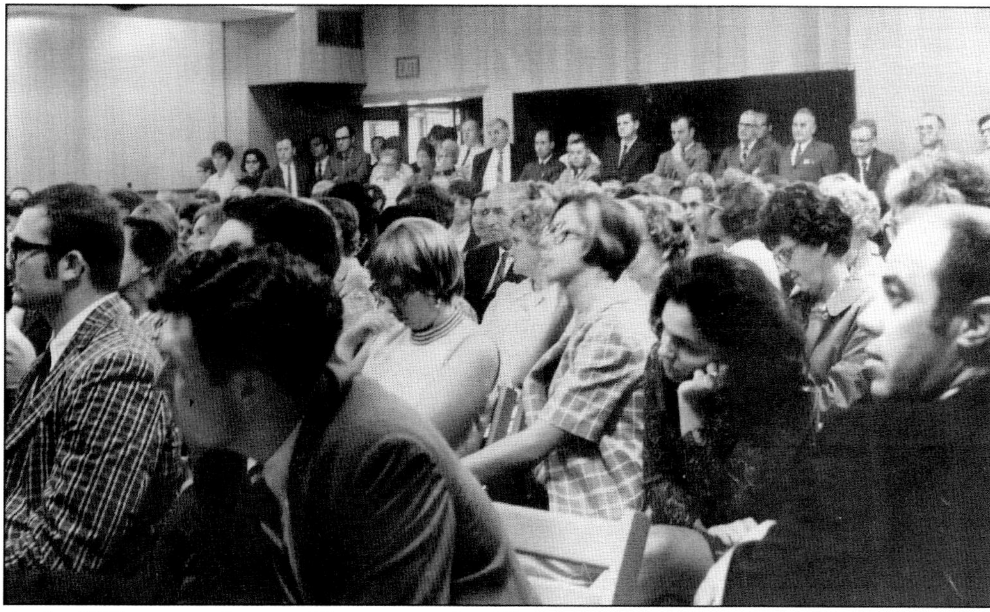

At the Willimansett Legion, Chicopee teachers listen as speakers report on the status of stalled contract talks with the Chicopee School Committee. The impasse was the catalyst for unprecedented public demonstrations and protests leading to union recognition and a first-time teacher's contract in Chicopee.

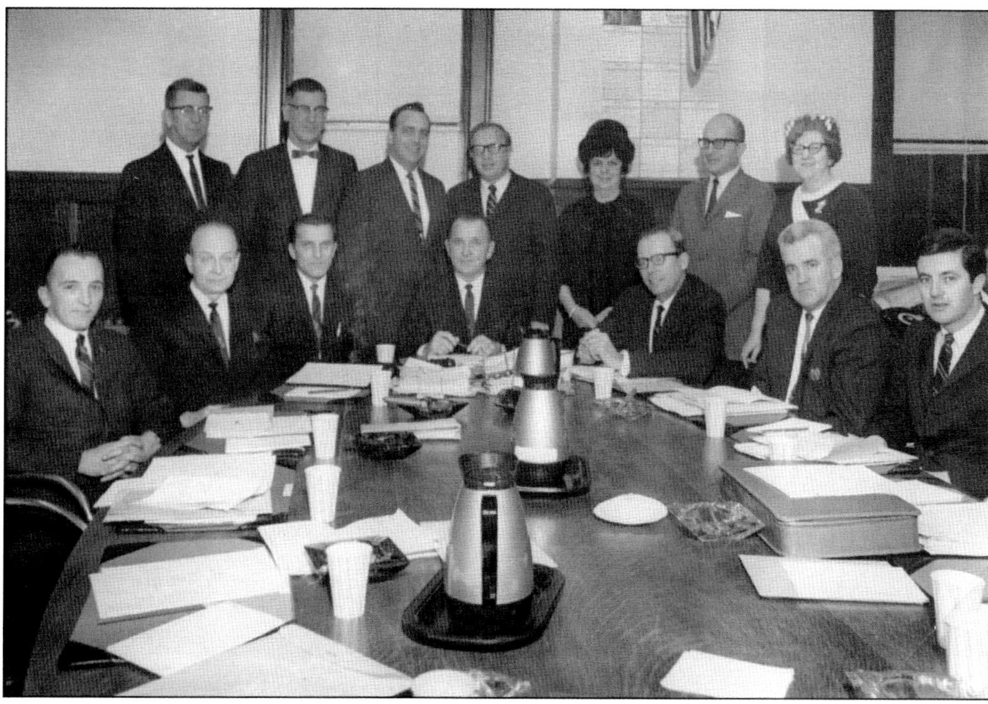

The superintendent of schools, the mayor, and the school committee pose for an official picture in 1968. The following year, the group would face student protests, antiwar demonstrations, and the state Supreme Court rulings that effectively threw out existing school dress codes for teachers and students.

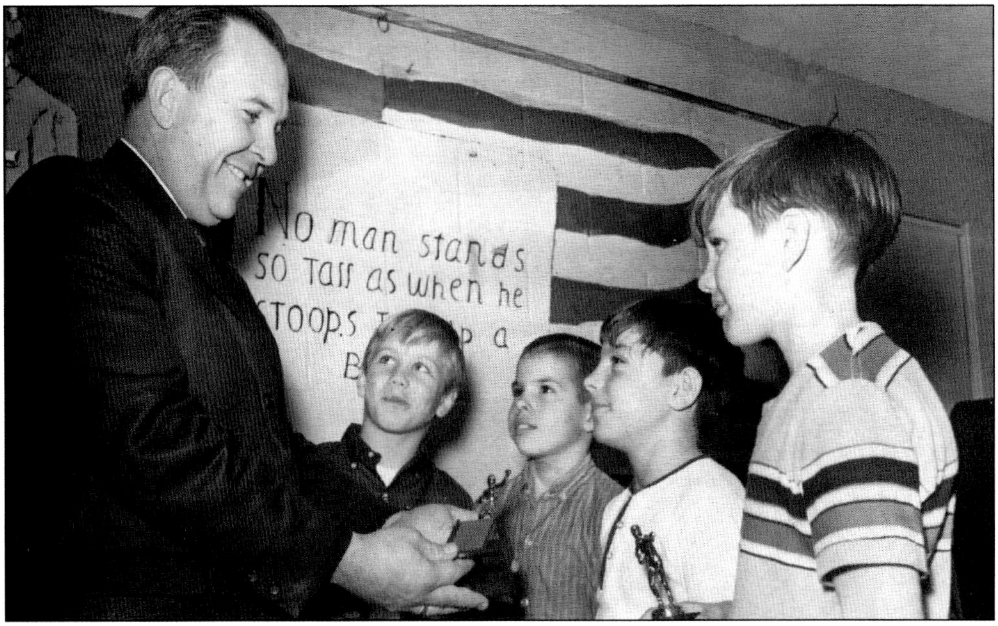

In Chicopee's 1927 mayoral election, Massachusetts representative Henry Cloutier organized the Franco-American Association and was elected. Anthony J. Stonina unified the Polish American groups two years later, making ethnic political endorsements a necessity for all candidates. Pictured here in 1969, in the city's last ethnic election, candidate for city treasurer Ernest Laflamme presents trophies to members of the Fairview Boys Club.

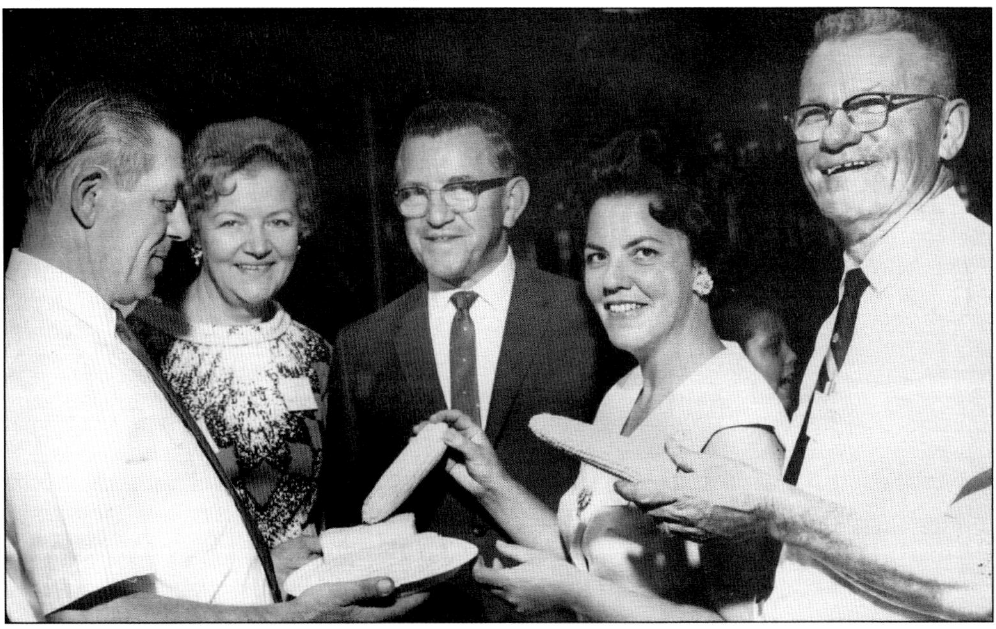

Laflamme's opponent in the treasurer's contest was Chicopee Falls businessman Matthew J. Rybak. Shown here is Rybak, surrounded by his supporters, who concentrated on the Polish American vote. Both Laflamme and Rybak were from prominent political families and were able to organize formidable volunteer support. Laflamme won in the "last hurrah" for what had been 40 years of ethnic voting in Chicopee.

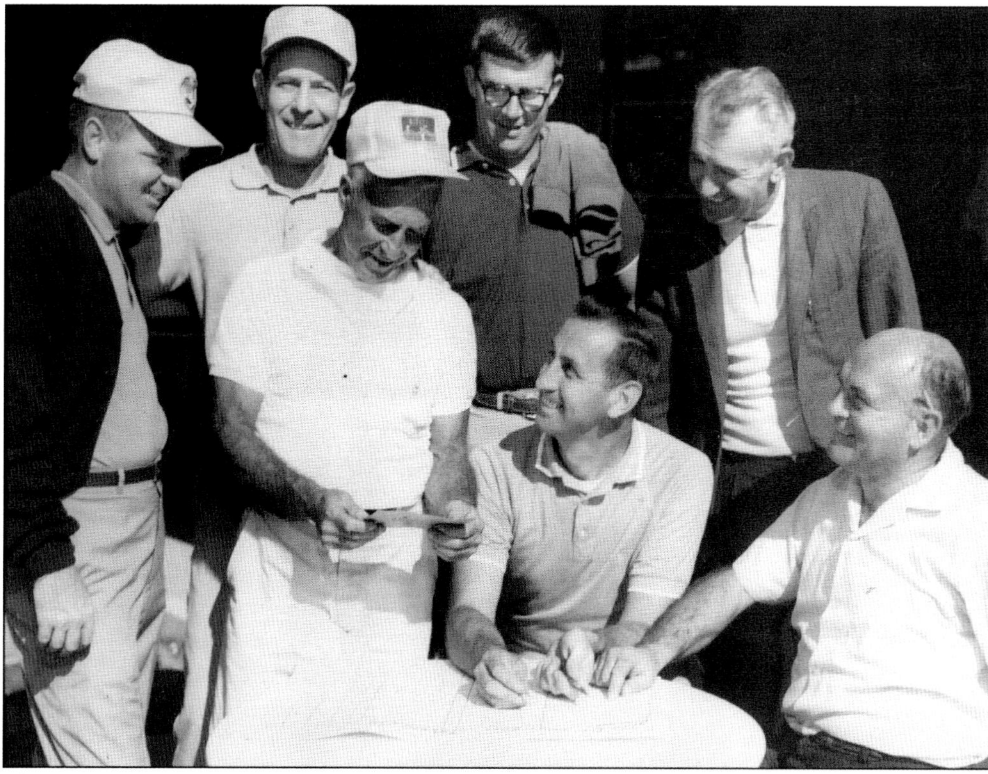

The new Chicopee Country Club was the site for the Polish American Veterans Andrew Balut Golf Tournament. The golfer with the lowest net score wins the Mayor Edward Lysek Trophy. Shown here preparing plans are, from right to left, Bill Maggie, Moe Charest, Sam Theroux, Wilbur Schoolcraft, Chet Jasinski, Walt Chwalek, and chairman Walt Tyburski.

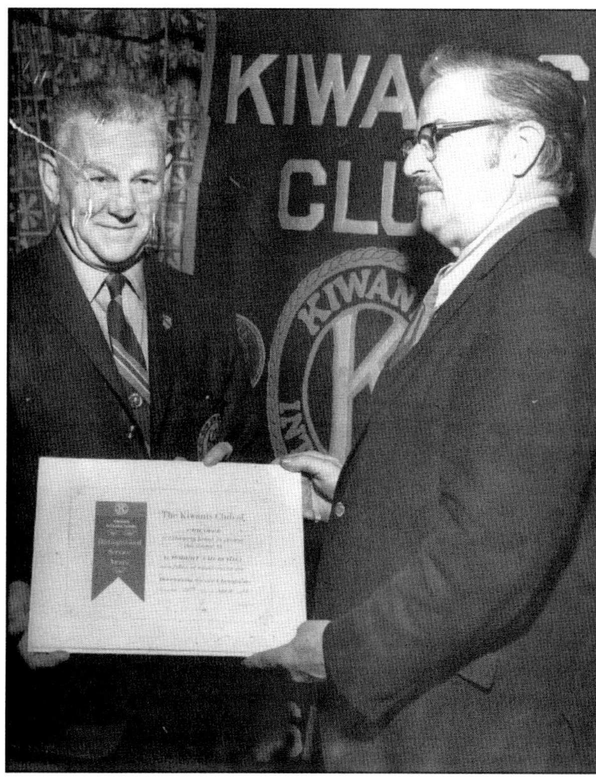

Attorney Eugene Blank, the president of the Chicopee Kiwanis Club, presents its annual distinguished award to Chicopee High School soccer coach G. Robert Churchill (left). At the end of the decade, Churchill's teams won two consecutive Massachusetts state division-one soccer championships.

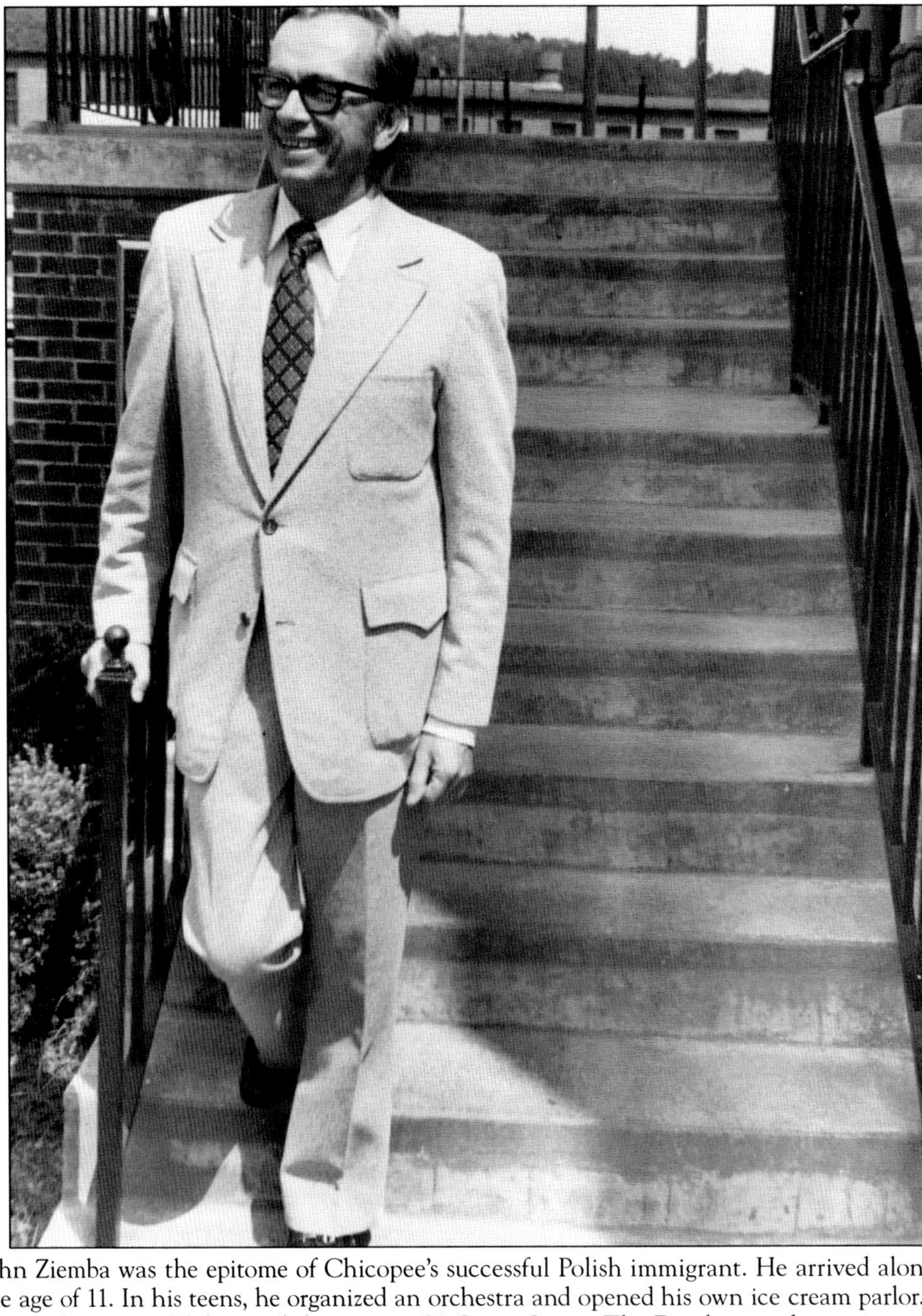

John Ziemba was the epitome of Chicopee's successful Polish immigrant. He arrived alone at the age of 11. In his teens, he organized an orchestra and opened his own ice cream parlor. He operated a successful dry goods business at 39 Grove Street. The Ziembas taught music to each of their seven children. The family included a teacher, two school principals, a medical doctor, and a mayor of Chicopee. Pictured on the steps of city hall, the new mayor was a graduate of New York University and Harvard Law School. Edward Ziemba was a practicing attorney, had served five terms as city treasurer, and was a member of the school committee. Ziemba was a member of a prominent local family with deep ties to the political establishment. His job at city hall was 35 years earlier as a member of the law department of Mayor Anthony J. Stonina, Chicopee's first Polish American chief executive.

Five

DEACTIVATION 1971–1975

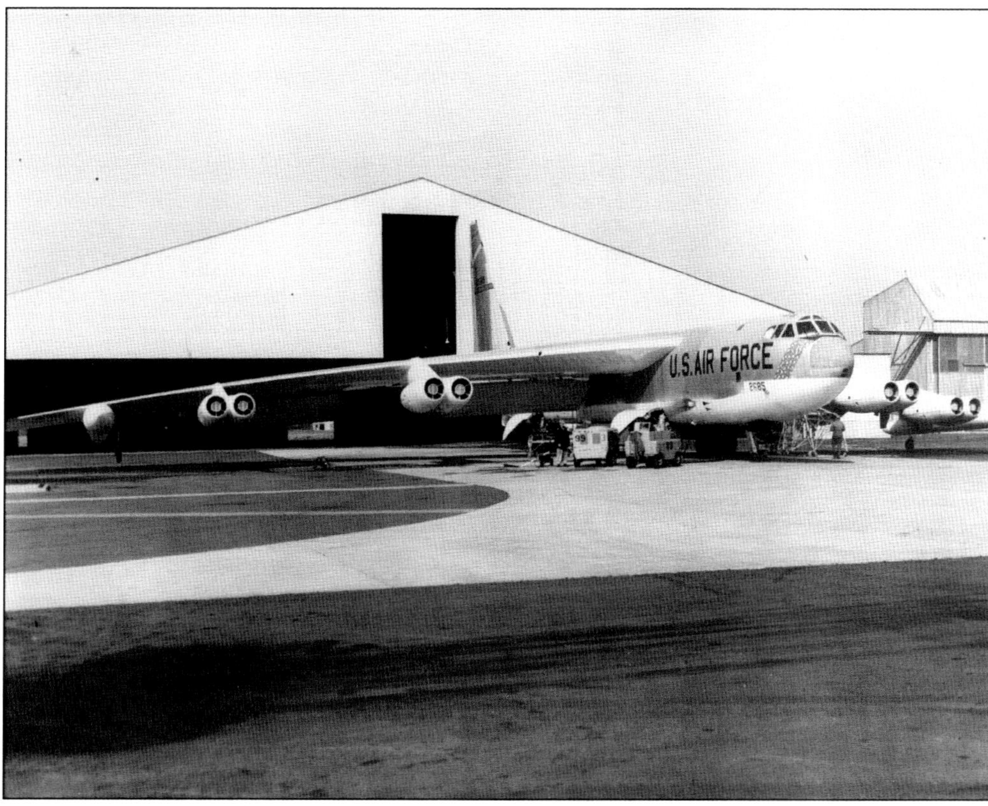

In 1971, Westover was the largest Air Force base on the East Coast. The base covered 4,717 acres of land. The facility had more than 1,000 buildings. The flight line area included 32 hangar structures for aircraft maintenance and storage. The Air Force was spending over $1 million a month in the region to purchase goods and services. The value of Westover's equipment and real property was more than half a billion dollars.

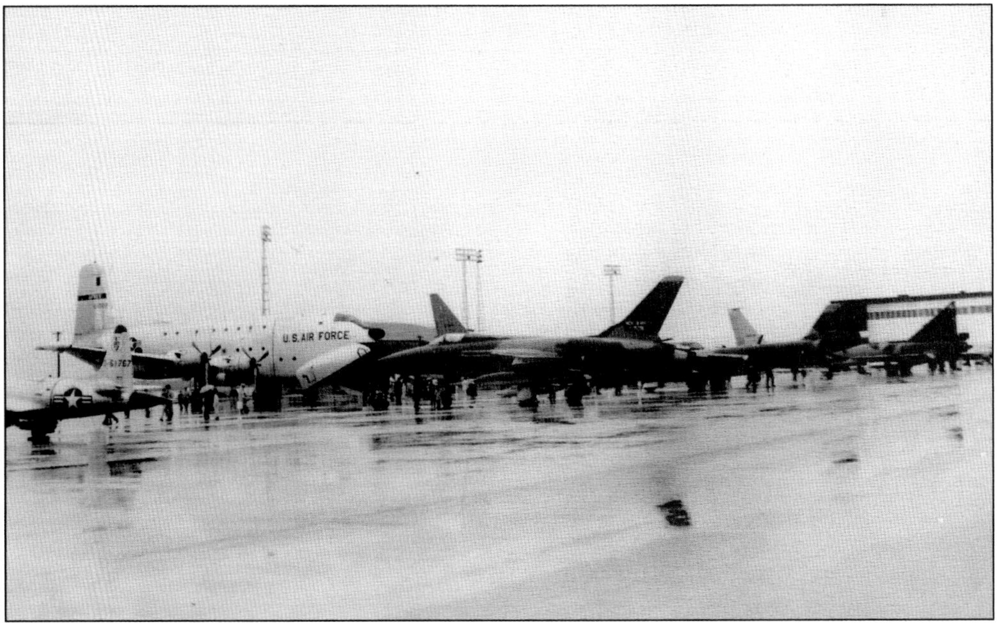

In 1972, the 99th Bombardment Wing returned to Vietnam. Remaining on base were 10 tenant units. The base was an integral part of the New England economic community. Employing approximately 5,000 military and 850 civilian personal, the base had an annual payroll of over $57 million. The total base community, including dependents, was almost 20,000.

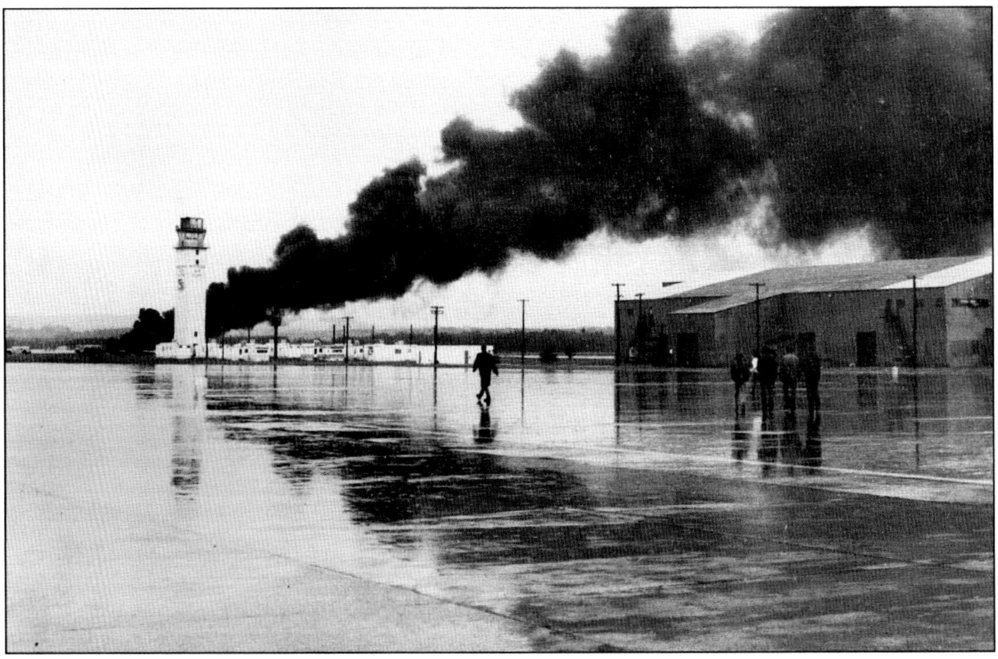

This dramatic picture of the Westover Control Tower engulfed in black smoke was the result of a minor accident. In 1972, the opposition to the war in Vietnam increased. Westover was the site of mass protests and arrests. Military police remained inside the base perimeter. The Chicopee Police Department was assigned the responsibility of keeping the roads leading to the base free of demonstrators.

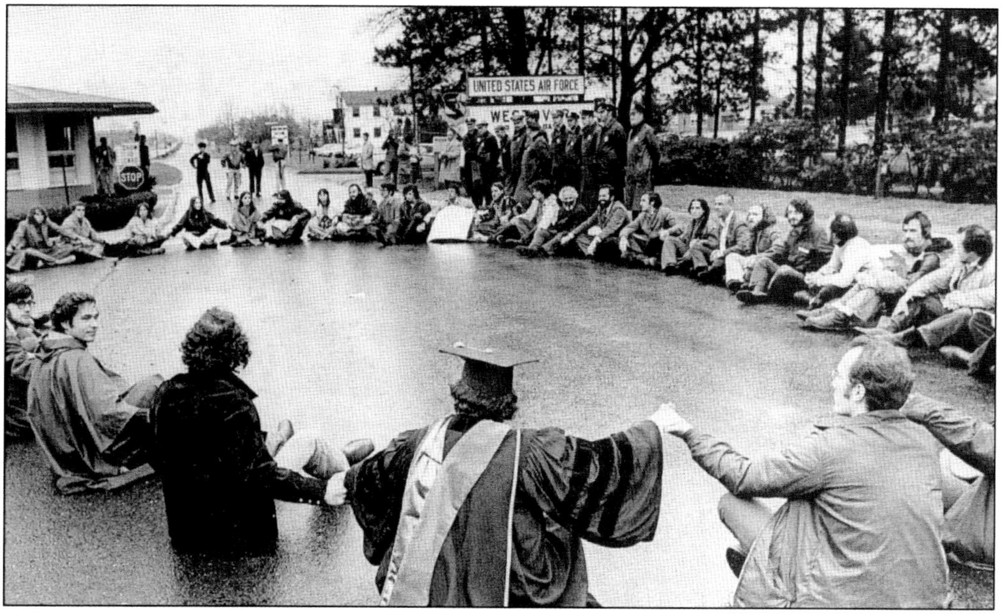

Students and faculty members from the nearby Hampshire County colleges and universities blocked Westover's main gate in ongoing coordinated antiwar protests. They would wait on nearby College Street until the buses carrying students to Chicopee Schools left the base. Business owners on James Street protested that customers were staying away, but the demonstrations were always peaceful.

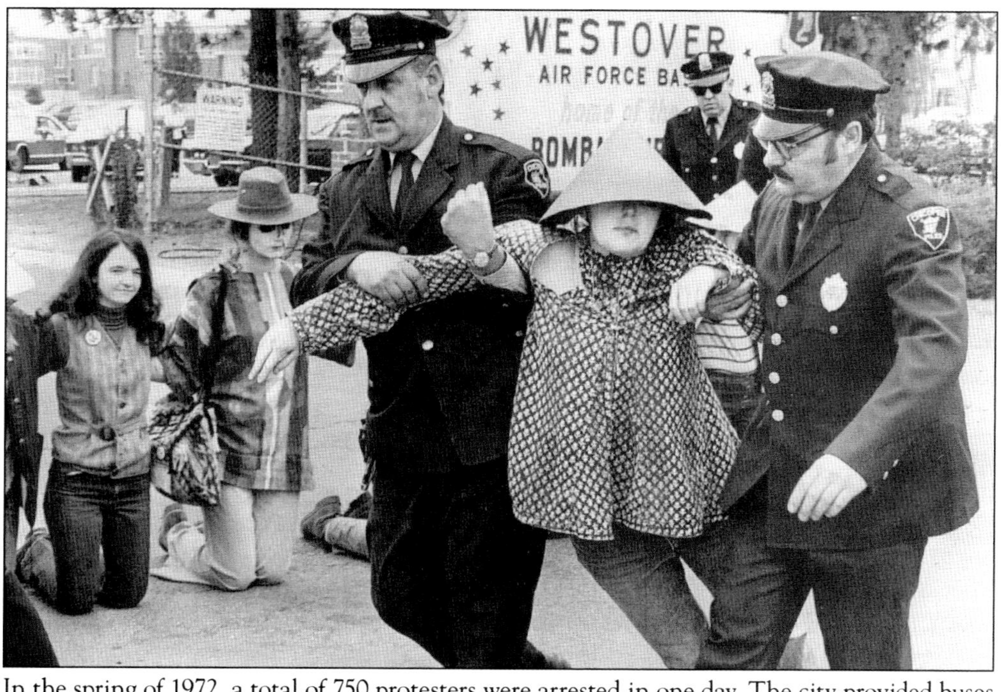

In the spring of 1972, a total of 750 protesters were arrested in one day. The city provided buses for the individuals who wished to be booked. Paying a modest fine was a way to indicate personal opposition. Mayor Edward Ziemba recognized that the demonstrators had a constitutional right to protest, but he reported the police overtime account was depleted.

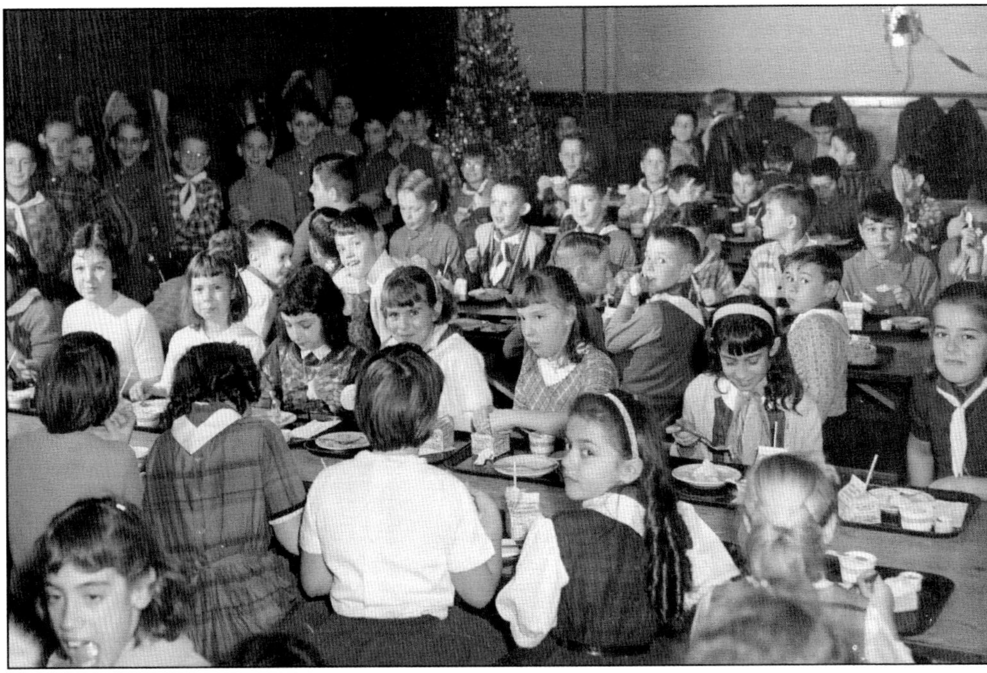

Students in the cafeteria of the St. Joan of Arc School in Aldenville peek at the camera. Christmas 1972 was a festive time. The main gate at Westover was quiet. Westover Field in Chicopee, Massachusetts, the region's most visible evidence of the American military, had returned to peacetime operations following the cease-fire in Vietnam.

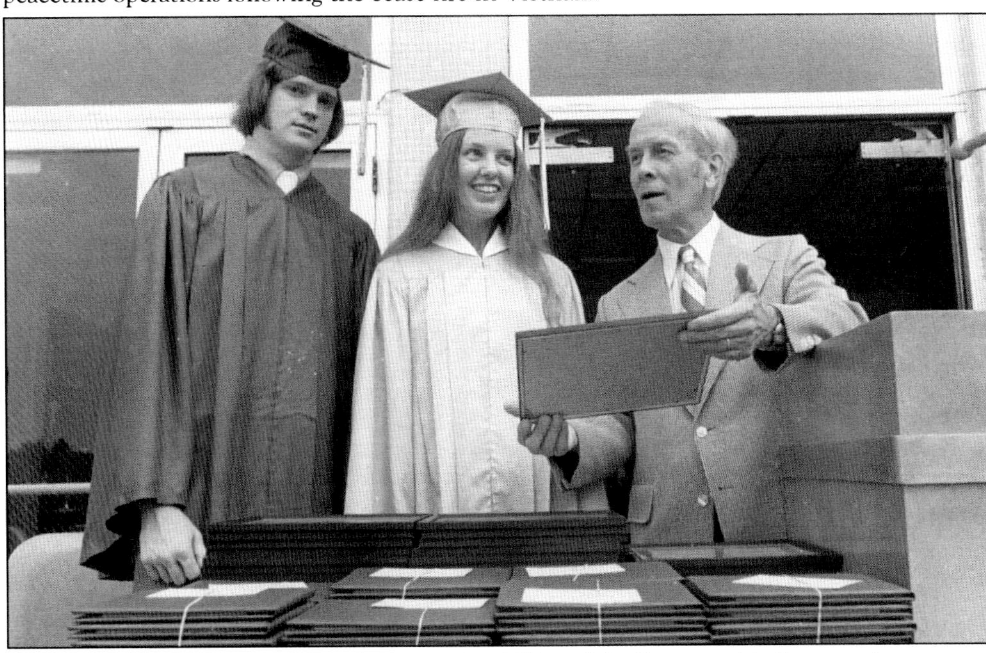

The 99th Bombardment Wing was deactivated in 1974, and the Strategic Air Command announced that the Westover Field was being turned over to the US Air Force Reserve. Several hundred students at Chicopee Comprehensive High School were military dependents. Valedictorian David S. McKissick and salutatorian Kathleen M. Loveridge look over the diplomas before graduation.

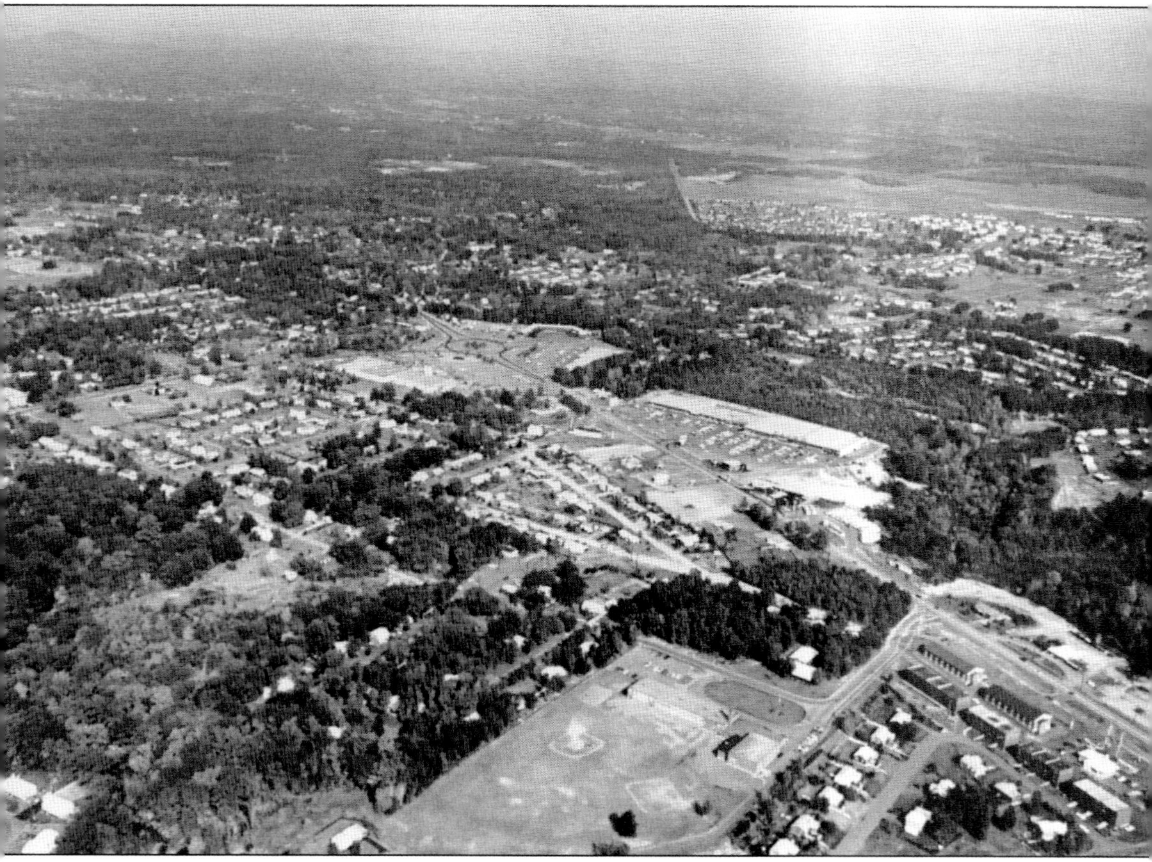

Looking at the Holyoke Dam and the bend in the Connecticut River from the top of James Street makes it easy to understand how the Fairview section of Chicopee got its name. The truly spectacular vista is probably the city's most scenic view. In fact, Fairview residents have beautiful views of Holyoke, South Hadley Falls, and the Connecticut River. In many ways, the history of Fairview is separate from the history of Chicopee. Fairview students used to ride home on something called the "rural bus." The region had close ties to the neighboring communities of South Hadley Falls, Granby, and Holyoke. The village called Plainville was first settled during the Civil War. In 1894, only 650 people lived in the village. The residential and retail development on Memorial Drive (Route 33) during the years 1950–1975 came about as a direct result of the expansion of the Air Force mission at Westover Field. Chicopee officials were cautiously optimistic about development plans for the soon-to-be surplus land on the military reservation.

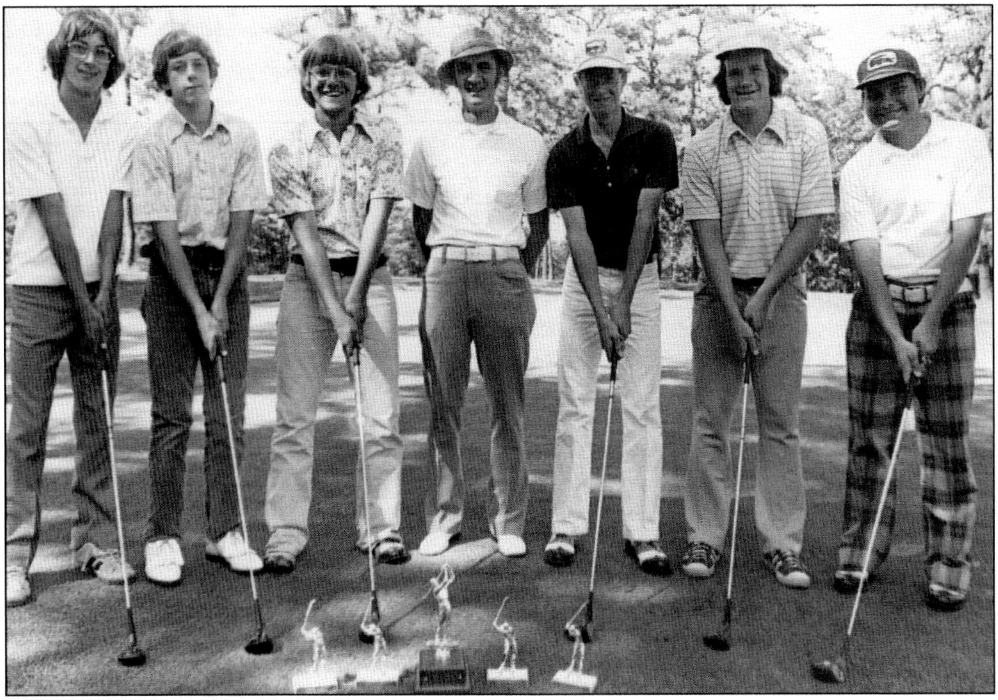

The new Chicopee Country Club was the site of the Western Massachusetts Schoolboy Tournament where the Chicopee High School golf team qualified for the State Schoolboy Tournament in Westborough. The team members are, from left to right, Paul Jamrog, Steve Bys, Clark Wojtowicz, Coach John Stewart, Tony Cyran, Jim O'Neil, and Joe Grochmal.

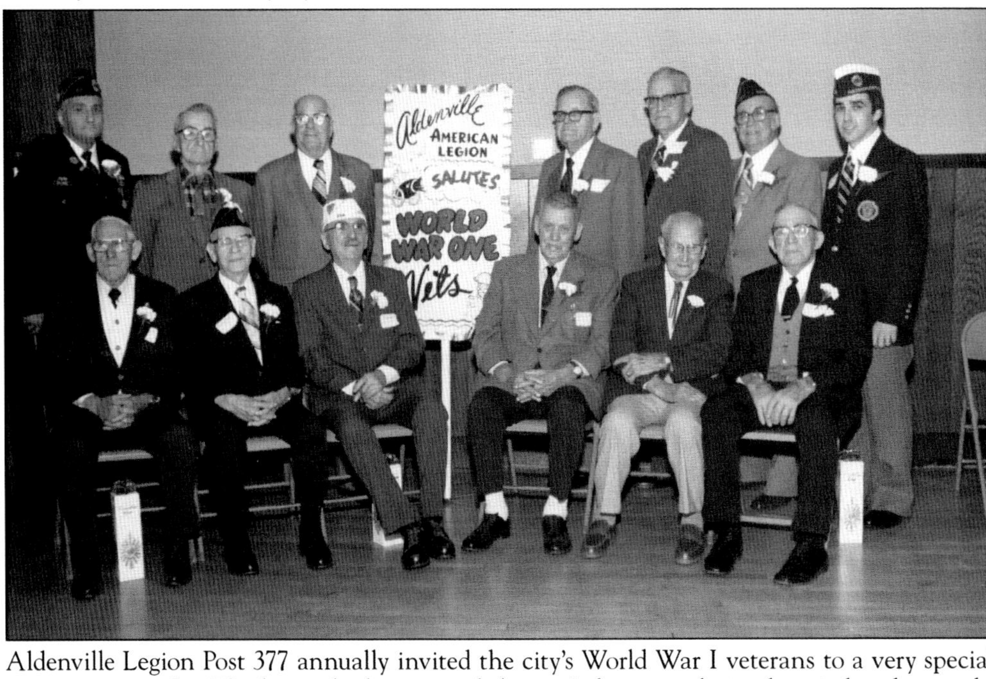

Aldenville Legion Post 377 annually invited the city's World War I veterans to a very special appreciation night. The legion had renovated the city's former isolation hospital and grounds, creating an attractive picnic and recreation area adjacent to the Ray Ashe Playground.

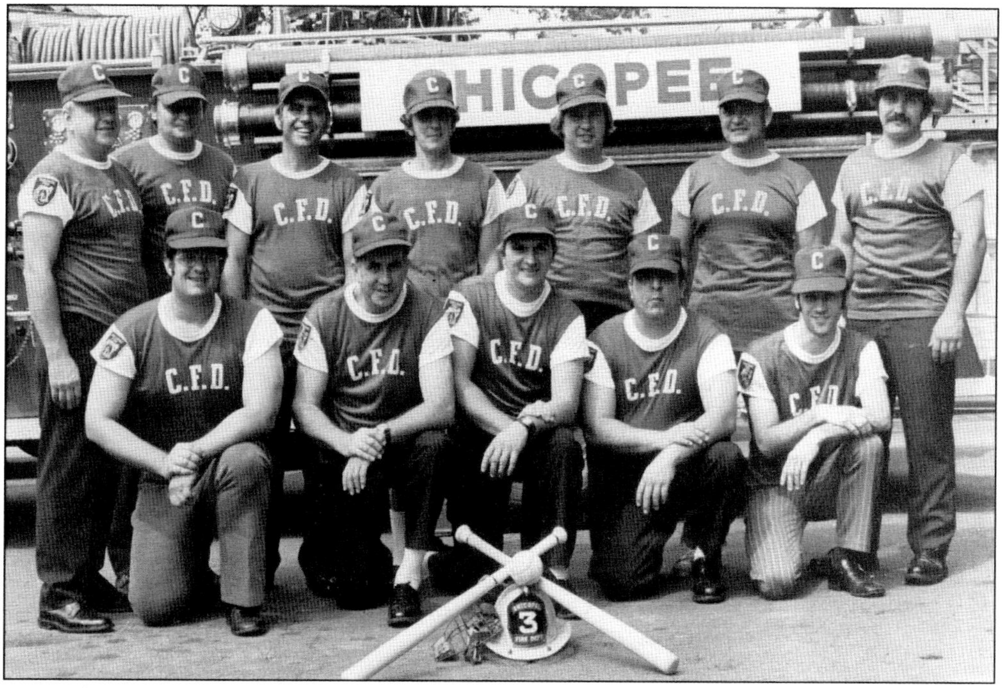

It was the golden age of adult softball with the big games being played under the lights at Szot Park. The colorful Chicopee Fire Department squad had their team picture taken with a vintage fire truck.

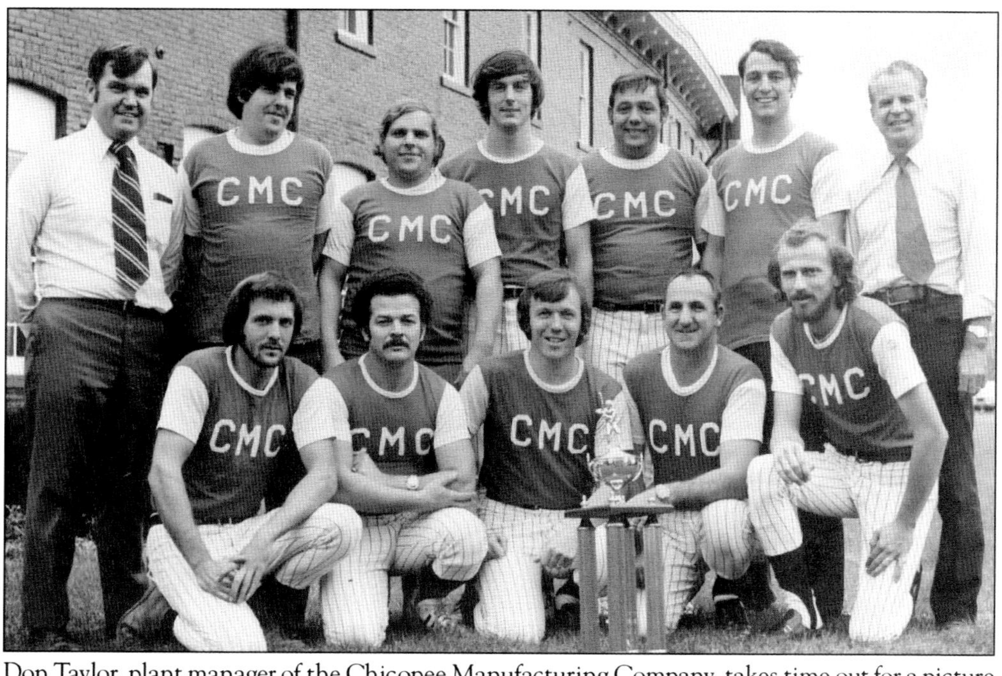

Don Taylor, plant manager of the Chicopee Manufacturing Company, takes time out for a picture with members of the company's championship softball team. While everyone was all smiles, it was known at the time that their parent company Johnson & Johnson, of New Brunswick, New Jersey, was in the process of trying to sell the Chicopee unit.

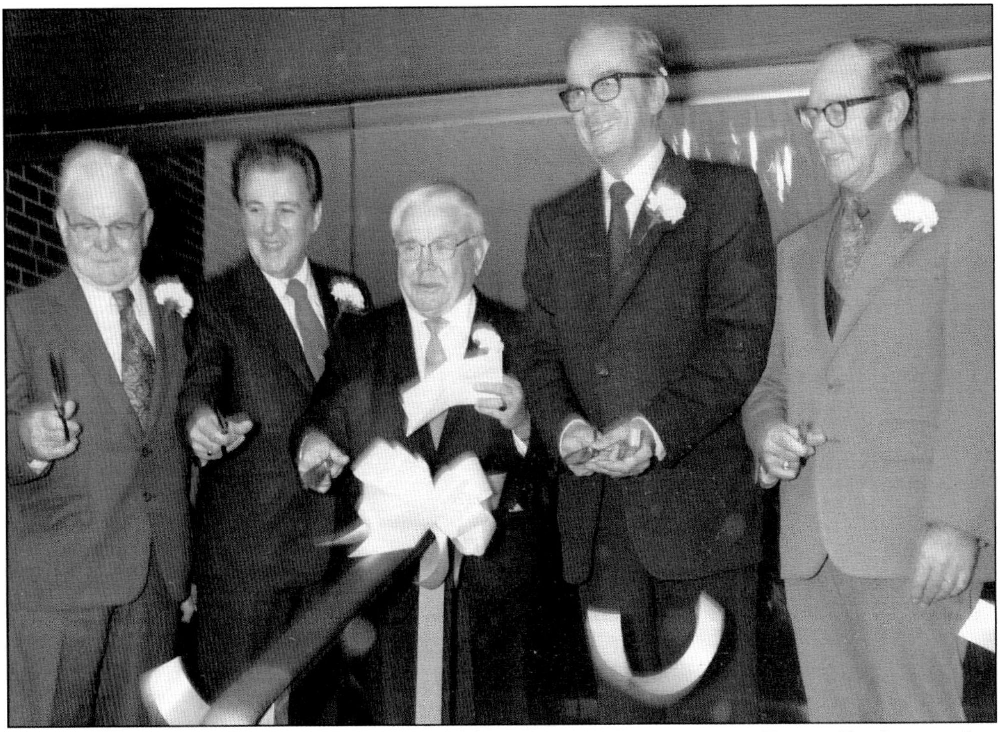

The Chicopee Savings Bank was the city's oldest continuous institution. Originally chartered in 1850, the bank had always been on Chicopee's Center Street. On October 29, 1973, a brand new bank opened. Cutting the ribbon at dedication ceremonies are, from left to right, Ernest Lavigne, Sen. Roger Bernashe, Pres. Stephen Zajchowski, and Mayor Edward Ziemba.

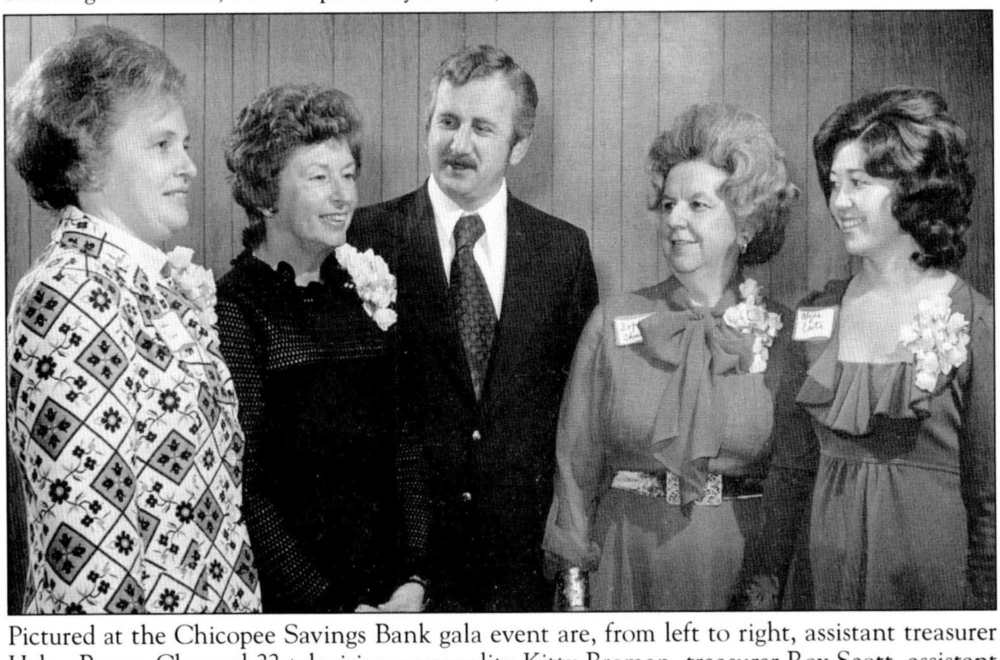

Pictured at the Chicopee Savings Bank gala event are, from left to right, assistant treasurer Helen Banas, Channel 22 television personality Kitty Broman, treasurer Roy Scott, assistant superintendent of Chicopee's schools Sophie Chmura, and Alizra Costa.

The most tragic event in the history of St. Stanislaus Parish was the fire that destroyed St. Stanislaus School on March 23, 1973. A new structure rose from the ashes as the parish family resolved to build a new school. On August 27, 1974, ground was broken for the new school. From left to right are Dr. John Luke, Mayor Edward Ziemba, and Bishop Christopher J. Weldon.

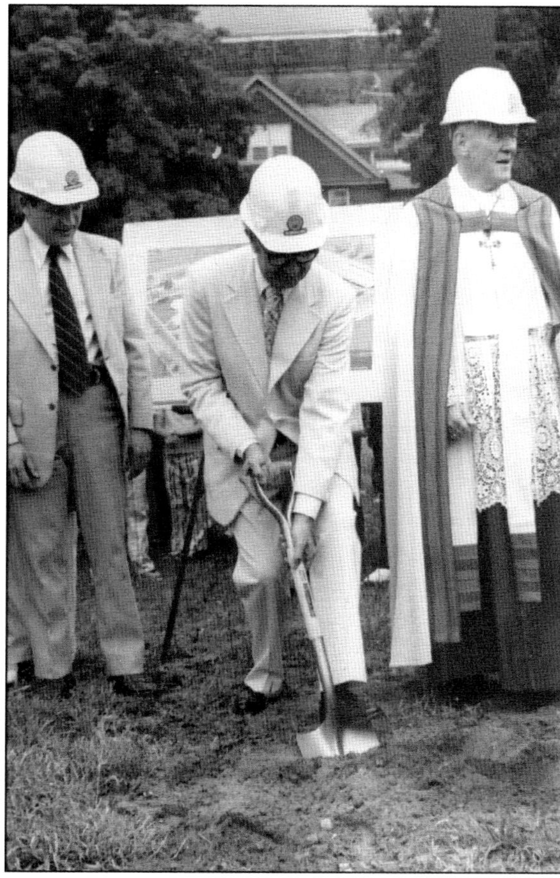

In 1974, the St. Stanislaus Parish Fundraising Committee was the first group to secure a tent for the Chicopee Chamber of Commerce's first annual Kielbasa Festival. The first festival was a makeshift affair on the grounds of the old Lamb Knitting Company in Chicopee Falls. The event had a cooking contest, the world's largest "King Kielbasa" on display, Golden Kielbasa Awards, Polish music, and a very popular kielbasa-eating contest.

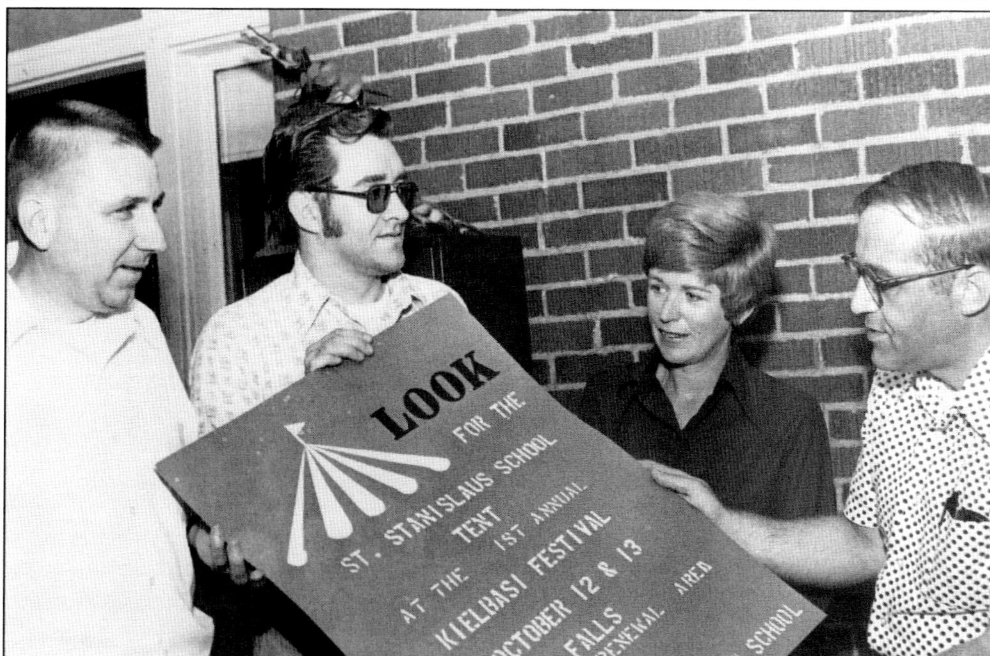

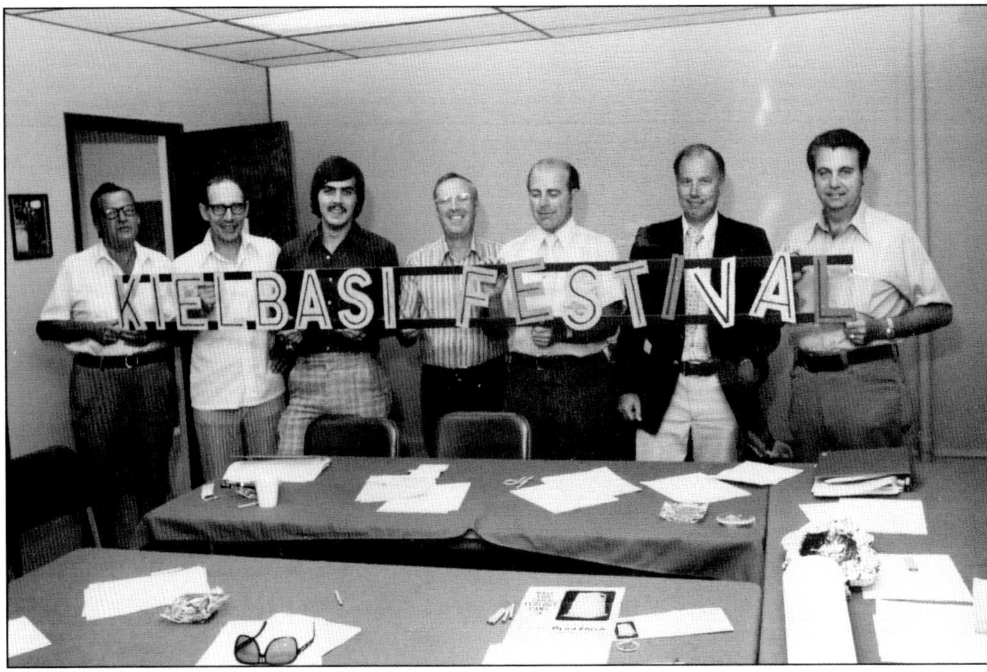

Pictured here is the original planning committee for the first K-Fest. From left to right are Ted Jarette, Frank Desmarais, Lou Denys, Irving Rosazza, Joe Roy, Marshall Hart, and Neil O'Leary, the man credited with coming up with idea for the festival.

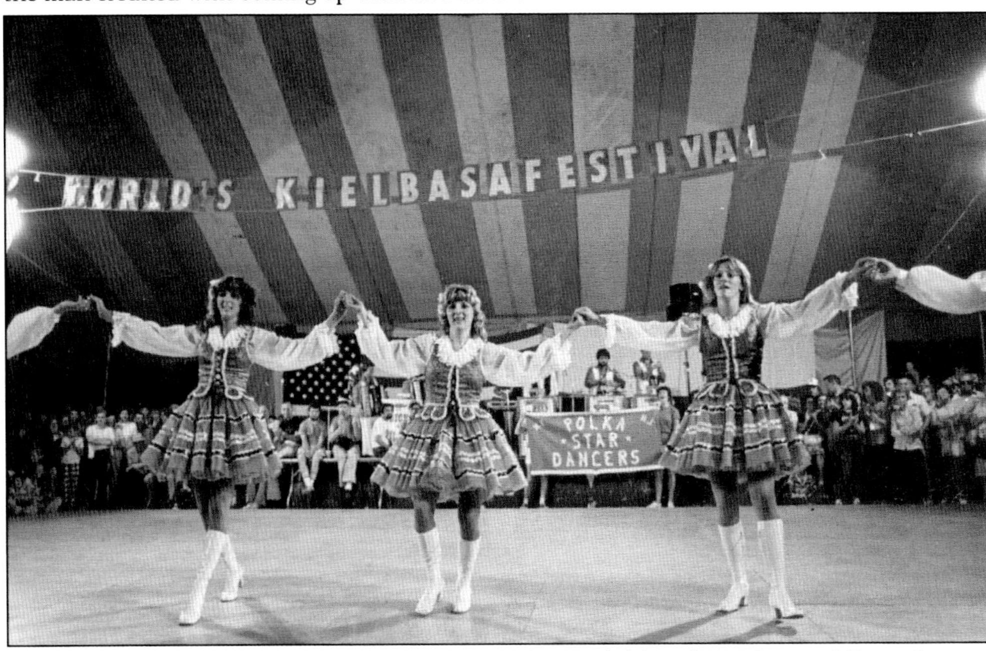

The following year, the event, located adjacent to the Fairfield Mall on Memorial Drive, became the World Kielbasa Festival. Each year, polka bands, some from as far away as Buffalo, New York, and Chicago, Illinois, thrilled area dancers who packed the giant tent on the midway. During the event's 22-year run, the festival added amusement rides, a casino tent, a Polka Mass, a Massachusetts Oldies Tent, and a very successful Miss Chicopee contest.

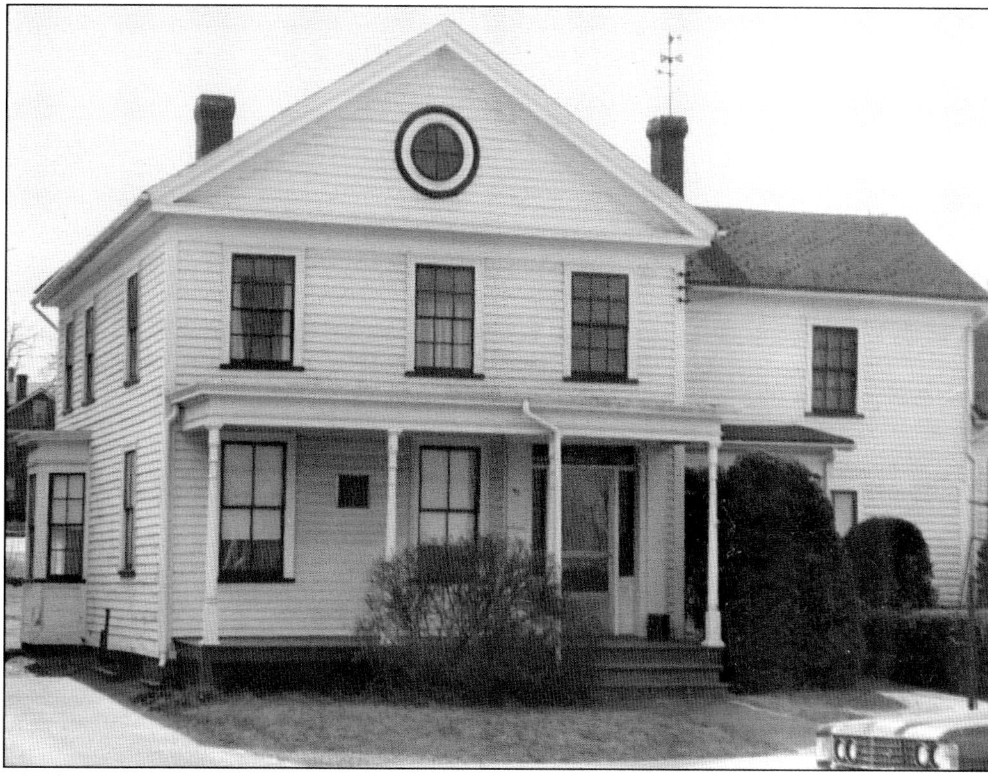

The home of Edward Bellamy in Chicopee Falls, Massachusetts, was designated as a national historic landmark by the US Department of the Interior on June 2, 1973. In 1888, Bellamy was the world famous author of the best-selling utopian novel *Looking Backward*. He had lived at 91 Church Street for most of his adult life.

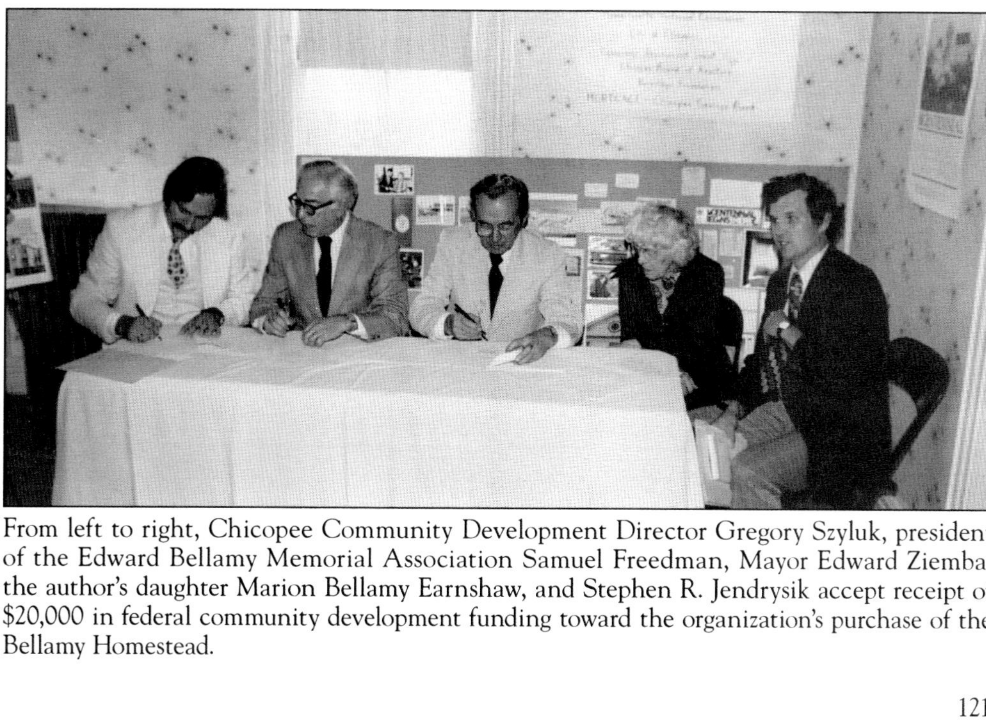

From left to right, Chicopee Community Development Director Gregory Szyluk, president of the Edward Bellamy Memorial Association Samuel Freedman, Mayor Edward Ziemba, the author's daughter Marion Bellamy Earnshaw, and Stephen R. Jendrysik accept receipt of $20,000 in federal community development funding toward the organization's purchase of the Bellamy Homestead.

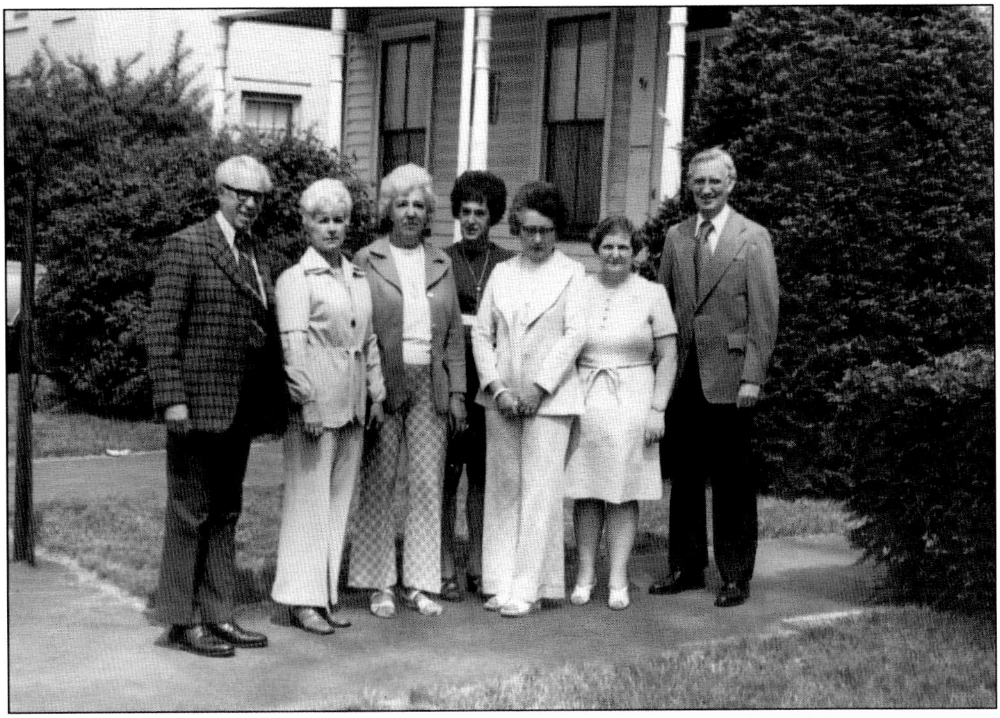

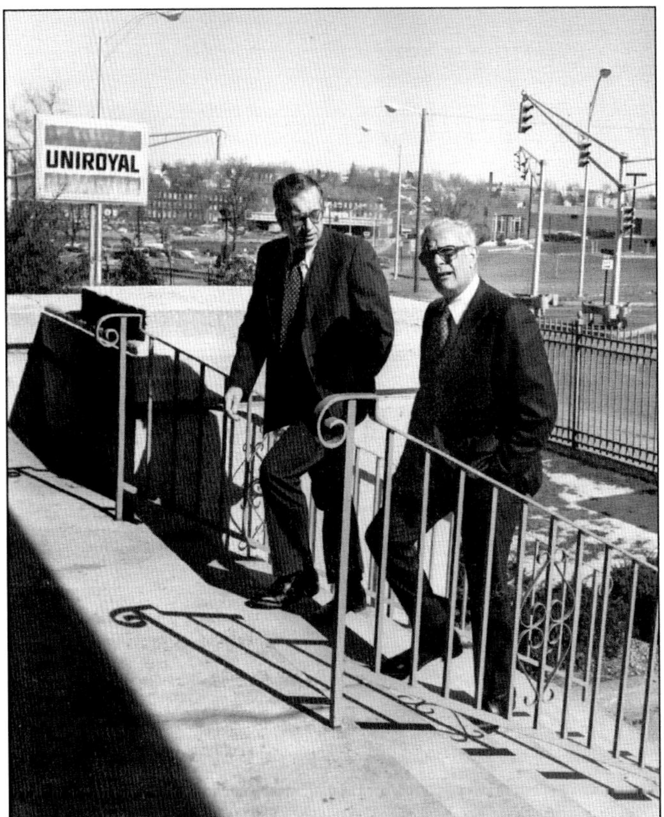

Members of the Uniroyalettes visit the Bellamy Homestead. The service organization at the Uniroyal plant pledged support for the planned restoration of the city's national landmark. They are joined by Bellamy Association president Samuel Freedman (left) and Uniroyal plant manager Robert Booton (right).

In the background is the Chicopee Falls Urban Renewal Project, shown as president and chief executive officer of Uniroyal David Beretta (left), and past factory manager of the Fisk Division in Chicopee Joseph Fontana (right), arrive on a fact-finding mission. A.J. Fontana managed the local facility during unprecedented labor unrest and a series of damaging strikes.

On the production line, Mary Zaskey, of Chicopee, seems to be greeting an old friend as she chats with George R. Vila, the chairman of the board of the Uniroyal Corporation of New York. He and Mary Zaskey had been in the tire business for almost 40 years.

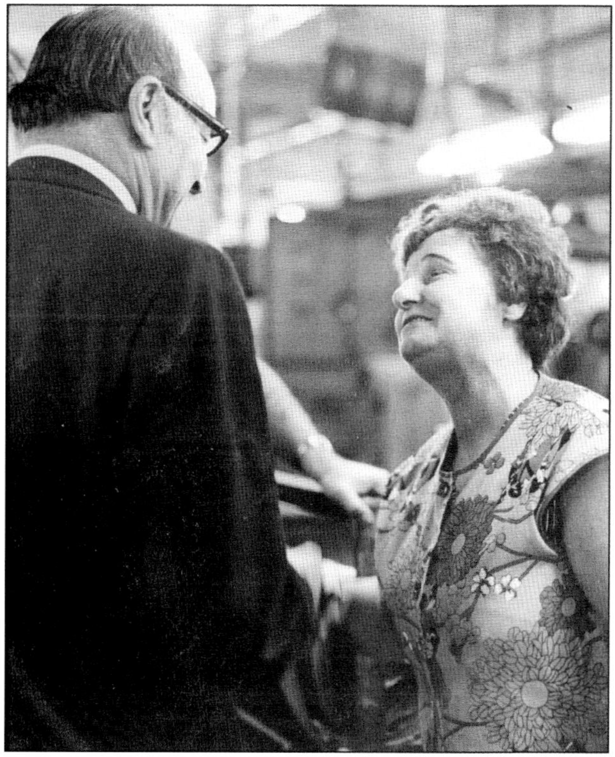

Laura Warchol worked as a splicer at the Grove Street tire plant for 40 years. Upon retirement, she received a handsome mantle clock and the heartiest congratulations from plant manager Robert Booton (center) and Uniroyal president George Beretta. In 1974, the trade papers in the tire industry were reporting that the Fisk Division of Uniroyal, the city's largest employer, would close as soon as the company's new radial tire plants in the South were ready.

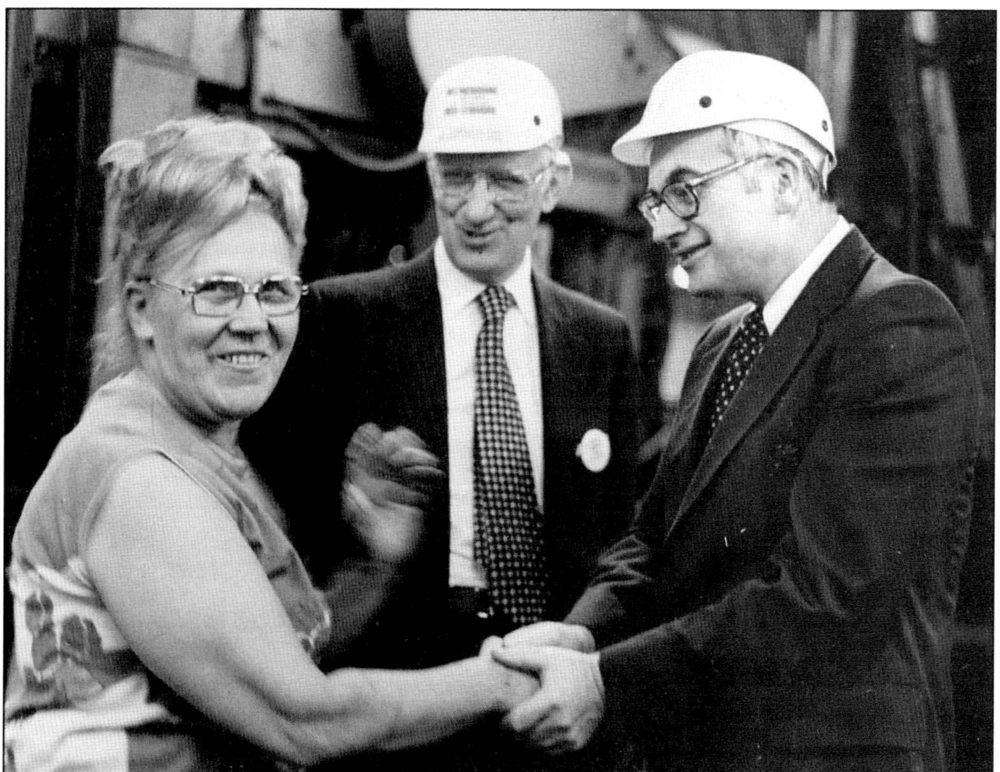

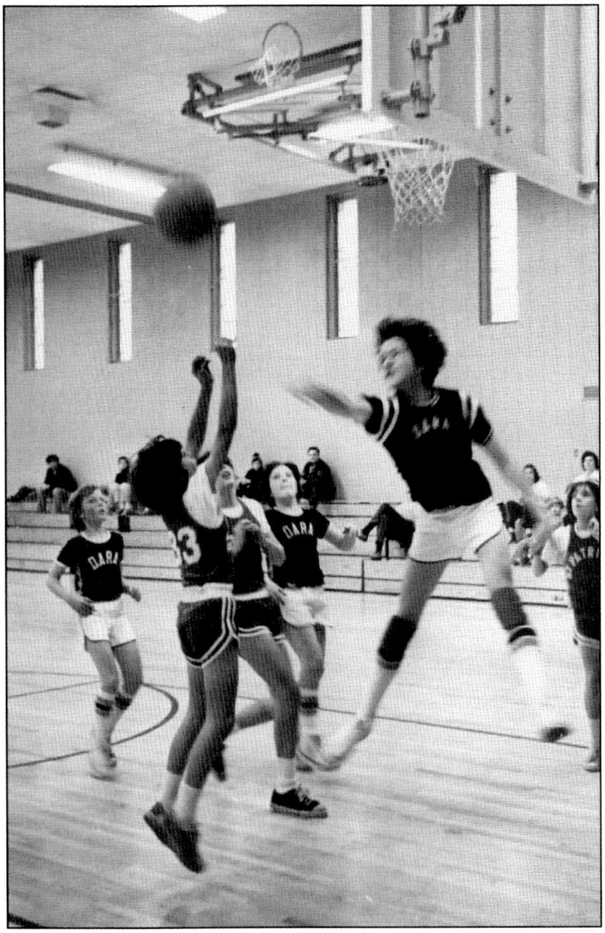

Chicopee's Park and Recreation Department's popular winter programs served a record number of boys and girls. The city's youth basketball program began to show positive results at the high school level. Shown here, Jimmy Roy, a future high school standout blocks a shot with DARA teammates Steve (right) and Paul (middle left) Plifka awaiting the rebound.

In 1974, the Chicopee Comprehensive High School basketball team defeated Springfield's Commerce High School to win the Western Massachusetts Championship. From left to right are (first row) Alex Mitchell, Bob Celatka , Rick Jasinski, Pat Holmes, Don Mitchell, and Tim Nelson; (second row) Coach Alex Vyce, Dan Cloutier, Mike Labrie, Gary Masse, Bob Mandreau, Dan Franczek, Tom Mistiv, and assistant coach Phil Airoldi.

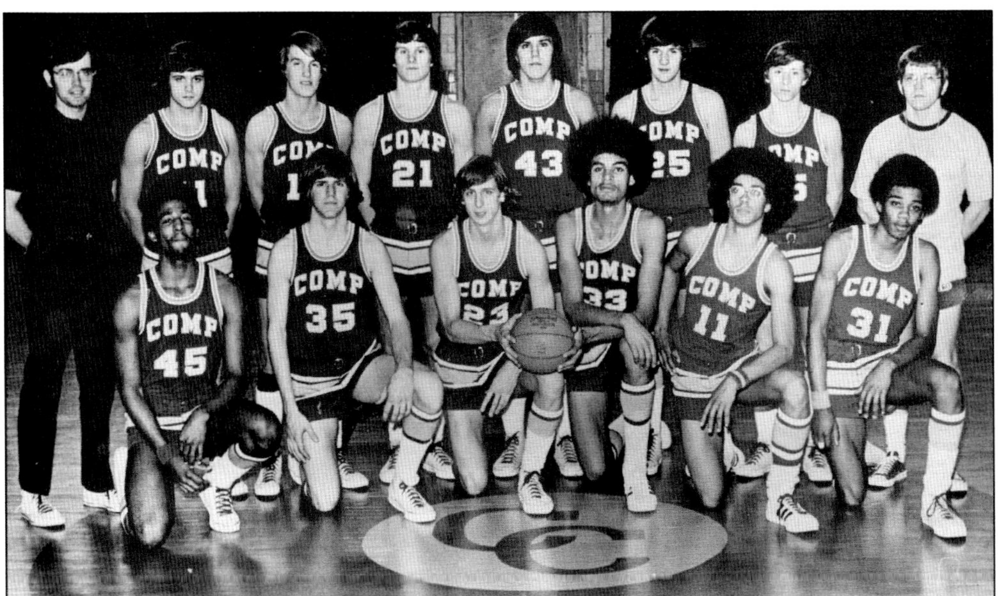

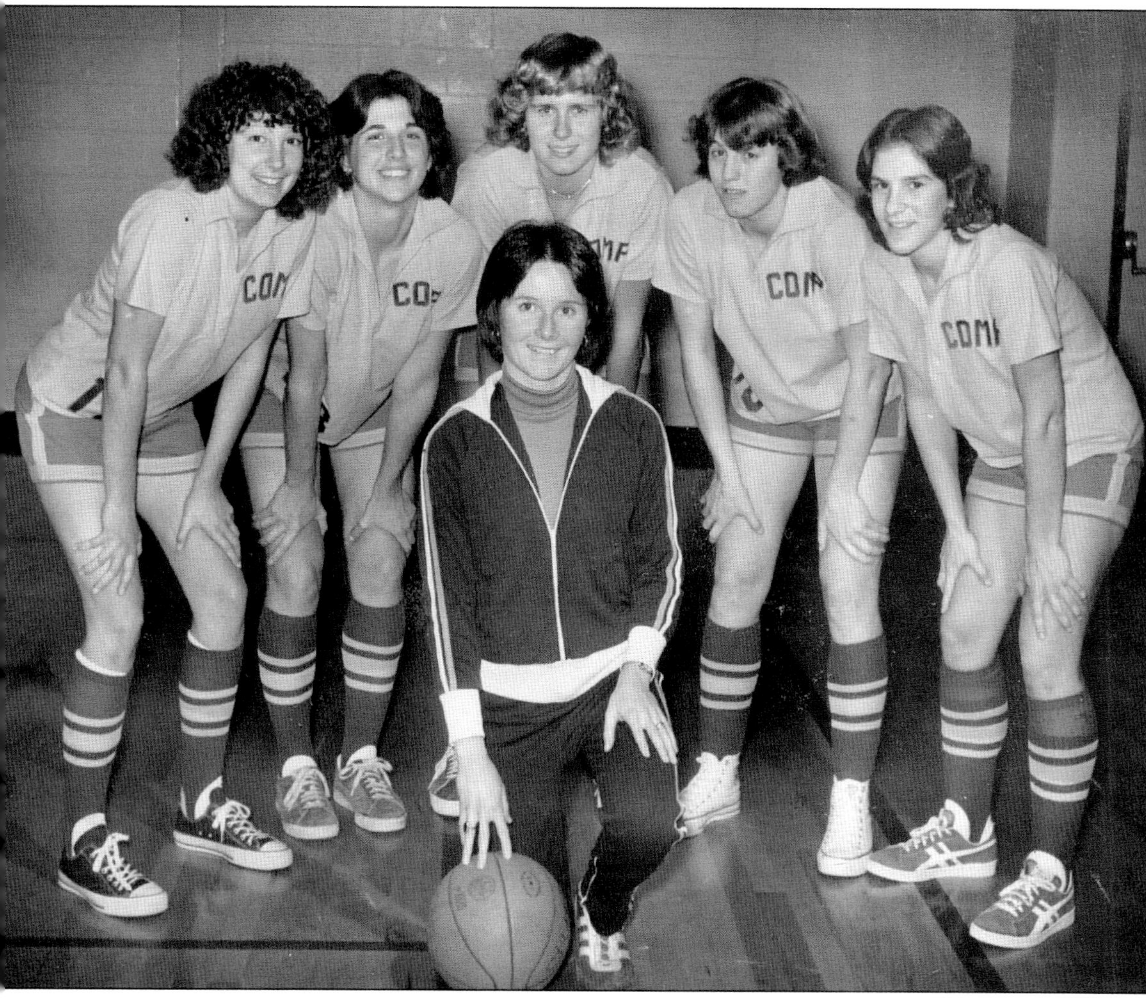

For generations, one half of the high school student body was exempted from participation in interscholastic high school athletics. At Chicopee High School and Chicopee Comprehensive High School, girls' varsity swimming and tennis were introduced, quickly followed by soccer, basketball, and softball. From the outset, the Pacers and the Colts would field highly motivated competitive squads. During the winter months, the gymnasiums were packed with a new generation of future players. They were learning the game and cheering on a group of trailblazers in sneakers. In 1975, Chicopee Comprehensive High School coach Joan Boratis was at the helm of the school's fledgling girls' basketball program. Freshman and sophomore players dominated her starting lineup and include, from left to right, extraordinarily talented Diane Murphy, Kathy Delisle, Gail Koziara, Marie Menard, and Laurie Duclos. They would win back-to-back division-one state championships for the school in 1977 and 1978.

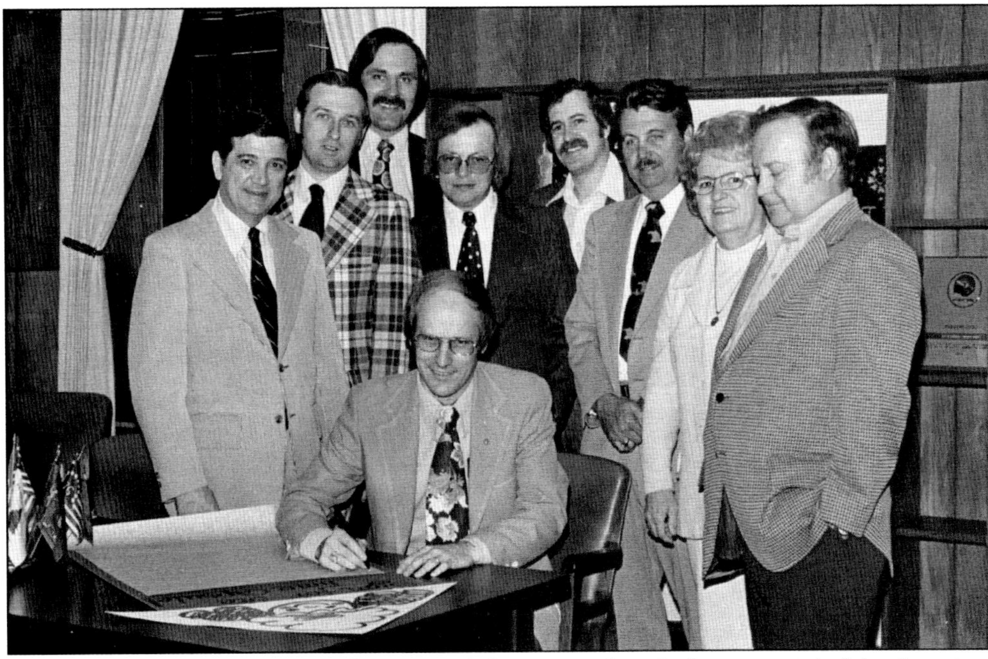

In Massachusetts, the bumper stickers reminded everyone that the bicentennial of the American Revolution begins here. Chicopee's new mayor Howard Redfern (seated) meets with bicentennial celebration planners. Pictured from left to right are Dr. John Luke, Paul Lebeau, Greg Szyluk, Paul Meroski, Marc Webb, Neil O'Leary, Ruth Campbell, and Bob Richards.

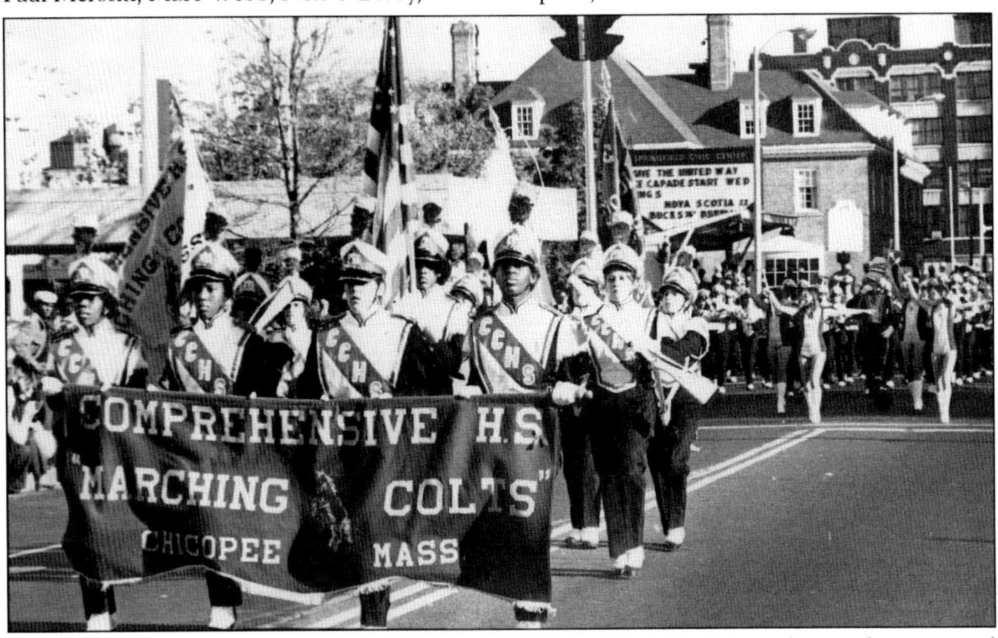

The Chicopee Comprehensive High School's Marching Colts were a Massachusetts bicentennial band representing their school, city, and state at bicentennial events all over the eastern United States. William Sittard, the school's outstanding music director, had high praise for the Chicopee Comprehensive High School Parents Booster Club, simply saying their volunteer efforts made it all possible.

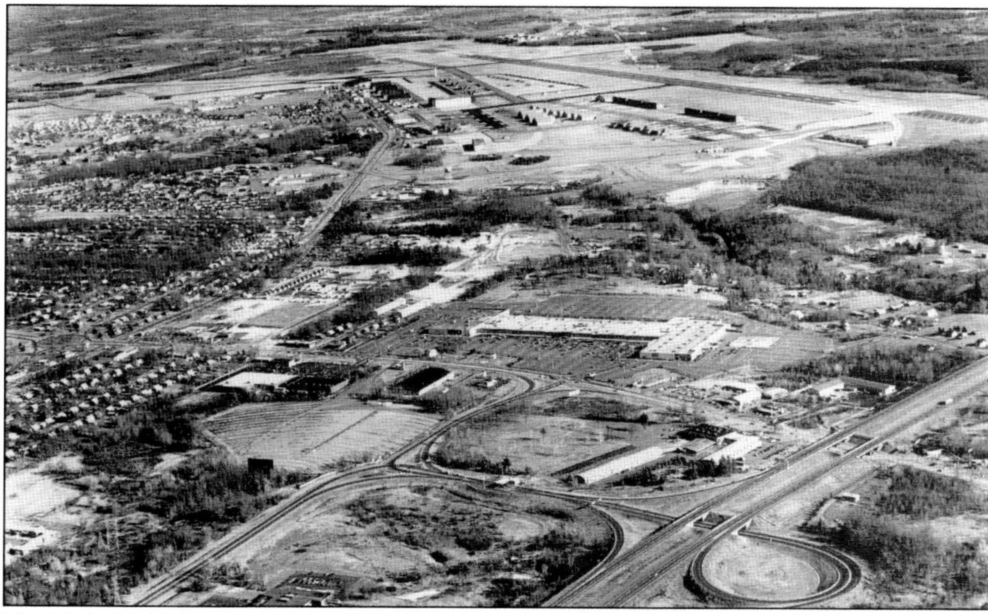

The Philadelphia developer of the proposed $10-million, 60-store Fairfield Mall (center) reported that his firm thoroughly investigated the possible effects of the deactivation of Westover Air Force Base on business along Memorial Drive, but found the closing of the base "will not affect us at all." George F. Rubin of Pan American Associates decided to move ahead with the project "because we think significant development will take place on the base."

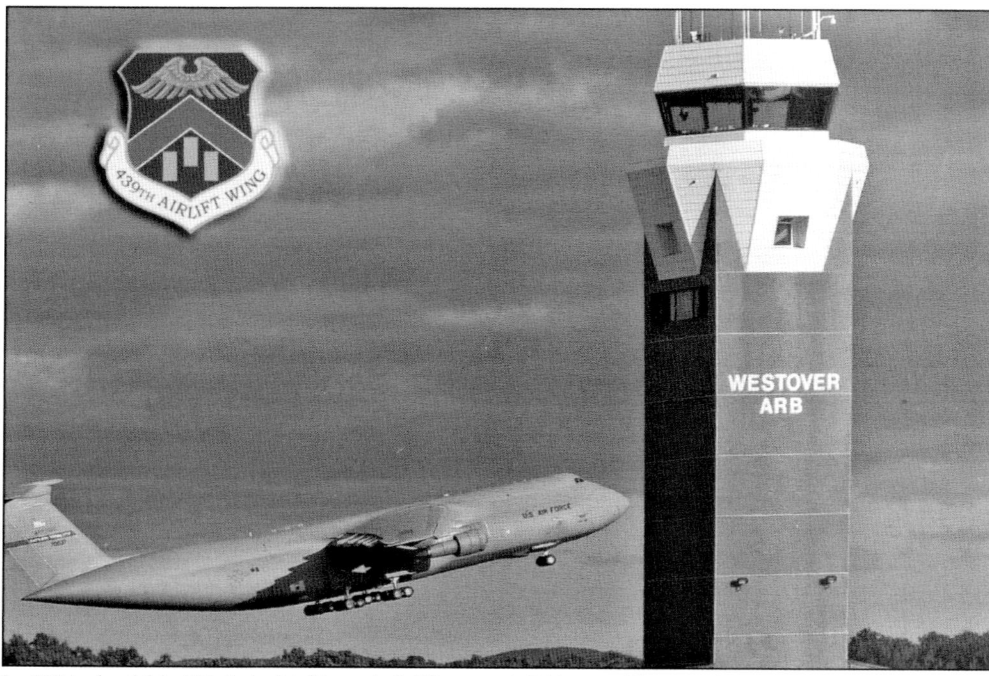

In 1974, the fabled Eighth Air Force left Chicopee's Tobacco Plains. The Strategic Air Command turned Westover Field over to the US Air Force Reserve. Today, Westover Air Reserve Base is the nation's largest Air Force Reserve facility—home to the 439th Airlift Wing and 16 giant C-5A Galaxies. Chicopee is a global transportation hub.